A HISTORY OF
MARGINAL UTILITY THEORY

A HISTORY OF
MARGINAL UTILITY THEORY

BY EMIL KAUDER

PRINCETON, NEW JERSEY

PRINCETON UNIVERSITY PRESS

1965

Publication of this book
has been aided by the Ford Foundation
program to support publication,
through university presses, of works in the humanities
and social sciences.

Printed in the United States of America
by Princeton University Press, Princeton, New Jersey

TO HELENE

ACKNOWLEDGMENTS

I GLADLY acknowledge my great indebtedness to an anonymous foundation which financed my work and the travel connected with it. My special thanks are due to many people for help in finding material and writing the text, for valuable comments, and for the ideas they inspired. My wife read, criticized, and typed a great part of the first draft. Mr. William Rogers, Miss Eva Maged, Mrs. Joan Irwin, and Mrs. Lois Willhoite typed the final draft. Richard Schüller and Karl Menger, Jr., told me all they remembered about Carl Menger the economist and his students. Ludwig von Mises, Oskar Morgenstern, Fritz Machlup, Gottfried von Haberler, Joseph Dorfman, and the late Otto Weinberger provided very valuable suggestions. Oskar Morgenstern, Karl Borch, Robert Meacham, Dudley South, Morton Davis, and Forrest Dristy helped me with the mathematical analysis. Of course these mathematicians are not responsible for any possible mistakes which remain and which are my own. The libraries here and in Japan did everything to further my work. I mention with gratitude especially Professor Taizo Takahashi, President of Hitotsubashi University, Dr. Foster Palmer, Librarian of the Widener Library, Professor Yamaguzi, Mr. Okasaki, and Mrs. Sunagawa from the Hitotsubashi Library, and the many others who have helped me.

CONTENTS

INTRODUCTION

OBJECT AND METHOD

THE problem of consumer valuation has displayed a strong persistency in the history of economic thought. Only a few economic systems omit consumer's estimation. What is the reason for this continuing interest? The theorists specializing in this field claim that the rationale of household strategy is an *eternal* element of economics. Economic actions under a communist system, a mercantilist control, capitalism, or under any other historical and geographical circumstances are conditioned by the consumer's needs.

The reasons for the choices of the household manager have been explained by observation and by theoretical analysis. Marginal utility is one of the most important discoveries in this field. Seldom have the theorists agreed on the character, function, and importance of their new device. Yet two considerations appear time and again in their descriptions. These common principles can be used for a preliminary orientation. First, the consumer deals with useful and scarce goods. Second, by the appropriation of these goods a critical point is eventually reached at the last good which the household manager can afford to use; the utility which this good creates is the marginal utility.

The clarification of this concept took about two thousand years. Ultimately, marginal utility became the basis of theoretical systems and the tool for the construction of rational consumer strategy. The discovery of this principle and the exploration of its consequences is described on the following pages.

This study had to be written before it was too late. New ideas have supplanted the marginal utility theory which was dominant for the last ninety years. The number of economists who are able and willing to use this theoretical tool decreases. By personal acquaintance and study I am in touch with the dwindling group of marginalists. Since my university days when I opposed Werner Sombart's elegant but inconclusive defense of Marxian Labor value, I have been interested in the marginal utility doctrine, especially in its Austrian formulation. Later I came in contact with leading members of the Viennese school. For quite a while I planned to write this history, but not before 1952 was I able to publish some preliminary papers. Sympathy, I hope, does not mean partisanship. This study is not a eulogy of things past, but rather it is intended to be a historical and critical investigation.

This book, written in the late twilight period of the marginalist schools, differs from older histories which were published during the period of general recognition. Some valuable contributions exist: Ricca Salerno, *La teoria del Valore* (Rome, 1892), Otto Weinberger, *Die Grenznutzenschule* (Halberstadt, 1926), Gaétan Pirou, *L'utilité marginale de C. Menger à J. B. Clark* (Paris, 1938), and François Perroux, *La Valeur* (Paris, 1943). Weinberger's book is very helpful for understanding the early history. In his analysis of recent developments he did not pay much attention to the Austrian achievements, because he rightly assumed that his German readers knew the Viennese discoveries. François Perroux has the great ability to clarify difficult problems with ingenious pedagogical devices, but he isolates each system and does not stress historical connections.

Few American studies exist: the best were written by George Stigler, "The Economics of Carl Menger," *Journal of Political Economy*, Vol. 45, 1937, and "The Development of Utility Theory," I & II, *Journal of Political Economy*, Vol. 58, 1950. I am very much indebted to Stigler's penetrating analysis. While I was preparing this book, R. S. Howey published *The Rise of the Marginal Utility School 1870-1889* (Lawrence, 1960). Howey grossly misunderstands the Austrian School.

For my study I had access to documents which were completely unknown to my forerunners. I made use of Carl Menger's voluminous notes which are kept in the Menger Library at Hitotsubashi University, Kunitachi, Tokyo. This material changes the traditional concept of Menger and his school.

Menger and his followers play a much bigger role in this study than do the other marginalist movements because the members of the Viennese group have probed deeper into the value problem than other economists. In my presentation, since I emphasize the logic and structure of the marginal utility theory and not its application, the price theory based on marginalism has been intentionally neglected. Obviously, the relation between prices and consumer valuation is very important, but a detailed discussion of this problem would detract attention from our central subject: to present the discovery and perfection of the marginal utility theories.

This book is planned as a progress report. Joseph Spengler wrote that the historian of economic analysis has to throw into relief "the imminent change," the development which originates "within itself."[1] The lack of continuity prevented me from following to the letter Spengler's design of writing history. Before 1870 the value theorists were often so much separated from each other that they had no information about the work that had been already done. After 1870 the language barrier nearly iso-

[1] Joseph Spengler and William R. Allen, *Essays in Economic Thought* (Chicago, 1960), Introduction, p. 2.

lated the different groups of marginalists. Continuing progress existed mainly inside the schools, and common ties
uniting the groups were sometimes weak. Even today language differences hamper the spread of information and
create misunderstandings. In spite of these obstacles I have
tried to follow Spengler's directions. To apply his advice
I needed an additional approach. The contents of the different theories, and the continuity and the discontinuity of
thought, will be better understood by describing the roots
of these ideas.

In general, the historians of economic thought have considered class interests and the intellectual climate (Zeit-
geist) as the two essential outside forces which molded
economic theories. Of these two roots only the second has
an essential bearing on the marginal utility theory.[2] The
intellectual climate is the result of humanities, science, and
religion in one age and in one society. More than any
other element of economic theory, marginal utility stands
in a complicated relationship to these cultural factors.[3] The
architects of marginal utility took their building stones
from philosophy, psychology, religion, mathematics, and
morals. Changes of these intellectual and cultural forces
were often accompanied by reforms of the marginal utility
doctrine. To understand its development it is therefore desirable to be acquainted with the history of ideas in adja-
cent fields.[4] However, a necessary and inevitable connection

[2] Below, p. 59ff. I intend to show that the ideological bias of the
ruling class had no bearing on the history of the marginal utility
theory.

[3] These lines are somewhat influenced by Dilthey and Troeltsch.
Wilhelm Dilthey, *Weltanschauungslehre*, Gesammelte Schriften,
VIII (Leipzic, 1931). Ernst Troeltsch, *Der Historismus und seine
Ueberwindung* (Berlin, 1924).

[4] Werner Sombart, *Die Drei Nationalökonomien* (Leipzic,
1930), p. 212. In America, Professor Boring, while investigating
the history of natural sciences came to similar results. Edwin G.
Boring, "Science and the Meaning of its History," *The Key Re-
porter*, XXIV, No. 4 (July, 1959), pp. 2, 3.

between intellectual climate and history does not exist. Too often the causal relation is interrupted by creative freedom, by the unexpected work of a great thinker.

The production of new thoughts and the perfection or rejection of old formulations are often determined as much by the refinement of economic thinking and observation and by the unexpected appearance of a gifted economist, as by the influence of outside forces. I use both approaches —the description of immanent changes, and the presentation of the impact of general ideas—to describe the development, the ninety years of domination, and the final decline of this theory. Whether or not the recent neglect of marginal utility theory is in the interest of economic analysis can be discovered only after the evidence on the following pages has been studied.

HISTORICAL LANDMARKS

The Development of the Utility and Marginal Utility	*History of Ideas and Value Theory*
I. VALUE-IN-USE	
Aristotle (384-322 B.C.). *Politics, Topics, Nicomachean Ethics.*	Public and Private Welfare.
1. The Schoolmen Thomas Aquinas (1225-1274) Buridanus (1295-1366)	Prevalence of Aristotelism and scholastic philosophy.
2. The Italian School Gian Francesco Lottini (fl. 1548), *Avvedimenti Civili.*	Late Aristotelism.

Ferdinand Galiani (1728-1787), *Della Moneta*, 1750 or 1751.	Enlightenment.

II. MARGINAL UTILITY

Daniel Bernoulli (1700-1782), "Specimen Theoriae Novae de mensura sortis." St. Petersburg, 1738.	Application of calculus to sciences.
Jeremy Bentham (1748-1832).	Hedonism.
William F. Lloyd (1795-1852). *A Lecture on the Nature of Value*, Oxford, 1834.	
Arsène Jules Dupuit (1804-1866), *De l'utilité et de sa mesure*, 1853.	
Hermann Heinrich Gossen (1810-1858), *Entwicklung der Gesetze des menschlichen Verkehrs*, Braunschweig, 1854.	Radicalism in the Rhineland influenced by French enlightenment (Helvetius) and Saint-Simonism.

III. THE TRIUMPH OF MARGINAL UTILITY 1870.

Carl Menger (1840-1921), *Grundsätze der Volkswirthschaftslehre*, Vienna, 1871.	Austrian Aristotelism. The Austrian School of psychologists (Franz Brentano, Christian Ehrenfels, Oskar Kraus).

William Stanley Jevons (1835-1882), *The Theory of Political Economy*, London, 1871.

John Stuart Mill's moderate Hedonism.

Léon Walras (1834-1910), *Eléments d'économie politique pure;* ... Lausanne, 1874.

Saint-Simonism. Étienne Vacherot, 1809-1897, French laicism.

1. The Austrian School from 1880-1947.

1880-1927. Systematization and consolidation.

Eugene von Boehm-Bawerk (1851-1914), *Kapital und Kapitalzins*, Innsbruck, 1884, 1889-.

Friedrich Paulsen (1846-1908): Aristotelian interpretation of social action. Max Weber (1864-1920): methodical investigation of rationalism in human action.

Friedrich von Wieser (1851-1926), *Der natürliche Werth*, Vienna, 1889.

2. 1920-1947

Neo-Marginalism. Hans Mayer, Ludwig von Mises, Paul Rosenstein-Rodan, Leo Schönfeld-Illy.

Alfred Schütz, *Der sinnhafte Aufbau der sozialen Welt*, Vienna, 1932; phenomenological interpretation of social sciences.
The Viennese circle ("Der Wiener Kreis"), Moritz Schlick (1882-1936), Richard von Mises, Logical Positivism.

3. 1943

Theory of Games	Introduction of the probability mathematics into the value theory.

John von Neumann (1903-1957) and Oskar Morgenstern (1902-), *Theory of Games and Economic Behavior*, Princeton, 1944.

4. The development of the indifference curves.

Francis Y. Edgeworth, *Mathematical Physics*, London, 1881.

Vilfredo Pareto (1848-1923), *Manuale d'economia politica*, Milan, 1906.	Positivism and empiricism.
John R. Hicks (1904-), *Value and Capital*, Oxford, 1938.	Behaviorism.

PART I

THE GENESIS OF MARGINAL UTILITY

CHAPTER I

THE PHILOSOPHICAL BACKGROUND

CONSUMER VALUE AND COST THEORY

THE first part of this study begins with the Greek philosopher Aristotle (384-322 B.C.), who already had some understanding of consumer valuation, and ends with the Prussian lawyer Gossen (1854), who wrote the first systematic treatise based on the marginal utility theory. An interval of 2,000 years lies between Aristotle and Gossen. During this period a crude concept was changed into a consistent theory. The explorers of the value-in-use were separated by time and space, by social status and profession. Nevertheless, a common element existed which joined together those theorists who wrote between 300 B.C. and 1800 A.D.

In writing my paper "The Retarded Acceptance of the Marginal Utility Theory,"[1] I discovered the strange fact that before the nineteenth century the writers interested in consumer value were Frenchmen and Italians, while the defenders of cost theory were of British origin.

Consumer value	Cost theory
Buridanus	Petty
Lottini	Locke
Davanzati	Adam Smith
Montanari	
Galiani	
Beccaria	
Turgot	
Condillac	

[1] *The Quarterly Journal of Economics,* Vol. 67 (1953), pp. 564ff.

THOMISM VERSUS PURITANISM

This could not be a coincidence. It seems likely that different religious backgrounds help to explain the fact that the French and Italian economists worked at cross-purposes with the British economists. Of course, the religion of their forefathers should explain only partly the thinking and writing of the mature authors. These latter can by no means be classified simply as either Catholics or Protestants without qualification, for some held religious convictions which were at variance with the faith of their youth. Thus the young Galiani, when he wrote his *Treatise on Money*, was influenced by Vico,[2] by Catholic theology,[3] and by the deism of the eighteenth century.[4] Condillac was one of the main interpreters of sensualistic philosophy. In the British camp Locke and Adam Smith combined deism with sensualism. But all these variegated views of sensualism, deism, etc., were grafted onto either a Catholic-Thomistic or a Protestant-Puritan pattern of thought. Early education leaves its permanent impression on our minds, regardless of how we may change our convictions at a later date. These indelible fundamentals created specific social outlooks which separated the two camps.

[2] See Fausto Nicolini, "Giambattista Vico e Ferdinando Galiani. Ricerca storica," *Giornale Storico Della Letteratura Italiana*, LXXI (10 semestre, 1918), p. 142.

[3] See especially his polemic against the Protestant theory of usury and his defense of Catholic censorship. Galiani, "Della Moneta," *Early Economic Thought*, ed. Arthur Eli Monroe (Cambridge, 1945), p. 300. A short time before, he wrote an essay on the Immaculate Conception. See S. G. Tallentyre (pseud. for Evelyn Beatrice Hall), *The Friends of Voltaire* (New York, 1907), p. 64. Apparently the young Galiani was not the skeptical freethinker of his later days.

[4] Galiani defends the theory of social harmony, one of the most important principles of deism. "Della Moneta," A. E. Monroe, *op. cit.*, p. 288.

THE GLORIFICATION OF LABOR

According to Max Weber, Calvin and his disciples placed work at the center of their social theology.[5] This earth is the place where man has to strive, by incessant labor, for the greater glory of God.[6] All work in this society is invested with divine approval. Any social philosopher or economist exposed to Calvinism will be tempted to give labor an exalted position in his social or economic treatise, and no better way of extolling labor can be found than by combining work with value theory, traditionally the very basis of an economic system. Thus value becomes labor value, which is not merely a scientific device for measuring exchange rates but also the spiritual tie combining Divine Will with economic everyday life.

Generally authors are not fully aware of the connection between their ideas and their early education. Locke and Adam Smith did not clearly see the relation between their theory of labor value and Calvin's glorification of work, although traces of it can be found in their writings. Locke wrote: "God . . . commanded man also to improve the world which God has given men for their own benefit."[7] Labor, divinely ordained, becomes the measure of market exchange. This conclusion had been drawn already by Locke and much more clearly by Adam Smith who, in

[5] Max Weber, "Die protestantische Ethik und der Geist des Kapitalismus," *Gesammelte Aufsätze zur Religions-soziologie*, I (Tübingen, 1920), p. 17. See also Talcott Parsons, *The Structure of Social Action* (Glencoe, Ill., 1949), p. 500.

[6] J. B. Kraus, S.J., *Scholastik, Puritanismus und Kapitalismus* (Munich, 1930), p. 243.

[7] John Locke, "The Second Treatise on Civil Government," Nos. 31, 33, in *John Locke on Politics and Education* (New York, 1947), p. 90. About Locke's Puritan family, see Alexander Campbell Fraser, *Locke* (Philadelphia, 1890), p. 5. Even as a student at Oxford, Locke had doubtless revolted against "Presbyterian dogmatism" and "Congregational fanaticism," but this revolution did not erase the social convictions of Calvinistic teaching.

spite of being a deist, showed during his entire lifetime, a
deep sympathy for Presbyterianism.[8]

The author of the *Wealth of Nations* believed that the
hidden hand of Providence must be guiding economic action in order to insure just prices. Fair prices are reached
if the amount of labor in the exchanged goods is the same.
Like many other defenders of the labor theory, Adam
Smith combined the Calvinistic glorification of labor with
the Aristotelian-Scholastic theory of the fair price. No
doubt Locke and Smith, both of whom studied in the British stronghold of Aristotelianism, Oxford, knew the writ-

[8] Adam Smith was born in the town of Kirkcaldy, whose inhab-
itants had fought for the Covenant in the battle of Tippermuir.
See Francis Hirst, *Adam Smith* (London, 1904), p. 1. He was
baptized in the Scottish Presbyterian church, not in the Anglican
church, as I falsely assumed in an earlier paper. See James Bonar,
A Catalogue of the Library of Adam Smith (2nd ed.; London,
1932), p. 208, registry of baptism. ("The established Church of
Scotland is called in this registry the "Kirk.") In the Burgh School
of Kirkcaldy he came into contact with young Scottish Presby-
terians, for instance, John Drysdale, who held twice "the helm of
the Scotch Church as Moderator of its general Assembly . . ."
(Hirst, *op. cit.*, p. 3). His mother wanted him to become an
Episcopalian clergyman; with the help of the Snell Exhibition, he
was sent to Oxford. However, he refused to become a clergyman
(*ibid.*, p. 8). He signed the Westminster Confession before the
Presbytery of Glasgow when he became professor at Glasgow in
1750 (*ibid.*, p. 23). His deep sympathy for the Presbytery is
plainly expressed in *The Wealth of Nations* (Oxford, 1928, II,
453): "There is scarce, perhaps, to be found anywhere in Europe,
a more learned, decent, independent, and respectable set of men
than the greater part of the Presbyterian clergy of Holland, Geneva,
Switzerland and Scotland." Already in his time his favorable attitude toward Presbyterianism was noted and unfavorably criticized
by one of his friends, Hugh Blair: "You are, I think, by much,
too favorable to Presbytery." (Letter of Hugh Blair to Adam Smith,
Edinburgh, April 3, 1776, quoted in W. R. Scott, "A Manuscript
Criticism of the Wealth of Nations," *Economic History*, III, 52.)
These remarks are not made to prove that Adam Smith was a
pious man in the sense of denominationalism, but to show how
far he was exposed to the Scottish brand of Puritanism.

ings of the Greek philosopher.[9] Thus they were able to combine Puritan social philosophy with the traditional Aristotelian theory of value. This combination was possible because Aristotle and the schoolmen had presented a value concept with two sides: the subjective utility aspect, which was explored by the Italo-French school, and the objective aspect, i.e., intrinsic value and just price, which fitted into the Puritan social pattern.

The Puritan theologians claimed that business is not only a morally acceptable, but also a divinely commanded, activity, with the condition that economic value is identical with the just price, and that just price is equal to the amount of labor in the commodities. This harmony between just price, valuation, and the full share of divinely commanded labor will be realized, they claimed, by free competition. The Aristotelian and Thomistic idea of fair price was not dead in the British camp, but by weaving just price together with a higher estimate of this world and the glorification of labor, a new social philosophy was originated. The Puritan philosophy was at variance with the social philosophy which was still dominant in Italy and France.

WELFARE, HEDONISM, AND ARISTOTLE

Until the middle of the eighteenth century the future authors of the Italo-French school were trained by professors of philosophy who often were also members of religious orders (Carmelites, Dominicans, and Jesuits). These teachers presented a combination of Aristotelianism and Thom-

---

[9] About English universities and their teachings in the seventeenth century see Fraser, *op. cit.*, pp. 10-11; in the eighteenth century: Leslie Stephen, *The English Utilitarians* (London, 1900), reprint of the London School, p. 43. Adam Smith must have acquired a very thorough knowledge of Aristotle. The existent fragment of his inaugural dissertation, "de Origine idearum," is proof of it. See Hirst, *op. cit.*, p. 23.

ism which generally was not touched by any modern "hereticism."[10] The young students were not exposed to ideas on the glorification of labor. Work, according to the schoolmen and their followers, is not a divine vocation but is necessary in order to maintain one's place in the given natural order of society. There was no compulsion to integrate labor costs into the social order, or into the philosophy of economic value.[11]

[10] Apparently Aristotelianism had a dominant position in the universities of France and Italy until the middle of the eighteenth century. Any attempt before that time to throw off the shackles of Aristotelian philosophy aroused the ire of religious orthodoxy and led to the persecution of the innovator. Aristotle was the only philosopher who could be taught according to the study plans of the Jesuits. ("*Commentariolus*" to the "ratio studiorum" of 1586.) See Paul Barth, *Geschichte der Erziehung* (5th and 6th ed.; Leipzic, 1925), p. 333. The Jesuits had an essential influence on Spanish and Italian education. Although French Jesuits and the Collège Royal de France were not on the best of terms, they joined forces against Descartes, Jansenism, and Quietism, and propagated the exclusive teaching of Aristotelianism during the whole seventeenth century. See Barth, *op. cit.*, pp. 349, 515, 735; Ernst von Sallwürk, "Bildung und Bildungswesen in Frankreich während des 17. und 18. Jahrhunderts," *Geschichte der Erziehung vom Anfang an bis auf unsere Zeit*, ed. K. A. Schmid and Georg Schmid (Stuttgart, 1896), Vol. IV, Part I, pp. 416, 431, 435, 437. A similar situation existed also in Italy during the seventeenth and the first quarter of the eighteenth century. During the lifetime of Giambattista Vico, the great Neapolitan philosopher, the inquisition tried to suppress Cartesians, Epicureans, and atheists (between 1683 and 1744). Max Harold Fisch and Thomas Goddard Bergin, *The Autobiography of Giambattista Vico* (Ithaca, N.Y., 1944), p. 34. N. Cortese, "L'Età Spagnuola," *Storia della Universita di Napoli* (Naples, 1924), pp. 428, 430. The attempts to break away from Aristotle were apparently successful only in the second part of the eighteenth century. In Pavia, under Austrian domination, Minister Kaunitz emphasized in a reform program of 1772 that philosophy should be taught according to Bacon, Locke, Condillac, and Bonnet. See Baldo Perroni, "La riforma dell' Universita di Pavia ne settecento." *Contributo alla Storia dell' Universita di Pavia* (Pavia, 1925), p. 147.

[11] Kraus, *op. cit.*, p. 72.

Instead of work, moderate pleasure-seeking and happiness form the center of economic actions, according to Aristotelian and Thomistic philosophy. A certain balanced hedonism is an integrated part of the Aristotelian theory of the good life.[12] If pleasure in a moderate form is the purpose of economics, then following the Aristotelian concept of the final cause, all principles of economics including valuation must be derived from this goal.[13] In this pattern of Aristotelian and Thomistic thinking, valuation has the function of showing how much pleasure can be derived from economic goods.

In Italy and France, Aristotelian "Good Life" and finalism formed the background for the development of one theory of value, whereas in Great Britain, moral recognition of economics and the glorification of labor led to quite a different theory of value. This, in my opinion, is the final reason why John Locke and Adam Smith were not interested in the work of their Italian and French contemporaries and vice versa.[14]

VALUE THEORY AND THE INTELLECTUAL CONVICTIONS OF THE NINETEENTH CENTURY

My theory has, however, an important limitation. The belated acceptance of marginal utility in the nineteenth

[12] Léon Robin claims that the place for pleasure is not clearly designated in Aristotle's ethics. "Three main ideas are presented: (1) pleasure is never a good (Speusippus); (2) some pleasures are good, but the majority are bad, all those which are neither true nor pure (Philebus); (3) even if all pleasures were good it still would be impossible that pleasure is the supreme good . . ." Léon Robin, *Aristote* (Paris, 1944), p. 215. (My translation.) It seems that most of our writers are interested in Aristotle's positive evaluation of pleasure seeking.

[13] W. D. Ross, *Aristotle* (London, 1930), p. 190.

[14] I presented this explanation for the first time in a paper read before the Midwestern section of the American Economic Association (Milwaukee, April, 1951).

century cannot be explained by the Aristotelian-Calvinistic dichotomy. Other conditions prevailed. Economists in general no longer thought consistently in accordance with their religious backgrounds. Only a dwindling minority was strongly influenced by religious convictions. To this small group belonged Alfred Marshall, to whom Talcott Parsons has drawn my attention.[15] The Evangelicalism of his dominating father left a strong imprint on the thinking of Alfred Marshall.[16] Evangelicalism was a Calvinistic revival movement which gained a foothold in many Protestant churches of America and Great Britain during the nineteenth century. The Evangelicals demanded the consecration of Christians to valuable and zealous action and condemnation of luxury.[17]

Marshall, as a mature personality, became an agnostic yet he retained a deep feeling for religious values,[18] and his welfare policy was patterned after the moral postulates of Evangelicalism. "Work in its best sense, the healthy energetic exercise of faculties, is the aim of life, is life itself"; comfort is "a mere increase of artificial wants."[19]

[15] In recent correspondence.

[16] His father was "cast in the mould of the strictest Evangelicals." John M. Keynes, "Alfred Marshall, 1842-1924," *Memorials of Alfred Marshall*, ed. A. C. Pigou (London, 1925), p. 1 (cited hereafter as *Memorials*).

[17] About Evangelicalism: *A Dictionary of English Church History*, eds. S. L. Ollard and Gordon Crosse (London, 1921), pp. 211, 215; *Encyclopaedia of Religion and Ethics*, ed. James Hastings (New York, 1920), v, 602.

[18] *Memorials, op. cit.*, p. 7.

[19] Quoted from *Memorials* and from Marshall's *Principles of Economics* in Talcott Parsons, *The Structure of Social Action* (Glencoe, Ill., 1949), p. 140, and p. 141, n. 1. Marshall's remark on his beloved chess game is typical of his Puritan abstinence from luxury. "We are not at liberty to play chess games, or exercise ourselves upon subtleties that lead nowhere. It is well for the young to enjoy the mere pleasure of action, physical or intellectual. But the time presses; the responsibility on us is heavy." *Memorials, op. cit.*, p. 2.

Transferring this Calvinistic appreciation of activity for its own sake and depreciation of comfort into economic theory produces a dilemma which has been ably analyzed by Professor Parsons. On the one hand, Marshall was one of the independent discoverers of marginal utility. On the other hand, his glorification of labor attracted him to the cost problem. The result was the unbalanced character of his price and value theory. He failed to make fullest use of the marginal utility theory,[20] and he valiantly defended Ricardo's objective value theory.

Marshall stressed costs and supply rather than demand in his famous explanation of price equilibrium. Calvinism in its evangelical form was still strong enough to minimize the marginal utility approach. But even the son of an evangelical father no longer suppressed scientific interest for the sake of religious postulates. Marshall's dilemma was rarely found.

Educational background was no longer a sufficient explanation of the trend in the nineteenth century. The tie between specific religious or philosophical convictions and a particular pattern of economic thinking became weaker and weaker. For example, most of the outstanding analysts of subjective value theory in the nineteenth century do not fit into the Aristotelian-Thomistic pattern. Lloyd and Longfield were Protestants; Gossen, the protagonist of marginal utility, was an outstanding anti-Catholic; Beccaria, Verri, and later Ferrara, who grew up in an intellectual climate which was still influenced by Catholic ideas, showed outspoken sympathies for the British cost theory.

The reasons for the delayed acceptance of marginal utility in the nineteenth century can be found mainly in the

[20] It is worthy of note that Marshall presents the whole marginal utility theory on two and one-half pages in his *Principles*, a book dedicated mainly to the explanation of price theory. See Alfred Marshall, *Principles of Economics* (8th ed.; London, 1930), pp. 92-94.

history of economic science itself. This statement contradicts customary explanations. Sociologists, philosophers, and economists claimed that either sensualism (Northrop and Gunnar Myrdal),[21] or the return to Kantianism (Stark),[22] or the changed interests of the leading social classes (Nikolai Bukharin and Fritz Behrens)[23] helped marginalism to establish its dominant position in economics. It seems to me that all three explanations are insufficient.

Most plausible is the first interpretation connecting hedonism with marginal utility. Marginal utility, according to Northrop and Myrdal, is a specific application of the hedonistic pain and pleasure calculus. It was when hedonism was adopted as a philosophical background by the majority of economists, Myrdal and Northrop claim, that the marginal value system got its central position in economic thinking.[24] This statement is an oversimplification. From the Middle Ages until the end of the eighteenth century the contact between hedonism and marginal utility was rather infrequent and accidental. Not even the young abbé Galiani can be considered a hedonist,[25] and only one of

[21] C. Northrop, *The Meeting of East and West* (New York, 1946), p. 131. Gunnar Myrdal, *Das Politische Element in der national-ökonomischen Doktrinbildung* (Berlin, 1932), p. 125. See Canina, "Valore e rarita nel pensiero di G. Montanari," *Istituto Lombardo di Scienze e Lettere* (Milano, 1943-44), LXXVII, p. 166, n.1.

[22] W. Stark, *The History of Economics* (New York, 1944), p. 3.

[23] Nikolai Bukharin, *The Economic Theory of the Leisure Class* (New York, 1927), pp. 8, 17. Fritz Behrens, "Hermann Heinrich Gossen oder die Geburt der wissenschaftlichen Apologetik des Kapitalismus." *Lëipziger Schriften zur Gesellschaftswissenschaft*, 1. Heft (Leipzic, 1949). Fritz Behrens, using the same approach as Bukharin, does not quote Bukharin at all.

[24] "The marginal utility theory adopts the hedonistic and psychological concept of valuation at a time in which the psychological experts all over the world are trying to eliminate hedonistic formulas and to establish more realistic methods." Gunnar Myrdal, *Das politische Element . . .* , p. 127 (my translation).

[25] See note 3.

his followers, Condillac, bases the value-in-use concept on the pain and pleasure principle.[26] But in the nineteenth century the situation was somewhat different. Bentham and Gossen were strict disciples of this philosophy. Already Jevons accepted only John Stuart Mill's diluted utilitarianism. Lloyd,[27] Menger, and Walras[28] were not sensualists. So the acceptance of marginal utility cannot be explained by the conversion of the majority of economists to sensualism.

Still less important than sensualism was the influence of the Kantian revival in spite of Stark's interesting thesis. He claims that, at least in Germany, both the acceptance of marginal utility and the contemporary renaissance of

[26] On sensualism, materialism, and enlightenment the following works were used: Friedrich Albert Lange, *Geschichte des Materialismus* (3rd ed.; Iserlohn, 1876); Baron Cay von Brockdorff, *Die englische Aufklärungsphilosophie* (Munich, 1924).

[27] No documentary proof can be given that Bentham had influenced his younger countryman, Lloyd. No doubt, Bentham and the Oxford professor of economics had much in common; Bentham knew the law of diminishing utility and so did Lloyd; Lloyd read the *Westminster Review*, the mouthpiece of the Benthamites. He did not, however, quote Bentham at all. Lloyd is a rather meticulous scholar; in his lectures he quotes each available source, even Daniel Defoe's *Robinson Crusoe* and some anonymous writers.

In a letter of October 22, 1951, Professor Roy Harrod, of Oxford, who is very familiar with local history, emphasizes that Lloyd cannot have been a Benthamite: "Lloyd was a clergyman and brother of a famous divine, and the circles in which he lived would hold Bentham in pretty good contempt . . ." (letter addressed to author).

[28] A fragmentary chapter intended for the second edition of his *Principles* makes it quite clear that Menger was not a sensualist. He distinguishes between physiological, egotistical, and altruistic wants. Carl Menger, *Grundsätze der Volkswirtschaftslehre* (2nd ed.; Vienna, 1923), pp. 4ff., note. See Emil Kauder, "Aus Mengers nachgelassenen Papieren," *Weltwirtschaftliches Archiv*, LXXXIX, No. 1 (Hamburg, 1962), pp. 1ff. About Walras' philosophy, see Léon Walras, *Eléments d'Economies Pure* (Paris, 1926), p. 16. Walras was apparently strongly influenced by Descartes, Comte, and Vacherot.

Kantianism are phenomena of the same kind, i.e., reaction to positivism and the reawakening of introspection and theory.[29] Yet Vienna, the center of the new theoretical studies in the German language area, was not touched by the new enthusiasm for Kant—instead of Kant, Aristotelianism and especially neo-positivism were taught.[30] The influence of the Austrian intellectual forces will be explained later. Also in another chapter the claims of the Marxists will be refuted. It is my conviction that during the nineteenth century philosophical, ethical, and religious forces did not any longer dominate the development of marginal utility theory; the need for a plausible value theory without contradictions guided the value theorists.

[29] Stark, *op. cit.*, p. 3.

[30] I have investigated the connection between Menger, Boehm-Bawerk, and the Austrian intellectual climate in "Menger and his Library," *The Economic Review*, x, No. 1 (Hitotsubashi University, Tokyo, January, 1959), pp. 58ff. See also Kauder, "Intellectual and Political Roots of the Older Austrian School," *Zeitschrift für Nationalökonomie*, xvii, No. 4 (Vienna, Austria: 1958), pp. 411ff.

CHAPTER II

VALUE-IN-USE: THE FORERUNNER OF THE MARGINAL UTILITY THEORY

A TIGHT connection between the intellectual climate and the study of economics existed before 1738. Marginal utility theory did not exist before that time. Economists before 1738 and even much later operated with a cruder concept, the value-in-use, which relates the economic importance of a good or service to utility and scarcity. Essential elements of the later marginal utility concept had been discovered in the framework of the value-in-use.

ARISTOTLE'S VALUE IN USE

It is generally accepted that Aristotle was the first who created the concept of the value-in-use. That he had a far-reaching knowledge of this field is generally unknown. Only Oskar Kraus of Prague, who was a student of Aristotle and of the Austrian school of economics, presented a complete picture of Aristotelian thought, which shows similarities with the Austrian theories of a much later date.[1] Economic goods, as Aristotle pointed out, derive their value from individual utility, scarcity, and costs. If the

---

[1] See Dr. Oskar Kraus, "Die Aristotelische Werttheorie in ihren Beziehungen zu den Lehren der modernen Psychologenschule," *Zeitschrift für die gesamte Staatswissenschaft,* Vol. 61 (Tübingen, Lauppsche Buchhandlung, 1905), pp. 573ff. As late as 1940, Kraus's investigations were neglected by Edmund Whittacker, *A History of Economic Ideas* (New York, 1940), p. 65. Whittacker apparently read only the *Politics* and the *Nicomachean Ethics* and did not pay any attention to the other works, especially the *Topics,* one of the main sources of Kraus's information.

amount of goods is increasing the value decreases and can even become negative.[2] Aristotle had at least some knowledge of the law of diminishing utility.[3] Even Menger's theory of imputation based on loss calculation (*Verlustgedanke*) can be found in Aristotle, as Oskar Kraus has pointed out. Aristotle claimed in the *Topics*—a work not often read by economists—that the value of one good can be best judged if we remove or add it to a given group of commodities. The greater the loss which we suffer from a destruction of this good, the "more desirable" is this commodity. Also, the more we gain by the addition of a thing, the higher is its value. The context makes it quite clear that Aristotle applies his argument to economic goods (example of the pruning-hook and saw in the *Topics*). Menger and Boehm-Bawerk used the same reasoning. Whether they read the *Topics* could not be found out.[4]

[2] "External goods, like all other instruments, have a necessary limit of size. Indeed, all things of utility (including the goods of the body as well as external goods) are of this character; and any excessive amount of such things must either cause its possessor some injury, or, at any rate, bring him no benefit." Aristotle, *Politics*, VII, I, p. 1323, b. 7 (Sir Ernest Barker's translation) quoted in Kraus, *op. cit.*, p. 582.

[3] Kraus, *op. cit.*, and Whittacker, *A History of Economic Ideas*, p. 65.

[4] To justify his claim Kraus quotes from Aristotle, Menger, and Boehm-Bawerk; Kraus, "Die Aristotelische . . . ," pp. 584ff. A complete English version of these quotations is given here.

"Moreover, judge by the destruction and losses and generations and acquisitions and contraries of things: for things whose destruction is more objectionable are themselves more desirable. Likewise also with the losses and contraries of things; for a thing whose loss or whose contrary is more objectionable is itself more desirable. With the generations or acquisitions of things the opposite is the case: for things whose acquisition or generation is more desirable are themselves desirable." Aristotle, *Liber Topicorum*, Book III, ch. 2, para. 8, p. 117a (translation W. A. Pickard-Cambridge; from the works of Aristotle, ed. Ross, Oxford, 1908-1952).

"Again, a thing is more desirable if, when added to a lesser good, it makes the whole a greater good. Likewise, also you should judge

BURIDANUS

Aristotle had laid the foundation for the later value discussion. His explanation was accepted by medieval schoolmen, by the theologians of the Reformation, and the Counter Reformation.[5] Buridanus and the Italian economists

---

by means of subtraction: for the thing upon whose subtraction the remainder is a lesser good may be taken to be a greater good, whichever it be whose subtraction makes the remainder a lesser good." Aristotle, *op. cit.*, Book III, ch. 3, para. 11, 12, p. 118b.

"The value of one concrete commodity of higher order [producers' goods] is identical with a difference of valuation, in which the higher value is determined by the want satisfaction created by a combination of goods of higher order including the concrete good in question and the lower value by the want satisfaction created by the same combination of goods of higher order without this concrete good." Carl Menger, *Grundsätze der Volkswirtschaftslehre* (2nd ed.; Vienna, 1923), p. 157.

"Value judgements take place mainly at two occasions: first if we dismiss a commodity from our fortune, e.g., either by making a present or by bartering or by consumption; second if we acquire a commodity to increase our fortune. . . . A commodity which is already in our hands will be appraised according to the *loss* which we suffer by giving it away. . . . A commodity which is still in our hands will be valued in the opposite way according to the *increase of utility* which its acquisition brings." Eugene von Boehm-Bawerk, "Grundzüge der Theorie des wirtschaftlichen Güterwerts," *London School of Economics and Political Science*, reprinted from "Jahrbücher für Nationalökonomie und Statistik," *Neue Folge*, Vol. 13, p. 33, n.2.

Kraus, *op. cit.*, compares this Boehm-Bawerk quotation with his first quotation from the *Topics*. The resemblance is rather farreaching.

[5] A selection of the works used for this period: V. Brants, "L'économie politique et sociale dans les écrits de L. Lessius," *Revue d'histoire ecclésiastique*, XIII, No. 1 (Louvain, January, 1912); Dr. Edmund Schreiber, "Die volkswirtschaftlichen Anschauungen der Scholastik seit Thomas v. Aquin," *Beiträge zur Geschichte der Nationalökonomie*, Vol. 1 (Jena, 1913), pp. 69, 70, *et passim*; George O'Brien, *An Essay on Medieval Economic Thinking* (London; Longmans, Green & Co., 1920); Selma Hagenauer, "Das justum pretium bei Thomas von Aquino. Ein Beitrag zur Geschichte der objektiven Werttheorie," *Beiheft 24 zur Vierteljahrsschrift für Sozial- und Wirtschaftsgeschichte* (Stuttgart: Kohl-

between the sixteenth and eighteenth centuries added new ideas to the Aristotelian heritage. In three directions Joannes Buridanus (about 1295-1366) improved the understanding of economic value. First, he explained the law of diminishing utility better than Aristotle. Buridanus wrote that the rich man attaches small value to goods with which he can even gratify his demand for luxury, while other people can only satisfy their most urgent desires.[6] Second, value and price (*valor commutabilium*) are not identical. Need alone does not determine the price, but need plus money does. The poor man who needs grain more than the rich cannot pay for his wheat, for he lacks money.[7] Third, on the market, not the needs of each individual but the needs of those persons who can afford to trade determine the price.[8]

Buridanus' three principles indicate an essential progress in the investigation of value; he separates value and price.

---

hammer, 1931). Hagenauer is of the opinion that Aquinas has only an objective theory of value. According to my thinking, this is a rather one-sided opinion. See also W. Seavey Joice, S.J., "The Economics of Louis de Molina" (Doctoral thesis, typescript, Harvard, 1948). The thesis contains in the appendix a translation of Molina's value theory.

[6] "Item multa sunt valde cura quibus modicum indigamus, et quibus divites utuntur non in eorum indigentiis, sed in eorum superabundantiis voluptatum et apparatuum." Joannes Buridanus. . . . *Quaestiones in decem libros Ethicorum Aristotelis ad Nicomachum.* "There are so many objects which we lack to a certain degree and which the rich people do not use for their bare necessities. They use them for superfluous luxurious and ostentatious consumption."

[7] ". . . sed plus pecuniae (pauper) non apponerat eo quod indiget ea, sicut frumento universaliter enim indiget exterioribus bonis." Buridanus, *op. cit.* "But the more the poor man is without money, the more he lacks goods, especially grain."

[8] ". . . indigentia istius hominis vel illius non mensurat valorem commutabilium; sed indigentia communis eorum qui inter se commutare possunt." Buridanus, *op. cit.* "The needs of this or that man do not measure value; but the needs of all those who are able to barter with each other."

Not the intensity of individual needs alone but the combination of personal wants and money income create efficient demand. He has also some understanding of the consumer's rent. The rich person could pay more than the market price for the satisfaction of his urgent needs. The money he saves, the consumer's rent, will be spent on luxuries. Buridanus had no immediate followers. The Italian economists from the sixteenth to the eighteenth century were less interested in the price-value relation than in a clearer understanding of value and utility.

The Italian Economists from Lottini to Galiani

Gian Francesco Lottini (fl. 1548), whose work was discovered by Augusto Graziani, was the earliest member of this Italian group.[9] Lottini, who was an Aristotelian scholar, a shady politician, and a leader of a Venetian murder ring as well,[10] wrote at the end of his colorful life a vademecum for a prince. Lottini's work "Avvedimenti civili," inspired by Machiavelli's "Il Principe," contains a number of shrewd political observations which are loosely strung together by the social philosophy of his great Greek teacher.[11]

[9] Augusto Graziani, *Storia critica della teoria del valore in Italia* (Milano, 1889), pp. 29f.

[10] About Lottini's somewhat unsavory character, see Cecily Booth, *Cosimo I, Duke of Florence* (Cambridge, England, 1921), pp. 131, 132, 199. Despite his reputation, he was known to the great historian Francesco Guicciardini. Exact dates about Lottini's life could not be acquired. He was secretary to Cosimo I, de Medici, Duke of Florence in 1548.

See also *La Bibliofilia, Rivista dell'arte* (Firenze, 1909), Vol. 10 (1908-1909), p. 368. About his style, see Bartholomeo Gamba da Bassano, *Serie dei Testi di Lingua* (Venezia, 1839), sec. xvi, p. 441, first column.

[11] Shortly after Lottini's death, several editions of his work were printed.

Gian Francesco Lottini da Volterra, *Avvedimenti Civili, Al Serenissimo D. Francesco Medici Gran Duca di Toscana,* In Firenze, Nella stamperia di Bartolomeo Sermatelli, 1574. (In

Lottini wrote as an elderly statesman, not as an economist; he touched upon economic subjects only incidentally. But even so, he mentioned economic principles of great importance.

Lottini's point of departure is the traditionally Aristotelian dichotomy between the common good (*il ben publico*) and the goods serving individual needs (*bene in particulare*).[12] Common welfare and individual well being, so explains Lottini, are not identical but are related. The common good is the foundation of the citizen's personal welfare; for instance, if the citizen loses his property, he can get it back with the help of the state.[13] Private needs

---

Houghton library, Cambridge, Mass., quoted *Avvedimenti*, edition Florence.)

PROPOSITIONI OVERO CONSIDERATIONI in materia di cope di stato sotto titolo di Auuertimenti, Auuedimenti, Civili & Concetti Politici, di M. Francesco Guicciardini, M. Gio (*sic*) Francesco Lottini, M. Francesco Sansouini, In Vinegia, Presso Altobello Salicato, 1588, Alla Libraria della Fortezza. (Also in Houghton library quoted *Avvedimenti*, edition Vinegia.) This copy belonged once to the English poet and theologian John Donne (1573-1631), whose marginal notes in ink stressed the connection between Lottini and Aristotle. The Houghton library has also an edition of 1583, of which the edition of 1558 is a reprint.

Lottini, *Avvedimenti Civili.* . . . In Venetia, Fabio & Agostino Zopini, 1582. (Rare book-room University library of the University of Illinois, Urbana-Champaign, quoted *Avvedimenti Civili*, edition Venice.)

All editions are identical in text and in paragraphs, but not in spelling and in pagination. The pagination is in folio.

[12] Folio 17v, para. 60, edition Venice. Folio 82, para. 178, edition Florence. For full quotation see n.13 below.

[13] "Il vero bene di ciascuna cosa, la quale sia parte d'un altra, non consiste in se stessa, ma hà il fondamento, in quell'altra, di cui essa è parte." (If a thing is a part of another thing, it has no true value in itself, but its value is established by that other thing of which it is a part [my translation], i.e., the individual good is a part of the common welfare and has therefore no value in itself.) The personal or individual good "ſta poſ to, e fondato nel ben publico della Città. . ." (is based and founded on the common welfare of the state) (my translation). If anything dangerous happens to

are satisfied with goods; these goods produce pleasure. His explanation of pleasures is typical for the transition between medieval and modern thinking. He moralizes as a schoolman and analyses as a modern scientist simultaneously. We feel pleasure by satisfying our needs, which are our desires for food and sex.[14] In satisfying our appetites, moderation, regulated by reason, is advisable. Reason should make men different from beasts.[15] Unfortunately, too many people do not find a limit for their insatiable appetites.[16] Man does not even pay enough attention to his future, *he overrates his present needs*, because he follows his senses which reveal his present wants, and not his reason with which he may plan for the future.[17]

---

the private goods. . . "possono tutta via sperare di potersi con l'aiuto del publico ageulomente riauere." (There is hope that one can regain these goods easily with the help of the state) (my translation). All quotations from edition Florence, Folio 82, para. 178.

[14] ". . . il mangiere & le cose di Venere. . ." (Folio 128, para. 278).

[15] ". . . il piacere in ciò non dee passar la misura, . . ." (Folio 87, para. 188, edition Florence)—pleasure ought to be moderate (my translation). In pleasure-seeking ". . . se non da colore, che non sanno far differenza dell'essere huomo all essere bestia. . ." (Folio 43v, para. 187, edition Vinegia)—do not pretend that there is no difference between man and animal.

[16] "Jo ho conosciuti molti, che sono stati insaziabili nel domādaré. . ." (Folio 70r, para. 195, edition Venice)—I have known many whose demand could not be satisfied.

[17] "Ben che le cos e future da gl'huomini saui antiuedute habbiano chiaris sime ragioni da douer succedere nel modo, che s'antiueggono, tutta via, perche le presenti sono dināzi à gl'occhi, esi toccano quasi cō mano, ell hāno houuto nō poche volte forza di tirarei medesimi huomini saui à pigliar piùtoſto la più uicina sodisfazzione, che aspettare la lōtana, . . ." (Folio 91r, para. 260, edition Venice)—Future things, as far as they can be foreseen by wise men, have the clearest reason to happen all the time in the way in which they have been foreseen. In spite of it the present, which is before our eyes and which can, so to speak, be grasped with our hands, has forced, more often than not, even wise men to pay

Behind the moralist Lottini is a shrewd observer of human foibles who sees the infinity of needs and who knows about the underestimation of future needs.[18] Like Molière's Monsieur Jourdan, who did not know that he was speaking prose, Lottini apparently was not aware of the fact that he was dealing with economic subjects; neither was this seen by his many readers. So it is understandable that it was not he but his younger contemporary Davanzati who started the Italian school of economists.

Davanzati and his followers, especially Montanari and Galiani, formed a school because they had a common program (the application of utility value to other economic subjects). Davanzati[19] and, following him almost

more attention to the nearest satisfaction than to hope for the far future.

The reason, according to Lottini, is that one pays more attention ". . . di ciò che il senso uede, che di quanto può far conoscere per uia di ragione. . ." (Folio 91v, para. 260, edition Venice)—to those things which one sees with his senses than to those which one can learn by reason.

See also "Di maniera, che pochi son quelli che delle deliberazione lunghe, e pericolose vogliano ostenataméte vederne il fine" (Folio 70v, para. 196, edition Venice)—only a few people follow a long-lasting and risky project stubbornly to its end.

[18] Graziani's valuable discovery of the *Avvedimenti* is somewhat marred by misunderstanding. Graziani claims that Lottini made all economic actions dependent upon needs. ". . . Che i bisogni sono il primo motore delle azione economiche . . ." (Graziani, *Storia critica*, p. 29). This is not quite correct because, as an Aristotelian, Lottini believes that pleasure-seeking should be restrained by moderation and reason, which, according to the author of the *Avvedimenti*, are the final rules of human action. Furthermore, Graziani asserts that Lottini has discovered the infinite character of needs. "Egli afferma che la soddisfazione d'un bisogno determina tosto il sogerne d'un altro . . ." (Graziani, *ibid.*)—He [Lottini] claims that after one want is satisfied another soon will come into existence (my translation). As I had pointed out before, Lottini had never characterized the interplay of want and satisfaction exactly in such a way. Lottini is rather inclined to consider the infinite character of needs as a moral aberration.

[19] Bernardo Davanzati (1529-1606) was a merchant, an econo-

verbatim, Montanari[20] explain the value of money on a completely subjective basis. Money reflects the value of commodities. ". . . tant' altre cose vale, tant oro vale. . . ."[21]

About one hundred years after Montanari, the brilliant young Neapolitan abbé Ferdinando Galiani (1728-1787) wrote his *Treatise on Money* (1751), in which he surpassed the older Italian economists.[22] Galiani was not very grateful for the ideas he received from his predecessors. His criticism of Davanzati is at least very unfair.[23] The abbé

---

mist, a famous translator of Tacitus, an historian of the English Reformation; he became, when seventeen years of age (1547), a member of the Florentine Academy. He is a typical representative of the Counter Reformation, a man of great classical erudition and at the same time a stern Catholic. This religious attitude is strongly expressed in his *Dello Schisma d'Inghilterra* (*About the English Reformation*). See Enrico Bindi (ed.), *Le opere di Bernardo Davanzati* (2 vols.; Florence: Monnier, 1852). Besides Bindi the following work about Davanzati was used: Gino Arias, "Les précurseurs de l'économie monétaire en Italie: Davanzati et Montanari," *Revue d'économie politique* (1922), pp. 733ff., especially p. 736.

[20] Geminiano Montanari (1633-87), Professor at Bologna and later at Padua. See Arias, "Les précurseurs," *op. cit.* The following work of Montanari was used: Geminiano Montanari, "Della Moneta, Trattato Mercantile," *Scrittori Classici Italiani de Economia Politica, Parte antica*, Vol. III (Milano: Destefanis), pp. 43-45, 58ff. The work was originally published in 1683 under the title: *La Zecca in Consulta di Stato* (*Money in the Affairs of Government*). It was republished with the original title in *Economisti del Cinque e Seicento*, Augusto Graziani, ed. Bari, 1913).

[21] As much as other things are worth, as much value has gold. Davanzati, *op. cit.*, p. 33. Gold is here used figuratively in the sense of money.

[22] *Della Moneta* (first anonymous edition of 1750 or 1751 was not in my hands). The following editions were used: Fausto Nicolini (ed.) (Bari: Laterza, 1915); Giorgio Tagliacozzo (ed.), *Economisti Napoletani del Sec. XVII e XVIII* (Bologna, 1937), pp. 93ff., and the English translation of Arthur Eli Monroe, *Early Economic Thought*, pp. 281ff. (cited hereafter as Monroe Translation).

[23] Monroe Translation, *op. cit.*, p. 288.

was in 1751 still a firm believer in the Catholic verities. But his later conversion to atheism is foreshadowed by his attempts to blend church doctrine with hedonism. The tradition of the early Italian economists and Galiani's peculiar brand of enlightened Catholicism are clearly discernible in his philosophical anthropology and his theory of utility. All things which bring happiness are useful. Happiness and passions are linked together. Man is motivated by passions. The satisfaction of passions brings pleasure, the feeling of pleasure means happiness. So far spoke the hedonist Galiani. But then the churchman Galiani cautioned that the only acceptable indulgence in those pleasures is the one which does not hurt others. Whosoever hurts his fellow man will be punished in the next life.[24]

This somewhat inconsistent moral theology forms the background for Galiani's value analysis. He repeated the traditional formula that value is dependent on utility and scarcity, but he broadened the field of application for this formula. It is not labor which determines value, Galiani wrote, but value-in-use which causes the price of labor.[25] Great generals like Prince Eugene and Marshall Turenne are so rare that they can receive high remunerations. Galiani's theory of interest has a great resemblance to Boehm-Bawerk's explanation of much later date. Interest according to Galiani is the difference between present and future money.[26] Lottini had already seen the value difference between present and future commodities but he did not connect this observation with the interest rate.

Einaudi, famous economist and one time president of the Italian republic, praised Galiani. "We Italians are proud of Galiani's two masterworks. . . . We claim his thought for Italy."[27] Einaudi hedged this eulogy. He said

---

[24] *Ibid.*, pp. 284-85.   [25] *Ibid.*, p. 292.   [26] *Ibid.*, p. 303.

[27] "Einaudi on Galiani." *The Development of Economic Thought*, ed. Hewy William Spiegel (New York, 1952), p. 62.

of Galiani that he "came near to the threshold of the discovery" of new ideas. This is very true, Galiani *almost* discovered the principle of marginal utility and—as we will see in the next chapter—he almost visualized the law of the equalizing of utility. Einaudi is wrong claiming that Galiani "attracted neither disciples nor followers." The abbé did not intentionally organize a school, but a group of writers followed his ideas.

THE FOLLOWERS OF GALIANI AND THE DECLINING INTEREST IN THE UTILITY DISCUSSION

Galiani's contemporaries appreciated the new vistas which he opened. The French economist and statesman, Anne Robert Turgot, in an unfinished paper "Valeurs et Monnaies,"[28] developed a price theory along Galiani's lines. Turgot uses a simplified model for the explanation of the exchange mechanism. Two men are living on an isolated island; one, A, has corn; the other, B, owns kindling wood.[29] A freezes to death if he has no kindling wood, and B is starving if he has only wood, but no food.[30] A is willing to barter his maize for kindling wood and

[28] Anne Robert Jacques Turgot, Baron de L'Aulnes (1727-81), "Valeurs et Monnaies," *Oeuvres de Turgot*, ed. Daire (Paris: Guillaumin, 1844), Vol. I, pp. 72ff. See also *Oeuvres de Turgot*, ed. Gustave Schelle (Paris: Alcan, 1919), "Valeurs et Monnaies," Vol. III, pp. 79ff. The following quotations are all from the Schelle edition, my translation. G. Schelle considers it possible that Turgot wrote the paper about 1796. It should have been published in Abbé Morellet's dictionary: *Dictionnaire du Commerce*. A prospectus of this dictionary was published in 1769, but the dictionary itself was never finished. See Schelle, *ibid.*, p. 79, n.(a).

[29] *Turgot*, ed. Schelle, pp. 89ff. I have added the letters A and B for the sake of simplification and clarification.

[30] But the kindling wood which can be consumed during one month becomes very unnecessary, when he (the producer of kindling wood) starves to death, due to lack of corn, and the producer of corn is not in a better position when on account of exposure he perishes due to lack of kindling wood.

B likes to exchange his wood for corn. Both plan to keep a maximum of their own commodity and to get a maximum of the other's good.[31] A wants to give 3 measures of corn for 6 armfuls of wood and B wants to exchange 6 armfuls of wood for 9 measures of corn. Since these personal estimations cannot be realized in exchange, A and B have to give more of their own product and/or to demand less from the other. Eventually a point of agreement is reached, where the individual value of the offered good is still lower than the value of the commodity received. If the exchange rate is 4 measures of corn to 5 armfuls of kindling wood, A prefers 5 armfuls of kindling wood to 4 measures of corn, and B prefers 4 measures of corn to 5 armfuls of kindling wood.[32] If we have two wood collectors and two corn owners instead of one the situation will not be essentially different from the isolated exchange between two persons. If one corn owner tries to undersell the other, the two who stored up wood will turn to him and he will raise his price. As in the case of an isolated exchange, the result will be one rate for all barters between the four partners.[33] According to Turgot, both exchange models prove that barter leads to a higher total utility for each partner than isolated production of one single commodity.[34] Any reader acquainted with our

[31] "Everybody has the interest to keep as much of his merchandize as he can and to acquire as much as possible of the merchandizes of the other."

[32] "When the barter is accomplished, the man who gives four measures of corn for five armfuls of kindling wood prefers without doubt the five armfuls to the four measures of corn; he gives them [the armfuls of kindling wood] a higher value estimation; but on the other hand, he who receives four measures of corn prefers them to the five armfuls of wood."

[33] *Turgot*, ed. Schelle, pp. 97, 98.

[34] "One has to understand here that the introduction of the exchange between two persons increases the wealth of the one and the other; that means, the same abilities give a much greater enjoyment. In the case of the two natives (the exchanging persons),

literature knows that Turgot's explanation is almost identical with the theory of isolated exchange presented by Menger and by Wicksell.[35]

With Galiani and Turgot subjective valuation becomes the keystone for a system of thinking. This theory had to be defended against the new classical system which was based on labor costs. The defense of Galiani, his followers, and his friends was taken over by Condillac.[36] According to him, costs are not the cause of value; rather, value is the cause of costs.[37] Condillac's counter-attack against the classical cost theory is the parting shot of an army falling back. Before 1800 Italian and French writers were already drawn into the orbit of British classical thinking. An attempted synthesis of utility value and cost theory was the main object of later Italian writers.[38] Yet before decadence

---

the area where the corn is produced and the place which produces the wood are remote. One native alone had to make two trips to get his provision of corn and kindling wood; therefore he loses much time and effort to navigate. If in opposition to the first case there are two, then one would cut the wood and the other would take care of the corn, instead of using time and effort for the second trip. The total amount of corn and kindling wood produced will be much bigger and therefore the part of each."

[35] Carl Menger, *op. cit.*, pp. 186ff. Knut Wicksell, *Lectures on Political Economy*, tr. E. Classen (London, 1946), I, 49.

[36] Etienne Bonnot de Condillac, Abbé de Mureaux (1714-80), "Le commerce et le gouvernement." *Oeuvres complètes de Condillac* (Paris: Houel), Vol. IV, Year VI (1798). Condillac, *Oeuvres Philosophiques*, Vol. I, Texte établi et représenté par George Le Roy. *Corpus Général des Philosophes Français*, Publié sous la direction de Raymond Bayer (Paris, 1947), "Traité des sensations" (1754), pp. 221ff.

[37] "Une chose n'a pas une valeur, parce qu'elle coute, comme on le suppose; mais elle coute parce qu'elle a une valeur." Condillac, *Oeuvres complètes*, pp. 14, 22.

[38] Graziani, in his *Le idee economiche*, mentions the following Italian economists of the beginning of the nineteenth century: Francesco Isola, Melchiorre Gioia, Adeodati Ressi, Carlo Bosselini, and Giovanni Romagnosi, who try to combine, in one way or another, utility value with cost theory.

set in, Galiani, Condillac, and Turgot had thoroughly explored the utility concept and its consequences, although they were still not able to explain the value of a concrete unity. Galiani can easily show why gold is normally more valuable than bread. Yet why one slice of bread has the same value as an infinitesimal amount of gold cannot be calculated with the help of Galiani's instruments.

Due to Adam Smith the Galiani school never went beyond the very promising start indicated in Turgot's unfinished work. Adam Smith had an unfortunate influence on the further development of the value explanation. After reading the *Wealth of Nations* many economists reached the conclusion that a further discussion of the value-in-use was meaningless. They accepted Adam Smith's verdict on the value-in-use: water has a great utility and a small value, but diamonds have a small utility and a great value. It is generally known that Adam Smith wrote down this paradox of value in his *Wealth of Nations*, but it is less known that in his lectures he taught that scarcity *and* utility are the determinants of the market price! He gave his students the right explanation, but in his *Wealth of Nations* he misled several generations of readers.[39]

In spite of Adam Smith a few economists continued the study of value-in-use. They were the outsiders and they were scattered throughout Europe. The most significant defenders of the value-in-use were the Earl of Lauderdale in Scotland, Louis Say in France, and the German Eberhard Friedländer, who taught in Russia. Also after 1800 the Italian economists attempted a synthesis of the utility value and cost theory.[40]

[39] H. M. Robertson and W. L. Taylor, "Adam Smith's Approach to the Theory of Value," *The Economic Journal*, LXVII (June, 1957), pp. 181, 187. As I indicate in the text, I cannot agree with their judicious criticism of my attitude toward Adam Smith.

[40] Augusto Graziani, "Le idee economiche degli scrittori Emiliani e Romagnoli sino al 1848," *Memoria della Regia Academia*

The German supporters of the value-in-use during the first six decades of the nineteenth century were mostly followers of Kant.[41] They rejected the cost value, because an intrinsic value apart from the evaluating mind does not exist. Value is an imagination of our mind.[42]

Other findings of these late supporters of the value-in-use theory will be discussed in connection with the marginalist schools after 1870. After the decline of the Galiani school the output of original ideas by the defenders of the value-in-use was somewhat small. Real progress, however, was achieved by the early marginalists.

---

de Science ed Arti in Modena, Serie IIme, Vol. x (Modena, 1893), pp. 431ff.

[41] Karl Heinrich Rau, Hufeland, Johann Friedrich Eusebius Lotz, Eberhard Friedländer, Friedrich Benedikt Wilhelm von Hermann, Albert Eberhard Friedrich Schäffle.

[42] Dr. Rudolf Kaulla, *Die Geschichtliche Entwicklung der modernen Werttheorien* (Tübingen, 1906). See also Rudolf Debes, "Ansätze zur subjektivistischen Wertlehre in der Darstellung älterer deutscher Autoren" (Doctoral thesis, Jena Waltershausen, Thuringia, 1934). Debes is strongly influenced by Kaulla.

CHAPTER III

THE EARLY MARGINALISTS BEFORE GOSSEN

BETWEEN 1738 and 1850 three groups of value theorists existed: British classicists instructed the majority of economists in labor or cost value; a minority of economists in Italy, Germany, and France studied the old-fashioned value-in-use; a third group discovered the essential elements of marginal utility. The most important pioneers of marginal utility are: Daniel Bernoulli (1700-1782), Ferdinand Galiani (1728-1787), Jeremy Bentham (1748-1832), William F. Lloyd (1795-1852), Augustin Cournot (1801-1877), A. Juvenal Dupuit (1804-1866).

REPETITION AND LACK OF COOPERATION

These six authors lived in a two-fold isolation. The majority of economists knew little or nothing about the new way of thinking, and the early marginalists knew still less about each other. The lack of communication led to a waste of intellectual labor. Unnecessary repetitions due to lack of information are typical in the history of all sciences. Newton and Leibnitz discovered calculus independently of each other. Langevin and Einstein formulated the theory of relativity in the same year.[1]

It seems that in its development marginal utility has suffered more from repetitions than have the natural sciences. The theory of marginal utility has been rediscovered more than six times! But each new attempt was not completely wasted. The writers saw new aspects of their

[1] I owe this information to Aaron Gurwitsch, Professor of Philosophy, New School of Social Research, New York City.

subject and came upon new approaches. Bernoulli, Cournot, and Dupuit applied calculus.

THE ROLE OF CALCULUS

Calculus was discovered during the last quarter of the seventeenth century. During the eighteenth century attempts to apply this new procedure to different fields of knowledge including economics became frequent.[2] The field of marginal utility is especially suited for this powerful tool of calculation. If $u(q)$ is the utility of a quantity q of goods, $u(q + \Delta q) - u(q)$ is the increase in utility corresponding to an increase in the quantity of commodities from q to $q + \Delta q$. Marginal utility is the limit of the ratio

$$\frac{u(q + \Delta q) - u(q)}{\Delta q}$$

as Δq goes to zero.[3]

Only one half of the early theorists used the new calculus; the other half, Galiani, Bentham, and even Lloyd, who was a trained mathematician, still adhered to the literary method. Thus begins the separation into two camps which is so typical for the history of the marginal utility theory. In this connection another general remark has to be made. Whether or not the one or the other method was more fruitful for the development of our concept is difficult to judge. More often than not the increase of our knowledge is not the result of an excellent method but is due to the originality of the thinker regardless of his approach. The mathematicians have worked with great exact-

[2] Leon Brunschvicg, *Les Étapes de la Philosophie Mathématique*, Bibliothèque de la Philosophie contemporaine (Paris, 1912), pp. 243ff. Chapter entitled: "La 'Métaphysique' du calcul infinitesimal." Carl Bower, *The Concepts of the Calculus* (New York, 1939).

[3] Lyman M. Kells, *Calculus* (New York, 1943). Ernst Cassirer, *Substance and Function* (New York, 1953), pp. 15-111, W. Stanley Jevons, *The Theory of Political Economy* (London, 1924), p. 51.

ness, but whether they added more depth and more new ideas than the literary authors is doubtful. Both groups have discovered the marginal utility concept and designed different models of household planning. How both subjects were treated will be discussed on the next pages.

BERNOULLI'S DISCOVERY

In 1738 Daniel Bernoulli discovered marginal utility for the first time.[4] He was especially endowed for such an investigation. Being a scion of a family of famous mathematicians and a great mathematician himself, he could skillfully use the new instrument of the calculus. Furthermore, he had a rather detailed knowledge of the contemporary achievements in the field. It is probable that his studies in Italy brought him in contact with economists who taught him the elements of the value-in-use theory. Like Buridanus he claimed that value and price are not identical. Value is determined by utility and *income*. Like later mathematical economists, Bernoulli substituted scarcity in general by the scarcity of the individual income. He recognized that the law of diminishing utility is not a theoretical law gained by reasoning, but is the offshoot of empirical observations; it is a rule with exceptions. "A rich prisoner who possesses two thousand ducats but needs two thousand ducats more to repurchase his freedom, will place a higher value on a gain of two thousand ducats than does another man who has less money than he." But Bernoulli

[4] Daniel Bernoulli, "Specimen Theoriae Novae de Mensura Sortis," *Commentarii Academiae Scientiarum Imperialis Petropolitanae*, Tomus v (1738), pp. 175-92. Two translations are available: an older German translation by Alfred Pringsheim, *Die Grundlage der modernen Wertlehre* (Leipzic, 1896), and an English translation by Louise Sommer, "Exposition of a New Theory on the Measurement of Risk," *Econometrica*, Vol. 22, No. 1 (January, 1954), pp. 23ff. Sommer produced an adequate and scholarly translation.

was of the opinion that these exceptions are so rare that he felt justified in neglecting them in his general conclusion. "The utility resulting from any small increase in wealth will be inversely proportionate to the quantity previously possessed."* Bernoulli developed the same principle more elaborately in mathematical language (see figure 1): *AC* is the fortune previously owned, *CD* the

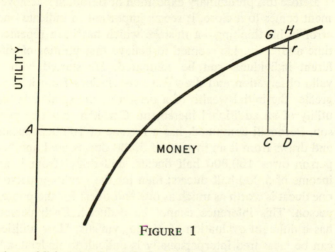

FIGURE 1

tiny additional gain, *CG* the total utility, and *rH* the small increase in utility. *AC* = *X*, *CG* = *Y*, *rH* = *DY*, *b* designates some constant data. These factors are included in the following equation:

$$dy = \frac{bdx}{x}$$

This means in geometrical terms that an additional amount *CD* of money will lead to an increase of utility *rH*. Bernoulli discovered the marginal utility of money under the condition of the law of decreasing utility, and it must be emphasized that Bernoulli deals with money and

* *David Bernoulli*, L. Sommer tr. p. 23ff.

not with goods. For Bernoulli this whole demonstration has only the character of an introduction. His main interest was the solution of problems connected with making decisions under risk. Economists finally discovered and discussed this part of Bernoulli's analysis two hundred years later. Therefore it seems appropriate to present Bernoulli's risk analysis in a later chapter.

Before this preliminary exposition of Bernoulli's achievement comes to a close, it seems important to indicate one error in his thinking—a mistake which has been repeated time and again. He seemed to believe that utilities of different individuals can be compared. He started with a valid observation and drew false conclusions from it. The greater the initial wealth of a person is, the smaller is the utility of an additional increment. Consider that one person, Bernoulli continued, has a fortune of 100,000 ducats and draws from it an income of 5,000 ducats, and another person owns 100,000 half ducats, and draws from it an income of 5,000 half ducats; then for the wealthier person one ducat is worth as much as one half ducat for the poorer person. This inference cannot be deduced. Each person has a different evaluation of his enjoyments. How utilities can be measured interpersonally is difficult to understand. The hunt for such an interindividual yardstick is still on, and the success is nil.[5]

Bernoulli had only a few followers and no one corrected his mistakes. The *Specimen Theoriae Novae* shared the fate of all the earlier books on marginalism. Natural scientists, like Buffon and Laplace, read and accepted it.[6] The only economist during the period of 1738 to 1850

---

[5] Morgenstern claimed quite recently that an interindividual comparison of utilities cannot be justified or proven, "but we live in making continuously such comparisons. . . ." "Anschauliche und axiomatische Theorie." ΑΝΤΙΔΩΡΟΝ, *Essays in Honor of Edgar Salin's 70th Birthday* (Tübingen, 1962), p. 86.

[6] My paper "Genesis," p. 659.

who understood Bernoulli's importance was Friedrich B. W. von Herrmann.[7] Galiani read Bernoulli, but was not aware of the fact that his own studies were related to the work of the Swiss mathematician.[8] Bentham, for whom Bernoulli's work might have been of importance, did not know the *Specimen Theoriae Novae*.

BENTHAM

Jeremy Bentham rediscovered marginal utility. He discovered it as a by-product of his reform projects. His central proposition, the balancing of pain and pleasure or the felicific calculus, was already known to Hobbes, Maupertuis, Beccaria, Hartley, and Helvetius.[9] The felicific calculus means: in the pursuit of pleasure man ought to watch that additional pleasure prevails over additional pain.[10] Marginal utility is an aspect of the pain and pleasure comparison. For striking a balance between these two

[7] Friedrich Benedikt Wilhelm von Herrmann, *Staatswissenschaftliche Untersuchungen* (München, 1832), p. 73. At the same time, Hermann T. Barrois mentioned Bernoulli in his "Essai sur l'application du calcul des probabilités aux assurances contre l'incendie," *Mémories de la Société Royale des Sciences de l'Agriculture et des Arts de Lille* (1834), pp. 85ff. I owe this information to Karl Borch. Kaulla claims that Gossen knew Bernoulli, or at least Bernoulli's student Laplace. For this claim, however, no documentary proof is available. Kaulla, *Die geschichtliche Entwicklung . . .* , *op. cit.*, p. 238.

[8] *Galiani*, Della Koueta Tagliacozzo (ed.), *op. cit.*, p. 209.

[9] Elie Halévi, *The Growth of Philosophical Radicalism* (New York, s.d. [1928?]), p. 33; Jacob Viner, "Bentham and John Stuart Mill. The Utilitarian Background," *American Economic Review*, Vol. 39 (1949), p. 365. "Pleasure and Pain are and always will be, the only principles of action in man." M. Helvetius, *A Treatise on Man . . .* , tr. W. Hooper, M.D. (n.p., 1810), p. 146. See also, pp. 125ff.

[10] Jeremy Bentham, *An Introduction to the Principles of Morals and Legislation* (New York, 1948), p. 1. As Halévi (*op. cit.*, p. 26) mentions, the pain-pleasure calculus is taken almost word for word from Helvetius.

emotions Bentham splits up pain and pleasure into small parts. The division of pleasure reveals the law of diminishing utility; ". . . the quantity of happiness produced by a particle of wealth (each particle being of the same magnitude) will be less and less at every particle; the second will produce less than the first, the third less than the second and so on."[11]

Like Bernoulli, his forerunner, Bentham was also interested in the possibility of measuring utility.[12] Besides the economist Stigler, the philosopher David Baumgardt described Bentham's efforts in this field.[13] Bentham knew that he was not the first writer in search of a yardstick, but neither Bernoulli nor other predecessors except Beccaria were known to him.[14] Bentham attempted several times to measure utility. Interpersonal measuring, Bentham wrote, is needed for purposes of practical legislation, for spreading happiness throughout society, but "the particular sensibility of individuals" and "diversity of circumstances" hinder the construction of a suitable yardstick.[15] In spite of these obstacles Bentham searched for the unity of measuring. He gave the number one to the smallest utility which can be felt. "Such a degree of intensity is an every day's experience; according as any pleasures are perceived to be more and more intense, they may be represented by higher and higher numbers."[16]

In another paper, which Baumgardt published com-

---

[11] *The Works of Jeremy Bentham*, ed. John Bowring (Edinburgh, 1843), 3rd vol., Pannomial fragments, ch. IV. 4, p. 229. See also, Oskar Kraus, *Zur Theorie des Wertes* (Halle, 1902), p. 59.

[12] George J. Stigler, "The Development of Utility Theory," *The Journal of Political Economy*, Vol. 58 (1950), pp. 307ff.

[13] David Baumgardt, *Bentham and the Ethics of Today* (Princeton, 1952). See especially "Measurement of Pleasure and Pain," pp. 223-36.

[14] Baumgardt, *Bentham*, p. 226.

[15] Quotations in J. Stigler, *op. cit.*, p. 309.

[16] Stigler, *op. cit.*, p. 310.

pletely for the first time, Bentham measured utility in money.[17] Bentham is aware of the essential obstacle, the law of diminishing utility. *"One Guinea*, suppose, gives a man *one* degree of pleasure; . . . it is not true by any means that a *million* of guineas given to the same man at the same time would give him a *million* of such degrees of pleasure."[18] But the law of diminishing utility is only efficient if great changes in the amount of money occur. It does not work with relatively small increases and decreases of income. Bentham is of the opinion that the marginal utility of money falls very slowly. If we deal with small quantities "the proportion between pleasure and pleasure" will be very near the relation between corresponding sums of money. For all practical purposes money is capable of measuring pleasure.

Would it have helped better understanding of measuring if Bentham had published these subtle reflections? It is very doubtful. Many economists of his time knew Bentham and no one saw that some of the theories of the great utilitarian can be applied in economics. David Ricardo, James Mill, and John Stuart Mill were Bentham's friends and devoted followers, but all three of them had their blind spot; it did not occur to them to apply the felicific calculus to economic value.[19]

The majority of later economists did not pay any more attention to Bentham than his contemporaries did. William Stanley Jevons was an exception. It is very unlikely that Gossen knew the British hedonist.[20] Neither Walras nor Menger had any contact with this discoverer of marginal utility.

[17] Baumgardt, *Bentham*, p. 554. Bentham MSS, University College, London, Portfolio 27, folder 5, sheet 32, pp. 1f.

[18] Baumgardt, *Bentham*, p. 559.

[19] Leslie Stephen, *The English Utilitarians* (London, 1950), Vol. 2, pp. 7ff. Elie Halévi, *op. cit.*, p. 107.

[20] See ch. IV on Gossen.

The neglect of Bentham's ideas left room for another round of discoveries. The new constructions created in the first half of the nineteenth century show different aspects, for scientific interests underwent a change. Mountiford Longfield in Ireland, Augustin Cournot and Juvenal Dupuit in France, and Mangoldt in Germany are more interested in the application of marginal utility to prices than in the deeper understanding of marginal utility itself.[21] Cournot, Dupuit, and Mangoldt independently discovered the demand curve.

This section of the study leaves out the most important contribution; Gossen's work is not mentioned. It will be discussed in the next chapter. Even without him and in spite of the wasteful repetition much progress had been made. The law of diminishing utility had been clearly formulated, final or marginal utility had been isolated, the connection between utility, income, and price had been seen, and even the measuring of utility had been investigated although with little success. But the main question was very seldom asked: what is the connection between the marginal utility of one good and the utility of other goods of equal quality? The building erected accidentally without a unifying plan and with many architects lacked its capstone.

GALIANI, LLOYD, AND CONSUMER BEHAVIOR

Lloyd raised this essential question in connection with his analysis of household planning, the blueprint that under-

[21] Mountifort Longfield, Fellow of Trinity College, Dublin, and Professor of Political Economy, *Lectures on Political Economy*, delivered in Trinity and Michaelmas term, 1833 (Dublin, 1834). Augustin Cournot, *Researches into the Mathematical Principles of the Theory of Wealth* (1838), tr. Nathaniel T. Bacon (New York, 1897). Juvenal Dupuit, "De L'Utilité et de sa Mesure," *Ecrits choisis et republiés par Mario de Bernardi, La riforma sociale* (Torino, 1933). H. V. Mangoldt, *Grundriss der Volkswirtschaftslehre* (Stuttgart, 1863), p. 48, especially.

lies household management. He, and before him Galiani, dealt with this problem. These two men, the Italian abbé and the Oxford don, came to similar results, although they were separated by eighty-five years and had different outlooks on life and divergent training in economics. Besides, there is reason to believe that the younger author never had read a line of Galiani's works.

I have already described how Galiani developed his own value-in-use theory. This is not his only achievement. He forms a bridge between the traditional value-in-use theory and a more modern understanding of consumer behavior. Galiani asked: What will happen when the consumer intends to satisfy several needs requiring diversified goods? He believed that in this case the needs of higher importance will be satisfied first; when these are satiated, suddenly (subito) the ones of lower rank become urgent; their saturation stresses the demands of still smaller intensity, and so forth.[22]

The rank of needs is determined by physiological and social considerations and not by personal decisions. The preservation of life, and the desire for food, clothing, and shelter hold the highest ranks. Next on this scale are marks of distinction, titles, honors, nobility, authority. The third station is occupied by beauty. We adorn our women and our children with gems, gold, silver, and works of art, Galiani wrote, to show our tenderness and love. So Galiani's "felicitá" (happiness or comfort) is dictated by the tastes of the good society of Naples. Galiani sketched a rough draft of a household plan. His explanation was original but not accurate. He believed that each consumer covers one class of needs completely before he starts to satisfy a lower group of desires. He did not see that in all classes of wants a similar degree of satisfaction can be reached. Lloyd avoided this error.

[22] Monroe, p. 285; Tagliacozzo, p. 96.

That William F. Lloyd's work remained unknown from 1833 to 1913, when Seligman found it, is a proof that modesty can go too far.[23] Lloyd published his Oxford lecture only because this was required by statute.[24] Even the great honor of being elected a member of the Royal Society of London could not induce him to spread his ideas around.[25] After his terms as lecturer had expired, he took over a parish, and died completely forgotten.[26] William F. Lloyd was a younger contemporary of Bentham, but the young clergyman, who was also the brother of a famous divine, was not influenced by hedonism. In his lectures he did not tell us who his intellectual mentor was, but he revealed his scientific opponents. Lloyd wrote mostly against Adam Smith, for the author of the *Wealth of Nations* mistook utility for value in his value paradox. Utility in Lloyd's terminology includes all the technical services which can be derived from a group of goods. Lloyd explains value as marginal utility; even the word *margin* is correctly used in this connection.[27] Man is aware of this margin by a feeling of "the loss of gratification contingent on the loss of the object."[28] The loss clarifies the essence of marginal utility better than earlier courses of reasoning. Lloyd anticipated one of Menger's main arguments.

Lloyd also improved Galiani's consumer preference

[23] E. R. A. Seligman, "On some Neglected British Economists," *Economic Journal*, Vol. 13 (September, 1913), pp. 353-67.

[24] William F. Lloyd, "A Lecture on the Nature of Value . . ." delivered before the University of Oxford in Michaelmas term 1833 (Oxford, 1834). Reprinted as an "Early Exposition of 'Final Utility,' " ed. R. F. Harrod. See also Harrod's introduction, "Economic History" (a supplement to the *Economic Journal*), Vol. 1 (1926-29), pp. 168-83. Quotations in text are from the Harrod edition.

[25] *Proceedings of the Royal Society of London*, 1833-34, No. 16.

[26] *Alumni Oxoniensis*, The Members of the University of Oxford (Oxford, 1888), Vol. 3, p. 475.

[27] Harrod, "Early Exposition," p. 174.

[28] *Ibid.*

scheme. Lloyd's theory of consumer strategy was developed out of his value and utility theory. A good such as water which satisfies very urgent as well as minor usages has a great technical usefulness. The technical utility of other classes of goods may be smaller. We feel the whole weight of utility if we lose at once a whole group of goods. But in most cases the consumer envisages only the loss of the last portions; he operates on the "margin of separation between the satisfied and the unsatisfied wants."[29] It can happen that the desire for the most useful good is lower than the desire for goods which serve demands of lower ranks of urgency. Speaking before students who were not used to this way of thinking, Lloyd compared for the sake of clarification the different utilities with the springs of a watch. The mainspring is extremely strong like the utility of objects which serve very important wants. The hairspring resembles a group of goods which satisfy wants of smaller importance. The wound-up hairspring is much weaker than the wound-up mainspring. "Yet when some play has been allowed" to the mainspring, "the force even of the hairspring of a watch shall be sufficient to keep it in its place."[30] Will Lloyd indicate that ultimately the last needs satisfied in a higher class are of the same intensity or value as those satisfied in a lower group? It seems so and yet, although Lloyd returns several times to the same question, he does not come out with a clear statement. Two years after Lloyd's death Gossen provided a consistent explanation.

[29] *Ibid.*
[30] *Ibid.*, p. 173.

CHAPTER IV

GOSSEN'S SYNTHESIS

INTELLECTUAL BACKGROUND

In his short life Hermann Heinrich Gossen (1810-1858) had more than his share of life's unkept promises.[1] He was neither successful as a civil servant nor as a business man. He hoped that his book *The Laws of Human Relations*[2] (1854) would bring him the fame of Copernicus, but he died unknown and neglected. Only later generations recognized his genius. It is easy to poke fun at his vainglorious self-advertisement; but one should not forget that he did not overrate himself very much. Gossen deserves the title of genius because he is the most original thinker and the only system builder in the whole group of early explorers in this field of economics. He claimed, not without exaggeration, that he designed all his scientific tools during "twenty years of reflection" without gaining any information from the other authors who worked in the same field. But it is very likely that he knew the French hedonists of the eighteenth century, especially Maupertuis

---

[1] Gisbert Beyerhaus, "Hermann Heinrich Gossen und seine Zeit," *Zeitschrift für Volkswirtschaft und Sozialpolitik*, N.F. v (Wien, 1927), p. 522; Karl Robert Blum, "Die subjektivistisch-psychologischen Wertlehren" (Doctoral thesis, Giessen, Germany, 1934); Hermann Riedel, "Hermann Heinrich Gossen, 1810-1858" (Doctoral thesis, Winterthur, 1953).

[2] Gossen, *Entwickelung der Gesetze des menschlichen Verkehrs und der daraus fliessenden Regeln für menschliches Handeln* (Braunschweig, Fr. Vieweg & Sohn, 1854). The so-called second edition of Berlin in 1889 is nothing but the first edition with a new title page and a new cover. In 1927 a third edition was also published in Berlin. If not marked otherwise, I quote from the second edition.

and Helvetius. He knew neither Bentham[3] nor the German theorists of subjective value. Gossen accused the economists of not knowing mathematics and of believing in the intrinsic value of goods.[4] Intrinsic value was a reminiscence from his academic training at the University of Bonn, where young Gossen heard the economist Peter Kaufmann (1804-1872).[5] Gossen's first and, perhaps, last mentor in the economic field indeed taught that economic values have

[3] About Bentham's influence on Gossen a controversy exists between the late Professor Oskar Kraus, Prague, and Gisbert Beyerhaus. Kraus denied that Bentham had any influence on Gossen. Kraus pointed out the great similarity between a Bentham and a Gossen quotation (*The Works of Jeremy Bentham*, ed. John Bowring [Edinburgh, 1843], Vol. 3, Pannomial fragments, ch. IV, 4, p. 229; Gossen, *der Gesetze*, p. 31), but, paradoxically enough, Kraus maintains that this similarity is no proof because Gossen claimed that he alone discovered his own theory. Beyerhaus and also Hayek (Hayek's introduction to the third edition of Gossen's book, p. xi, n.1) believe that Gossen was influenced by Bentham. Beyerhaus assumed that Gossen may have read Bentham's *Principles of Moral Legislation*, which was published in a German translation in Cologne in 1833. This does not prove that Gossen read Bentham. Besides, marginal utility is explained in the Pannomial fragments which were *not* translated. I think Kraus is right for the wrong reason. Gossen's declaration of his own originality must not be accepted without a grain of salt. Gossen's character does not exclude bragging. But it is much more likely that an intellectual from the Rhineland knew the French hedonists, especially Maupertuis and Helvetius, than that he read Bentham. French ideas had a decisive influence on Rhenish liberal and radical thinking, but not British ideas.

[4] Gossen, *Gesetze*, pp. 46-47, 87. Gossen's knowledge of mathematics apparently was not flawless. Gossen "may seem somewhat deficient in the quality of mathematical elegance." F. Y. Edgeworth, "Gossen" in *Palgrave's Dictionary of Political Economy* (London, 1923), II, 232.

[5] See the "Quästurakten" (registration files), the University of Bonn, quoted in Beyerhaus, "Gossen," p. 527, n.1. Gossen took in the winter semester of 1829-30 a social science survey course (Enzyklopädie der Staats—und Kameralwissenschaften) under Peter Kaufmann.

an intrinsic character.[6] Gossen did not adhere to the views of his master; he created his own theory of value.

ECONOMICS AND RELIGION

Gossen's economic theory is interwoven with a new religion. His book is partly homily, partly mathematical theory. His faith grew out of the intellectual and spiritual situation of his native Rhineland in the early nineteenth century. This most western part of the Germanies was a meeting ground of French and German ideas.[7] Catholic clericalism joined forces with political romanticism to fight against enlightenment. The opposition centered around Saint-Simonism.[8] Gossen took part in this fight of ideas. He was an ardent critic of the Roman Catholic church and had strong leanings toward Saint-Simon and Comte, because he believed in the salvation of mankind by science, and he considered himself the priest of this new scientific religion.[9] An essential part of this faith is the Hedonist

[6] Dr. Peter Kaufmann, *Untersuchungen im Gebiete der politischen Oekonomie betreffend Adam Smith und seiner Schule staatswissenschaftliche Grundsätze* (Erste Abtheilung, Bonn, 1829), pp. 15, 29, 89, 155ff. Roscher considered Kaufmann's criticism of Adam Smith very valuable. Wilhelm Roscher, *Geschichte der Nationalökonomik in Deutschland* (München, 1874), pp. 993-94. It is noteworthy that Kaufmann's book contains a mathematical explanation of the quantity theory of money.

[7] Justus Hashagen, "Das Geistesleben im Wandel der Zeiten" in *Geschichte des Rheinlandes von den ältesten Zeit bis zur Gegenwart* (Essen an der Ruhr, 1922), especially p. 334. Gisbert Beyerhaus, "Ludolf Camphausen. Staat und Wirtschaft 1848," *Deutsche Rundschau*, Vol. 205, pp. 24ff. Beyerhaus, "Gossen," *op. cit.*, pp. 522ff. Johanna Köster, "Der rheinische Frühliberalismus und die soziale Frage" (Doctoral thesis, Berlin, 1938).

[8] Johanna Köster, *Frühliberalismus*, p. 37.

[9] "Priester dieser Religion sind die Menschen, denen es gelingt, ein neues Gesetz zu entdecken, oder ein bekanntes näher zu bestimmen, oder seine Erkenntnis weiter zu verbreiten, und sie verkündigen mit jeder neuen Belehrung mit Posaunenschall stärker als der, der die Mauern von Jericho zum Einsturz brachte, die Macht, Weisheit und Güte des Schöpfers." English translation E.K.

Deism of the enlightenment. Gossen was convinced that God has created a harmonious world in which everybody can enjoy his life. The average man knows only vaguely, but Gossen, the self-appointed secretary of the joy-spending divinity, sees clearly the plans of God.[10] For the benefit of his fellow men he wrote down rules for the right conduct for happy living. The motto of the book, Friedrich Schiller's "Ode to Joy," prepares the reader for Gossen's message.

These new tidings are revealed in economic laws which Gossen expounds in words, in algebraic equations, and in geometrical figures. He rediscovered theories like the law of decreasing utility and the balance of pain and pleasure, which already were known to his forerunners. What is more important, he tackled problems which were not seen before him, such as the equalization of different want-satisfactions, imputation, etc. Because Gossen wrote as a moralist and an economist, these theories are prescriptions in a guidebook to the happy life as well as being related parts of an equilibrium system that embraces the whole economy.

Man seeks the maximum of happiness; this is the central thesis for the moralist and for the economist Gossen.[11] The degree of happiness can be expressed in quantities.[12] Under given social circumstances the quantities that one person has cannot be compared with the quantities en-

---

"Priests of this religion are those people who succeed in discovering a new law or in giving a better explanation of a known law, or in broadcasting the knowledge of this law and each new doctrine which they proclaim, announcing more strongly than the trumpet which destroyed the wall of Jericho the power, wisdom and kindness of the creator." Gossen, *Gesetze*, p. 188.

[10] Helvetius also crusaded against Roman Catholicism and preached a natural religion of happiness. Helvetius, *Treatise on Man*, pp. 52ff.

[11] Gossen, *Gesetze*, p. 3.

[12] *Ibid.*, p. 71.

joyed by another human being, for the king, the beggar, the rake, and the monk are worlds apart in terms of happiness.[13] Gossen hoped that education would equalize the pleasure feelings of everybody, so that eventually quantities could be compared.[14] He was not satisfied with this postponement to a future and more propitious date. Later in his book he suggested that one pleasure can be arbitrarily chosen as unit of measuring. Like Bentham, he selected money.[15]

GOSSEN'S ECONOMIC THEORY

The intensity of pleasure-feelings is regulated by the well-known law of diminishing utility, which Gossen rediscovered, and following Wieser, has been called, with doubtful justification, "Gossen's first law." Gossen emphasized the psychological and physiological aspects of this principle. The more a person eats of one kind of food at one sitting the less he enjoys his meal. The more the artist looks at the same beautiful work, or the scientist returns to the same trend of thought, the less he will enjoy his activity.[16] Whenever the saturation point is reached, boredom and disgust set in. These obnoxious consequences can be avoided if man pays attention to the following factors: time, the variety of needs, the pleasure-pain relation, and money.

The lack of available time forbids the complete satisfaction of all needs,[17] of which a variegated multitude exists. The problem of how to plan the best gratification

---

[13] *Ibid.*, p. 1.   [14] *Ibid.*, p. 85.

[15] Page 123. George J. Stigler, *Utility Theory* . . . , p. 315.

[16] Gossen, *Gesetze*, pp. 4ff.

[17] Gossen does not explain his meaning of the time element. According to the whole context, it may be a time interval in which a given income is consumed. That Gossen meant the psychological time interval, as Baggiotti claims, is rather doubtful. Tullio Baggiotti, "Reminiszenzen anlässlich des hundertsten Jahrestages des Erscheinens des Buches von Gossen," *Zeitschrift für Nationalökonomie* (Vienna, 1957), XVII, 40.

of divergent needs which have different intensities had interested Galiani and William F. Lloyd. Both observed that the less powerful needs become more urgent after the stronger wants are satisfied.

Gossen surpassed his forerunners: he offered a conclusive explanation because he balanced the marginal utilities in different classes of wants; that had not been done before him. Consumption in different groups of wants (e.g., food, living quarters, clothing, etc.) need not be satisfied entirely, as Galiani assumed; it can be broken off anywhere, because the whole consumption process can be chopped off into small "atoms." This fractionalization of enjoyment allows the consumer to break off satisfaction, so that in each class of needs Gossen's last atom brings the same enjoyment.[18] This law of the equalization of marginal utilities, of maximalization of utilities, has been called by Wieser "Gossen's second law." Gossen's discovery provided a satisfactory answer for several generations of economists, until Wieser himself and his followers challenged the validity of this theory.

Gossen explains this law with a geometrical figure. In figure 1, time is represented by the horizontal and pleasure

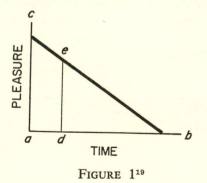

FIGURE 1[19]

[18] Gossen, *Gesetze*, pp. 12, 33.   [19] *Ibid.*, p. 29.

by the vertical. If the available time is *ad*, then *ed* is a possible enjoyment. In all fields of enjoyment men will reach *ed*. Gossen uses variations of this figure to explain the balancing of pain and pleasure.[20]

Next to time it is labor which prevents absolute satisfaction in all fields of wants. Gossen's theory of labor greatly resembles Helvetius' and also Bentham's balancing of pain and pleasure; the geometrical presentation was new.

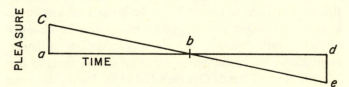

FIGURE 2[21]

The horizontal *ad* (figure 2) represents time in which labor is applied. As in figure 1, the vertical measures pleasure. In the beginning work does not create pain, but rather pleasure *ac*. With the increase of work, pleasure decreases and eventually changes to pain. At point *b*, a situation of indifference is reached where neither pleasure nor pain is felt; at the time limit *d*, the pain is equal to *de*.

To compare the feelings caused by production and consumption, Gossen used an ingenious device which has

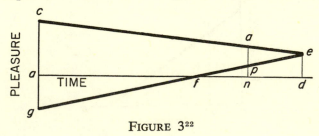

FIGURE 3[22]

[20] *Ibid.*, pp. 38, 45.   [21] *Ibid.*, p. 37.
[22] *Ibid.*, p. 41. Figure simplified.

often been imitated. He reversed figure 2, and superimposed it on figure 1, which remains in its original form.

In figure 3, *ag* is pleasure derived from work at its initial stage, *ge* marks pain and pleasure in relation to the horizonal *ad*, and *f* is a point of indifference between pain and pleasure. The elevation *ce*, over *ad*, represents pleasure in the field of consumption. To the time interval *an*, corresponds the pain *np*; at *an*, the total pleasure is *gfpqc*. The maximum of pleasure is reached at the time limit *ad*, where pleasure is represented by the triangle *gec*. This balance of pain and pleasure is valid for the isolated Robinson Crusoe, who works only for himself, and for the man who produces for the market. In the exchange economy enjoyment is calculated by comparing the marginal utility of the good bought with the marginal disutility caused by the production of the good offered for sale.[23] Buying and selling presuppose the existence of money, which, so Gossen points out, reflects the pleasure-pain calculation. The last atom of money has to bring the same pleasure in different classes of wants.

Gossen carried the equalization of marginal pleasures rather far. He was not satisfied with the balancing of the last atoms in *one* household; he even claimed that two people will exchange as long as "the value of different objects for both exchanging individuals are the same." Although he added the restriction that both traders must act under the same conditions,[24] Walras, the founder of the school of Lausanne, objected to Gossen's conclusions. According to Walras, the situation described by Gossen could exist only under the conditions of a communist state.[25] Gossen believed that the market economy under certain circumstances can achieve this balancing.

[23] *Ibid.*, p. 90. [24] *Ibid.*, pp. 82, 83, 85.
[25] See Léon Walras, *Études d'Économie Sociale* (Lausanne, 1896), pp. 209-11. Gossen stressed much more than Walras the

With the introduction of the market economy Gossen, the moralist, loses out against Gossen, the economist. In the money economy, competition will equalize marginal enjoyment for each and everybody. The maximum of utility will be accomplished behind the back of the individual. The hortatory pages in which Gossen calls on every reader to follow the laws of God's creation become superfluous, because the individual can rely on the market mechanism and not on his own decision.

Another riddle lies in his concept of an economic system. Side by side with the functional system which explains how the individual will be maneuvered into a position of maximal utility is a causal organization which does not dovetail with the first structure. The gist of the first fabric of thought is that an equilibrium is reached whenever pain and pleasure balance. In Gossen's mathematical system pain and pleasure are two independent variables. Pains are costs, but when Gossen changes from a functional to a causal explanation, costs (i.e., pains) are no longer independent variables; they are the effect of consumer valuation. Gossen, using the functional and the causal approach, becomes inconsistent. Gossen applied causality mainly for explaining the relation between costs and consumer goods.

The value derived from the finished goods is transferred to the factors of production.[26] Gossen was very possibly the first author who discovered subjective imputation or the theory of psychological accounting which balances the enjoyment derived from the finished goods with the costs of the factors of production. He saw the main difficulty inherent in such a value transfer: the enjoyment is one

---

idea of equality, while Walras paid much more attention to freedom. It is possible that Helvetius convinced Gossen that all men are equally well organized and "have an equal disposition for understanding." Helvetius, *Treatise on Man*, p. 95.

[26] Gossen, *Gesetze*, pp. 25ff.

undivided psychological experience; the factors of production are many. How is it possible to split up the value unit into many particles and assign them to the produced goods? A few decades later the Austrian economists developed many ingenious patterns attempting to give satisfactory answers to this question. Contrary to his followers, Gossen expressed a healthy skepticism about the possibility of finding the "right" key for such a distribution. He emphasized that no fast and fixed rule can be offered. Like later Austrian writers, he believed that loss of the factor and the difficulty of its replacement determine the rating of one separated factor of production. But he did not construct a general scheme, for cases are too much at variance with each other.[27] With the discussion of imputation Gossen's causal system comes to a close. In comparison with the functional analysis Gossen's causal system is somewhat sketchy.

Gossen worked with two different methods. Later generations used either the one or the other approach. One group thought mainly in the relation of cause and effect while their opponents constructed economic theory as a functional system of equations and curves. Both schools could have grafted their work on Gossen's findings, but in the next two decades the *Laws of Human Relations* was almost forgotten.

[27] Gossen describes one case which reappears also in Boehm-Bawerk's system. The comfort of a well-heated room is dependent on the oven, the heating material, and the fire. If the fire cannot be kindled, but oven and heating material are available, then the whole value will be contributed to the fire. If one factor of the combination is missing, then the lacking piece can have the value of the whole combination. See Gossen, *Gesetze*, pp. 25ff.

PART II

THE ACCEPTANCE OF
THE MARGINAL UTILITY THEORY

CHAPTER V

THE RISE OF MARGINALISM

THE FORGOTTEN GOSSEN

BEFORE 1870 Gossen's work had not been read by prominent economists. Only Gyula Kautz, an Hungarian economist, and Friedrich Albert Lange, a German philosopher, mentioned it.[1] After 1870 the *Laws of Human Relations* became famous. An abrupt change had occurred. Marginal utility was no longer a subject described by a fringe group of isolated scientists but rather was the central problem of economic thinking. Menger, Jevons, and Walras rediscovered marginal utility; now at last the consumer value theory was discussed and interpreted. The triumvirate of rediscoverers even established schools.

THE CLASSICAL VALUE CONCEPT

The state of economic science during the second half of the nineteenth century and the strange role of economic value explain the great and rising interest in the theory of marginal utility. John Stuart Mill had published in 1848 his *Principles*, the last great work of the classical school. About that time economists became tired of theory. They found economic analysis inconsistent. The inconsistency was partly due to the development of the value concept. From the end of the seventeenth century until the first

---

[1] See Julius Kautz, *Die Nationalökonomie als Wissenschaft* (Wien, 1858), p. 9; also Kautz, *Die Geschichtliche Entwicklung der Nationalökonomie* (Wien, 1860), p. 704. Jevons did not know him before 1879. William Stanley Jevons, *Theory of Political Economy* (London, 1879), pp. xxxv-xlii. Walras wrote a paper about Gossen, "Un économiste inconnu Hermann-Henri Gossen," *Journal des Économistes* (April-May, 1885).

decades of the twentieth century the value idea played an exaggerated role in economic thinking. All that time value had the same position in economics as the atom and the electron have in modern physics. Lauderdale had already understood the situation when he sneeringly called value the philosopher's stone.[2] Much later Gottl-Ottlilienfeld characterized value as a "veiled" dogma.[3] For many economists value became the building material with which economic systems were constructed, the final cause for exchange, the purchasing power of money, and distribution. Value even ought to measure the economic significance of goods. To satisfy these and other functions Sir William Petty, Locke, Smith, and Ricardo selected the labor value theory. This was an inconsistent construction indeed. Adam Smith already knew that; he formulated, according to Wieser's interpretation, a philosophical theory in which labor alone determines the exchange of goods, and an empirical theory in which goods exchange according to wages, profit, and rent. From the publication of his *Principles* to the last days of his life, Ricardo was irritated by the discrepancy between theoretical and empirical exchange. Following his general assumption, commodities ought to be exchanged according to embodied labor, but they were not in reality, because profits interfered grossly with his law of value. Nassau-Senior did not settle the question when he substituted labor by two elements of costs: labor *and* abstinence. He gave up the uniformity of value so that measuring was no longer possible. Neither he nor John Stuart

[2] James Maitland, the eighth Earl of Lauderdale, *An Inquiry into the Nature and Origin of Public Wealth* . . . (2nd ed.; Edinburgh, 1819), p. 21. See also Emil Kauder, "The Retarded Acceptance of the Marginal Utility Theory," *Quarterly Journal of Economics*, LXVII (1953), p. 574.

[3] Friedrich von Gottl-Ottlilienfeld, *Der Wertgedanke ein verhülltes Dogma der Nationalökonomie* (1897), reprinted in *Wirtschaft als Leben* (Jena, 1925), pp. 2-15.

Mill improved the situation when they tried to glue together a value concept with the divergent elements: costs and utility. After Mill the construction of value along classical lines was abandoned.

LETHARGY AND OPPOSITION

After 1850 a certain lethargy was setting in. Gossen was not read. Neither Dupuit nor Cournot had many followers. The historical school had a dominant influence in Northern Germany. Lorenz von Stein, the brilliant but confused Hegelian, taught economics at the University of Vienna. The European West still clung to the remnants of classical thinking. Even after 1870, this state of indifference was not disturbed by the appearance of three books on marginal utility. They were read, book reports were written, but not until after 1880 did the majority of economists seriously study the new principles to discover that ten years before three young economists had wrecked the foundation of classicism and had begun to build a new theory.[4] This slow and faltering recognition was in sharp contrast with the sudden revolution created by Keynes in 1936, when, after a short resistance, the majority of Anglo-American economists became Keynesians. In 1880, older established schools did not capitulate before the new value philosophy. Historians like Schmoller, defenders of classicism like Heinrich Dietzel, and the Marxists fought against the marginal theory. Knies, one of the founders of the older historical school, did not accept Menger's theory although he was generous enough to let Wieser speak about it in the Heidelberg seminar.[5]

The avant-garde of the young marginalists had read

[4] R. S. Howey, *The Rise of the Marginal Utility School*, pp. 139ff.

[5] Friedrich Freiherr von Wieser, *Gesammelte Abhandlungen* (Tübingen, 1929), pp. viii-xi, 377ff.

Menger. Six years passed, 1870 to 1876, before two of Menger's followers, Wieser and Boehm-Bawerk, were sufficiently imbued with the new doctrine to defend the thesis of their master before Knies, and another six years passed before their first original works were published.[6] In England, Switzerland, and Italy the situation was similar; the new doctrine was not seriously studied before 1880. Marshall's conciliatory attitude combining classicism and the new ideas prevented in England the heated arguments which were so typical for Germany.

Much later, in 1907, Wieser spoke about his reason for accepting Menger's value. "Political economy cannot be explained without having the value explained first. And so I started here and, riding on the plank of the value theory, I drifted into the boundless ocean of social phenomena."[7] In a similar vein, Boehm-Bawerk spoke about value as the pass key for solving economic problems. It is very probable that these words also expressed the convictions of others who joined the new group.

This rather unexciting explanation is based on the known facts set forth here. Other explanations disregard the historical facts; the favorite Marxian interpretation unmasks the new value theory as a defense for the interests of the ruling classes. As Marxians and many non-Marxians have claimed time and again that marginal value theory is nothing but an ideology, it seems appropriate to discuss this thesis in the following appendix.

[6] Wieser was not Menger's student at the university but accepted Menger's book as foundation for further work. See Hayek's letter to Wesley Mitchell of April 16, 1924, Wesley Mitchell Collection (Columbia Library).

[7] Friedrich von Wieser, "Arma Virumque Cano," *Gesammelte Abhandlungen*, p. 239.

APPENDIX TO CHAPTER V

THE MARXIAN INTERPRETATION OF
THE MARGINAL UTILITY THEORY

FOR the Marxists the schools of marginal utility are an an-
noying stumbling block.[8] Karl Marx had explained the
"true" laws of capitalism in *Das Capital,* and just three
years after its publication new non-Marxian theories
emerged. The new marginalists, the Viennese Fuchs com-
mented, could not be guided by scientific curiosity; if this
were the case, only socialist systems could have come into
existence.[9] The supporters of marginal utility must have
been motivated by the economic interests of the ruling
bourgeois class. The hunt for these presumed class interests turned up two hidden ideologies. Marginalism is a
propaganda for the consumption habits of the decadent
bourgeois classes, and a weapon in the fight of the middle
classes against communism.

Bukharin denounced the new economists as advertising
agents of the bourgeois class. He claimed that the marginalists, especially the Austrian economists, described only
the psychology of a bourgeoisie which is "distinctly para-
sitical, . . . has already lost its function of social utility"
and is "concerned only with riding mounts, with expensive
rugs, with fragrant cigars, and the wine of Tokay."[10] This
portrait whose colors are *borrowed* from his older con-

8 Nikolai Bukharin, *The Economic Theory of the Leisure Class*
(New York, 1927); Albert Fuchs, *Geistige Strömungen in Oesterreich, 1876-1918* (Wien, 1949); Fritz Behrens, "Hermann Heinrich Gossen oder Geburt der wissenschaftlichen Apologetik des
Kapitalismus," *Leipziger Schriften zur Gesellschaftswissenschaft*
(Leipzic, 1949), 1 Heft.
9 Albert Fuchs, *Geistige Strömungen . . . ,* p. 27.
10 Nikolai Bukharin, *Economic Theory . . . ,* p. 25.

temporary Veblen is undoubtedly closer to a caricature than to a serious description. But this is not the essential point. An ideology in the sense of Karl Marx should *conceal* and not *advertise* the true interests of the leading class. The adherents of marginal utility claimed quite openly that man's main interest in economics is consumption. Besides, are only the rich capitalists interested in eating and drinking? Are not the lower classes much more concerned with their needs for subsistence than the affluent group? Marginal utility applies to the behavior of all consumers regardless of social rank.

The argument that the members of the new schools used their theories for combating Marxian ideas makes more sense than Bukharin's artificial construction. Some empirical evidence can be offered: Wieser and John Bates Clark did oppose Marxism, and Boehm-Bawerk wrote a famous repudiation of the Marxian system. But this would prove ideological bias only if these authors had attacked Marxism *mala fide*, if they were secretly convinced that labor value, the law of exploitation, the theory of increasing misery were correct, if they wrote against their better conviction as paid handmaidens of the bourgeois class. No proof for such dishonesty can be offered. The supporters of marginal utility wrote against Marxism because they were convinced that Karl Marx had created theories inconsistent in logic and contradictory to the facts.

Whoever accuses the marginalists of dishonesty neglects essential facts of history. First, he mixes up the time table. Walras, Jevons, and Menger worked out their solution of the value problem between 1860 and 1870, at the time when Marx was writing *Das Capital*. It was not until 1880 that the standard work of Marx entered the general discussions. How could the triumvirate Jevons, Menger, and Walras criticize *Das Capital* before they had read it? Second, Menger, Walras, and Wicksell were politically unsuited to support bourgeois interests. Walras' appointment to the University of Lausanne was opposed by a minority of the nominating committee because he was allegedly a communist.[11] Menger was a typical Austrian liberal trained in the Josephinic tradition.[12] He was against bigotry and anti-semitism; he opposed militarism and dueling; the glory of war, he said, is not the high point of man's achievement. He wrote into one of Knies' books: "The prevailing historiography is not satisfactory. The historian teaches battles but not those factors which determine the progress of man."[13] Although his family belonged to the petty nobility (Carl von Menger, Edler von Wolfesgrün), he was very critical of the feudal pillars of the Hapsburg monarchy—clergy, army, and nobility.[14] In 1878 Crown Prince Rudolf, with the help of Menger, his former tutor and trusted friend, wrote an anonymous paper about the Austrian high aristocracy in which he criticized their luxury, their life without responsibility, and their insipid amusements.[15]

[11] Marcel Boson, *Léon Walras* (Paris, Lausanne, 1951), p. 94.

[12] See Emil Kauder, "Menger and his Library," *The Economic Review*, edited by the Institute of Economic Research, Hitotsubashi University, Kunitachi, Tokyo, Vol. X, no. 1 (January, 1959), p. 63.

[13] Karl Knies, *Die politische Oekonomie vom Standpunkt der geschichtlichen Methode* (Braunschweig, 1853), p. 11. Menger's remark in his copy: "Die Geschichtsforschung (die herrschende) befriedigt nicht. Sie lehrt Schlachten etc.; aber nicht die den Fortschritt der Menschen bestimmenden (dauernd nachwirkenden) Entwicklungen."

[14] See his remarks in Karl Friedrich Rau, *Grundsätze der Volkswirtschaftslehre* (7th ed.; Leipzig, 1863). More in my paper, "Freedom and Economic Theory," second research report on Menger's unpublished papers, *Hitotsubashi Journal of Economics*, Hitotsubashi University, Kunitachi, Tokyo, Japan, Vol. 2, no. 1 (September, 1961), pp. 67ff.

[15] *Der österreichische Adel und sein konstitutioneller Beruf. Mahnruf an die aristokratische Jugend* (Von einem Oesterreicher, München, 1878). This pamphlet was published anonymously. In 1906 it became known that crown prince Rudolf was the author.

In the field of political economy, economic freedom is Menger's ideal. Men are free if they are ends and not means nor economic goods as the slaves of classical times.[16] But not all people as Menger sees them have reached this stage. Married women and especially the members of the lower classes are still half-slaves. They are somewhat better off than they were in earlier times. Their chains are longer than previously. A poor girl has often only the choice between becoming a prostitute or a seamstress.[17]

Economic progress will improve the situation of the poor. The luxury of the rich hinders the advancement of the lower classes. Here the young Menger finds the root of social evil.[18] "The more the rich people consume, the merrier one lives in the present disregarding future development. If the rich people did not live a gay life, all the workers would have good living quarters; there would be

Neue Freie Presse (Wien), April 10, 1906, N. 14959, p. 11. See also Oskar Freiherr von Mitis, *Das Leben des Kronprinzen Rudolf* (Leipzic, 1928), p. 37. Heinz Gollwitzer, *Die Standesherrn* (Stuttgart, 1957), p. 188. Reading this pamphlet, I came to the conclusion that Menger cooperated widely in the writing. First, the writer had an exact knowledge of the legal and economic studies at the University of Vienna. One cannot expect that the crown prince was informed about all these details (Mahnruf, pp. 37ff.). Second, the author or authors demand that the studies in the history of law must be shortened (pp. 38ff.). This is Menger's hobby horse, the eternal war against historicism.

[16] It is amusing that Menger, who had such strong sympathies for the poor, has been accused by Bukharin of being a defender of bourgeois class interests. Nikolai Bukharin, *Economic Theory . . . ,* pp. 25ff.

[17] See Menger's own notes to his *Grundsätze der Volkswirtschaftslehre.* These notes are at the Menger Library, Hitotsubashi University. A mimeographic transliteration has been published in Tokyo, 1961, under the title, *Carl Menger's Zusätze zu Grundsätze der Volkswirtschaftslehre;* pp. 28, 59.

[18] Menger's notes to Karl Friedrich Rau, *Grundsätze der Volkswirtschaftslehre* (7th ed.; Leipzig, 1863). These notes written in October, 1867, may well be the first attempt to write his principles.

brick layers and carpenters instead of hairdressers and whores." But the youthful reformer is at a loss to find well-defined targets for his attacks. What is luxury and who are the rich people? His definition of luxury has some resemblance with Veblen's conspicuous consumption. "Luxury is the application of more means than are necessary for achieving a purpose."[19] But this kind of waste is not the exclusive vice of the rich; Menger must concede that poor people especially indulge in reckless spending.

It is wrong to give these remarks a social revolutionary meaning. Menger recommends substituting for luxury the old "capitalist" virtue of "abstinence." Saving steers consumption away from luxury to those consumer goods which are necessary for life. It is a consequence of his faith in freedom that Menger during his whole lifetime believed in the efficiency of private production and opposed socialism. This does not mean, however, that for Menger undiluted free competition was the cure-all for social evils. From Menger's scientific postulate of "the methodical individualism" the conclusion was drawn that he is an unconditional defender of laissez faire. But his atomism forms the sociological basis of his economic analysis and not a political program.[20] He agrees with Cairnes that laissez faire is not a *scientific* principle but only a *practical* guide whose application is limited by many exceptions.[21] Menger demands that private egotism, the driving power behind free competition, must be prevented from encroaching on public welfare. He exclaims that society cannot en-

---

[19] Menger's notes to Rau, p. 437.

[20] *Zusätze*, p. 5. See also, Menger, *Untersuchungen über die Methode der Socialwissenschaften und der Politischen Oekonomie insbesondere* (Leipzig, 1883), pp. 288-89.

[21] Menger's *Zusätze*, p. 5, "dass das Princip des laissez faire keine wissenschaftliche Basis habe." Menger quotes here J. E. Cairnes, *Essays in Political Economy. Theoretical and Applied* (London, 1873), pp. 244-51.

dure "the last consequences of private individual egotism."[22] One of the many examples of Menger's personal additions to his *Principles* which illustrates this discrepancy between egotism and welfare is quoted here: "Who produces rice powder or whiskey during a famine may earn a huge profit, but the welfare of the community will not be improved."[23] In the *Errors of Historicism* Menger emphatically denies that he is a defender of the Manchester doctrine; he declares that in spite of his opposition to Schmoller he is in favor of social reform (Kathedersozialismus).[24] Carl Menger was no defender of the leisure class; he has an outspoken resemblance to the welfare economists of today. He was not a consistent defender of free competition, and he was not a socialist, although his brother, the famous socialist Anton Menger, had some influence on him. Regardless of what Bukharin wrote, socialists or socialist sympathizers have also accepted the marginal utility theory.

Knut Wicksell, Strindberg's friend and a famous marginalist, was the champion of all the radical causes that were bitterly opposed by king, court, nobility, and the middle classes of Sweden. Once the Swedish socialist party considered his nomination as a candidate to the Parliament.[25]

It seems necessary to write at some length against these Marxian interpretations.[26] In spite of all my arguments I

[22] Menger's notes to Rau, p. 435, upper right margin.

[23] Menger's *Zusätze*, pp. 202-203.

[24] Carl Menger, *Die Irrthümer des Historismus in der deutschen Nationalökonomie* (Wien, 1884), p. 83.

[25] Torsten Gardlund, *The Life of Knut Wicksell* (Stockholm, 1958), p. 234.

[26] Neither Wicksell nor any other leading marginalists were at the beck and call of the bourgeois class. The Marxian claim is dependent on an oversimplified reconstruction of the European power structure. In the semifeudal Hapsburg monarchy, the pillars of the realm were the clergy, the army officers, the high aristocracy and, since the time of Joseph II, the upper ranks of the civil service, including the university faculty. Bankers and factory owners could join the group, especially if they were ennobled or became

am sure that the case for ideological bias will be reopened time and again, for the general suspicion of ideology (allgemeiner Ideologieverdacht, Mannheim) has taken hold of many historians.[27]

---

members of the house of lords. But a professor with the title "Hofrat" felt superior to the owners of rolling mills and blast furnaces from Morava Ostrava. Professor Richard Schüller told me about Boehm-Bawerk's polite but uncompromising refusal to change his opinion in the question of the sugar subsidy, when he encountered the opposition of the owners of sugar factories. A book about the social structure of the Hapsburg monarchy is still not written, but parts of the class organization are very ably discussed in Nikolaus von Preradovich, *Die Führungsschichten in Oesterreich und Preussen*, Veröffentlichungen des Instituts für Europäische Geschichte Mainz (Wiesbaden, 1959), II.

[27] Karl Mannheim, *Ideologie und Utopie* (Bonn, 1930), pp. 15ff.

CHAPTER VI

THE ACHIEVEMENTS: A COMPARISON OF MENGER, JEVONS, AND WALRAS

WALRAS, Jevons, and Menger wrote their books at the right moment. This may be only their good fortune. It is their merit that they surpassed their forerunners. Menger saw the connection between marginal utility and value. All three improved the theory of household planning; only Gossen's theory of imputation remained unchanged.

MARGINAL UTILITY AND VALUE

If a consumer owns a number of goods which have the same quality and form, then one of these units will gratify the least important desire. Earlier Bernoulli had discovered this unit. The other early marginalists repeated this discovery. They investigated some consequences of the new theory, but only one of them asked the question: what is the influence of marginal utility on the *value* of each good in a group where each commodity has the same quality and form? Lloyd touched this question and gave a vague answer. Carl Menger saw the problem clearly and produced an original solution.

Menger's new theory of value contains two basic concepts: the indivisible smallest unit of household calculation, and the law of diminishing utility. Galiani had claimed that the smallest unit of goods that can gratify a desire is created by physiological and cultural forces. Menger worked on similar lines. For Menger man's ultimate goal is his welfare which is planned for the whole of his life.[1] To secure this goal man must take care of his physiological desires: life and health; and his cultural needs: comfort and entertainment. A host of different goods from the first glass of water to the hunting lodge may be acquired for securing and improving welfare. Menger's "single concrete acts of satisfaction" are welfare gains added to the saturation already existing.

The size of the welfare gain depends on the units of goods used for the purpose. Menger does not fractionalize the goods into infinitely small parts; his last irreducible portion is that piece which social convention and market relation considers a unit. It can be a piece of bread but not a crumb of bread; it can be a game table but not a tenth of a game table. How much satisfaction such a piece creates is determined by duration and satisfaction of enjoyment. Menger distinguished between the size (duration plus satisfaction) and the importance or rank of satisfaction. The goods which are used for the preservation of life rank before those which are needed for the conservation of health. Commodities for comfort and for amusement occupy the lowest places in the welfare scale. Due to the objective character of this scale, one could assume that welfare gains are measurable. Each utility has its marked place in one of the four layers of the welfare hierarchy. But Menger is against measuring, at least in his unpublished notes. He clearly indicates another consequence: if the welfare scale has a general character, then it is possible to develop the law of diminishing utility from this pyramid of needs and satisfactions.

The consumer who owns a number of commodities equal in quality and form will distribute his supply starting with

[1] Carl Menger, *Grundsätze der Volkswirthschaftslehre* (Wien, 1871), pp. 90-91. See also Menger's remarks to Gossen mentioned before.

the highest welfare gain and going down to lower and lower utilities until he reaches the end of his stored up wealth. The individual disposes of his units following the declining slope of welfare gains. Menger's version of diminishing utility reflects the objective character of his welfare hierarchy. He described the farmer who uses wheat first for the preservation of his life; then he secures the life of his family. Afterwards he takes care of the following goals which are ranked in an order of declining importance: conservation of health, seedcorn for the next crops, production of beer and brandy, fattening of cattle, feeding of luxury animals.[2] None of these objectives has any connection with the physiological reactions following man's indulgence in food. But these reactions are not completely omitted. Menger blends cultural and physiological elements. Diminishing utility is also a consequence of increasing saturation. Intake of food, acquisition of houses, etc., is limited by satisfaction, indifference, and even disgust.[3]

Goods of the same kind create a variety of welfare gains, but each good can only have the value of the last application which still can be satisfied. This last usage is the dependent utility, which has been called later marginal utility. *Value is marginal utility.*[4]

This is Menger's baffling statement, which gives his theory its unique character. Menger's proof lies in the combination of three arguments, substitution, loss calculation, dependent utility. Substitution: each good of the same kind

[2] According to my knowledge, George Stigler is the first author who understood the objective element in Menger's law of diminishing utility. George Stigler, "The Economics of Carl Menger," *Journal of Political Economy*, LXV (1937), pp. 229ff.

[3] Graziadei did not understand that these physio-psychological elements are only one side of Menger's explanation. He falsely considers Menger's theory a derivation of Weber-Fechner's law. Therefore his criticism of Menger is based on a misunderstanding. Graziadei, *La Teorie sull'utilita marginale* . . . , p. 209.

[4] Menger, *Grundsätze*, p. 97.

can be employed for any usage, for which the good is technically suited; therefore one unit can be replaced by the other. Loss calculation: the consumer who loses one piece will rearrange his consumption, omitting the smallest welfare gain or marginal gain. Dependent utility: only the smallest welfare gain is dependent on each piece in a stock of goods. Dependent gain, value, marginal utility are identical.

If Robinson Crusoe, the beloved example of many Austrian economists, owns a well which delivers daily one hundred pails of water, then he may comfortably take care of all the needs he can satisfy with water.[5] If for any reason the daily output of this well is reduced by ten pails, he will not ration his drinking or the watering of his animals, but he may use less water for his flower garden. Any change of the water supply and of the needs leads to a new organization of Robinson's plans. With this example Menger clarifies his deductions and shows the significance of the time element. Like Gossen he knew that consumer valuation can not remain stable if the control over goods changes.

Menger's whole chain of reasoning found only a weak echo in the publications of Walras and Jevons. There is, however, some resemblance in the conceptual framework. What Menger called the dependent utility was Jevons' final degree of utility,[6] and Walras' rarity (rareté).[7] Menger's concrete utility is Jevons' degree of utility and Walras' intensive utility.[8] Walras' extensive utility is that amount of goods which is necessary to satisfy needs to the zero

[5] *Ibid.*, p. 102.

[6] William Stanley Jevons, *The Theory of Political Economy* (London, 1871), pp. 52, 53.

[7] Léon Walras, *Éléments d'économie politique pure; ou, Théorie de la richesse sociale* (Paris, Lausanne, 1926), p. 22.

[8] Walras, *Éléments*, p. 73.

point.[9] In Menger's book, no parallel for the last concept can be found.

The three discoverers had almost the same concepts, but they used them differently. Menger searched for the nature of value, Jevons and Walras for its function. Menger tried to find the correct definition by deduction and by a general appeal to observation. Jevons and Walras were interested in the interdependence of marginal utility and the market economy. They believed that the forces of the market tend towards a stage of rest or an equilibrium. This stage is best described in the form of equations. Jevons begins to unfold his system with the mathematical definition of marginal utility. In opposition to Menger he did not emphasize the loss but the gain of goods. A small increase can be expressed with the differential coefficient $\dfrac{du}{dx}$,[10] where u is the utility and x the amount of an available good. In other words, utility changes with the rate in which the amount of goods changes. Walras agreed with Jevons in this respect.[11] Neither the definition nor the formula was new. Bernoulli knew about them. Yet Jevons drew a new conclusion from the old formula which is at variance with Menger's opinion. Jevons dealt only with changes around the marginal zone. Excluding famines, increases and decreases of supply and utility take place only at the lower end of the utility curve. In this region only insignificant changes of utility occur. Jevons had no intention of explaining the value of those units which are used for higher enjoyments, or the total value of goods. He had not read Menger's identification of value with marginal utility, and

[9] *Ibid.*, p. 72.

[10] Jevons, *Theory*, 4th ed., p. 51.

[11] "La dérivée de l'utilité effective par rapport à la quantité possédée, exactement comme on definit la vitesse: la dérivée de l'espace parcouru par rapport au temps employé à le parcourir." Walras, *Eléments*, p. 103.

it might not have interested him. He was satisfied that he had explained the ordinary commercial transactions which are concerned only with the lower degrees of utility. But Jevons' construction of a lower area contradicted his other statements. He had claimed that utility is a personal experience not comparable with the evaluation of another individual. Therefore he could not delineate a region of transactions where people deal only with their lowest degree of utility. The consumers participate in the market with very different degrees of utility. A common zone of utility presupposes men of equal character, habits, and income. Jevons excluded the search for total utility because he used the wrong reasoning. He admitted that it would be quite interesting to know "the total value enjoyment of a person," but he considered it more interesting to estimate the subtractions and additions to a given enjoyment.[12]

The difference between Menger and Jevons can best be demonstrated by adapting for this purpose a figure drawn by Jevons himself. (See figure 1.)

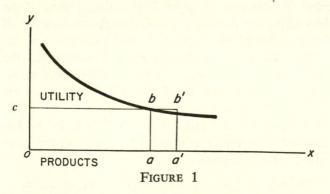

FIGURE 1

Consider that the vertical axis indicates utility and that the horizontal line shows the amount of goods available.

[12] Jevons, *Theory*, 4th ed., p. 52.

If we take an additional amount of the commodity $a\,a'$, then the degree of utility corresponds to the line $a\,b$, the utility of $a\,a'$ will be the product "of $a\,a'$ and $a\,b$ very nearly, and more nearly the less is the magnitude of $a\,a'$."[13]

Menger's theory can be poured into the same mathematical mould, although Menger would have resented it. If $a\,a'$ is the marginal piece, $a\,a'\,b'\,b$ is the marginal utility of $a\,a'$, and the line $O\,a'$ is an addition of ten fractions each equal to $a\,a'$ in length, then the value of each fraction is equal to $a\,a'\,b'\,b$. The line $c\,b'$ is the locus that satisfies in all points the height of the value of all ten pieces. The utility curve left of b soars above the value line $c\,b$. The discrepancy between the value line and the utility curve illustrates the difference between Menger and Jevons.[14]

The contrast between the two theories can also be expressed as follows: for Jevons the degree of utility u corresponds to the quantity of commodity x as $\dfrac{d\,u}{d\,x}$; Menger, if he did know enough mathematics, could not have denied this statement; he went further than Jevons. If the utility of the last particle is given, then the "values" of all other particles of the same good must have the same intensity as the utility of the last piece. Consider that the utility of the last piece a_n is 5 and the other pieces a_1, a_2, a_3, a_4, . . . a_n have utilities of 100, 95, 90, 85 . . . 5 respectively, then the value of each a till a_n is only 5, although the individual utility is much higher. In the following table the utility is in round brackets and the value is given without brackets.

Pieces:	a_1	a_2	a_3	a_4	. . . a_n
Value:	5	5	5	5	. . . 5
Utility:	(100)	(95)	(90)	(85)	. . . (5)

[13] *Ibid.*, p. 49.   [14] Walras, *Eléments*, p. 103.

It is interesting that the three authors did not know each other sufficiently to become aware of their differences in the treatment of value. Before Hans Mayer, the Austrians did not investigate Jevons thoroughly.[15] Mayer's criticism dealt only with the equalization of utilities. Recently Schönfeld-Illy investigated critically Jevons' utility formula.[16] The formula $\frac{d\,u}{d\,x}$ means according to Jevons that "the degree of utility is . . . the differential coefficient of u considered as a function of x, and will itself be another function of x."[17] Schönfeld-Illy claimed that Jevons' formula is only meaningful if the total utility u of the quantity x can be measured and if the consumer can tell what is the utility of 100 ounces of fat, of 500 cigarettes, of 10 pounds of tea. Schönfeld-Illy rejected the possibility of measurement. The Austrian economist could have strengthened his hand by quoting Jevons himself, who claimed that we are "ignorant of the total utility,"[18] and even denied that utility can be measured. "To speak simply of the value of one ounce of gold is as absurd as to speak of the *ratio of the number seventeen*."[19] The value of a ton of iron does not express an exchange ratio. Jevons, however, did not question that "the value of a ton of iron is equal to the value of the ounce of gold, or that their values are as one to one."[20]

For Jevons and Walras value meant a ratio of exchange. This relation is strongly influenced by consumer planning.

[15] Hans Mayer, "Der Erkenntniswert der funktionellen Preistheorien," *Die Wirtschaftstheorie der Gegenwart* (Wien, 1932), II, p. 165ff.

[16] The author's name was originally Leo Schönfeld; when the Nazis occupied Austria they forced him to change his name to Illy. I take the liberty of calling him Schönfeld-Illy. Illy (recte Schönfeld), *Das Gesetz des Grenznutzens* (Wien, 1948), pp. 71ff.

[17] Jevons, *Theory*, 4th ed., p. 51.

[18] *Ibid.*, p. 52. [19] *Ibid.*, p. 77; Walras, *Eléments*, p. 103.

[20] Jevons, *Theory*, 4th ed., p. 78.

THE HOUSEHOLD PLANNING

When Menger wrote his *Principles*, the rational planning of the budget was already an old standby in the marginalist literature. Galiani, Lloyd, and Gossen had studied the question. Menger did not follow the path traced by his forerunners; his theory was a by-product developed while pursuing quite a different object. Ludwig von Mises correctly pointed out that Menger wanted to show the error in Smith's value paradox.[21] In his *Wealth of Nations* Adam Smith considered only the abstract, not the concrete utility (see page 28). For Menger the abstract utility contains all the acts of consumption which serve the same or a similar purpose. The concrete utility is the act of consumption itself. The abstract utility food, for instance, embraces breakfast, lunch, and dinner, or the concrete acts of consumption. In his *Wealth of Nations*, Adam Smith claimed that the abstract utility determines the value in use, whereas Menger believed that the last concrete act of consumption determines this value. At this point arises a difficulty of demonstration which Menger overcame by drafting a blueprint of household planning. Many classes of desire exist, and each class contains many concrete acts of consumption. The manager of the household has to create order in this diversity. He allocates the items of concrete consumption to their respective classes of abstract utility. The class with the highest concrete utility comes first, and the class starting with a very low concrete act of consumption occupies the last place. In Menger's table the Roman numbers beginning with I refer to the classes of utility, number I having the highest significance. The Arabic numbers represent the concrete acts of satisfaction. The higher their utility the higher is the number. Following the law of diminishing utility each class in itself contains successive

[21] Ludwig von Mises, *Human Action* (New Haven, 1953), p. 123.

utilities arranged according to decreasing importance. Menger combined these scales in the following table which has been reprinted in many German textbooks.[22]

I	II	III	IV	V	VI	VII	VIII	IX	X
10	9	8	7	6	5	4	3	2	1
9	8	7	6	5	4	3	2	1	0
8	7	6	5	4	3	2	1	0	
7	6	5	4	3	2	1	0		
6	5	4	3	2	1	0			
5	4	3	2	1	0				
4	3	2	1	0					
3	2	1	0						
2	1	0							
1	0								
0									

This table illustrates the strategy of the household manager. If he has the means to acquire fifteen units, he will not satisfy all ten needs in column I and five needs in class II, but he will gratify concrete needs regardless of classification, so that he breaks off the satisfaction of his wants with the same or a similar intensity of utility. In our table he always will reach units with the utility index 6.

It might seem that Menger only repeats Gossen's second law. This is not completely true. Some disagreement between Gossen and Menger remains. In Gossen's model the last atoms carry the same utility under the condition of free competition. Menger avoided such an outright commitment. He spoke about equilibrium, and he explained how the individual balances his needs, but in the very end of his involved explanation he stated that the consumer reaches only an approximate state of equilibrium, because the individual deals with more or less utility, and not with

[22] Menger, *Grundsätze*, p. 93.

equality of satisfaction, with goods of different value (die Verschiedenheit des Werthes der Güter).[23] This uncertain tone which prevails in Menger's whole presentation left the door open for further revisions. Later Austrian economists increasingly disparaged the thesis of equilibrization.

Menger himself was not satisfied. In his author's copy he crossed out the table. No reason is given; most likely, Menger, the ardent opponent of mathematical treatment, questioned his own semi-mathematical interpretation. Even in the original stage, mathematics plays only a subordinate role; the Arabic numbers are just illustrations. James Bonar, in his evaluation of Menger's achievements, had shown that his budget plan can be rewritten without numbers.[24]

	I	II	III	IV
Degrees	*Food*	*Clothing*	*Lodging*	*Smoking*
First	Necessary for life			
Second	Necessary for health	First suit necessary		
Third	Agreeable	Second suit convenient	1 room	
Fourth	Less keenly agreeable	Third suit desirable	2 rooms	4 pipes a day
Fifth	Still less keenly agreeable	Fourth suit not unacceptable	3 rooms	8 pipes a day
Sixth	Satiety	Fifth suit satiety	4 rooms satiety	Satiety

[23] *Ibid.*, pp. 94-95.

[24] James Bonar, "The Austrian Economists and their View of Value," *Quarterly Journal of Economics* (October, 1888), p. 7. In the Menger Library, I found a copy of this paper dedicated to Menger. Apparently he did not read it.

THE EQUALIZATION OF UTILITIES

James Bonar, contrary to Jevons and Walras, showed a deep understanding of Menger's ideas. Jevons and Walras were not interested in Menger's consumer strategy. They investigated the interdependence of three variables: consumer preference, price, and income. They asked, how will the consumer evaluate goods and services when he bids for goods with his income in the market?

The explanation suggested by the two Western marginalists had been anticipated by Gossen, and even by Turgot, but three improvements were added. In the first place, the marginal utilities are leveled for each person separately. Second, Jevons and Walras rejected Gossen's interpersonal equalization of utilities.[25] Third, they offered a more exact deduction than Gossen.

For the case of two goods the maximum of utility will be reached, Walras pointed out, when the relation of marginal utilities is equal to the price relations.[26] Walras, commenting on Jevons, illustrated this principle as follows: Two traders, *A* and *B*, exchange meat for wheat. The exchange stops when for *A* the last pound of wheat has a utility of 7 and the last pound of meat has a utility of 14, and for *B* the respective utilities are 3:6, and when the price relation is 1:2. It seems now that the leveling of marginal utility has been abolished, for the pounds of meat and wheat have different utilities. This is not so, for Walras does not figure in pounds but in money. For *A* one dollar

[25] "The reader will find, again, that there is never in any single instance, an attempt made to compare the amount of feeling in one mind with that in another." Jevons, *Theory*, 4th ed., p. 14. Walras accepted Jevons' system of exchange and rejected Gossen's theory. Léon Walras, *Études d'économie sociale* (Lausanne, 1896), pp. 208ff. George J. Stigler, "The Development of Utility Theory I," *Journal of Political Economy*, Vol. 58 (Feb.-Dec., 1950), p. 318.

[26] Walras, *Eléments*, p. 82; Walras, *Études d'économie sociale*, p. 208.

meat money has the same utility 7, as one dollar wheat money. In an exchange economy not the units of goods, as Menger assumed, but the last units of money carry the same marginal utility. Walras had already discovered what Pareto later called the weighted utility (ophelimité ponderée).

If the marginal utility of the last unit of the commodity is divided by the price $\frac{M\,U}{p}$, we receive as a result the marginal utility of money. The marginal utility of money is $M\,U$, if p is the price and $p = 1$. When the consumer deals with an infinite number of goods, a chain of equations can be established, $M\,U_2 \ldots M\,U_n$. The number of equations is M-1, if one good is the "numéraire" or money.

Walras claimed that under three conditions these equations are valid. First, every person marketing his goods satisfies the maxima of his needs; the relations of "raretées" (marginal utilities) are equal to the prices. Second, if only one price exists for each good on the market and if the total demand is equal to the total supply, every one receives in proportion to what he gives. Third, all the prices are in the stage of equilibrium.[27] This mathematical explanation of the price structure will be valid for realistic situations if free competition prevails.

These equations are the basis of Walras' famous mathematical system. This mathematical structure also contains a theory of imputation which is not as well developed as other parts of his system. Walras claims only that the productive services of the factors labor, land, and capital will be rewarded by prices which free competition will keep on the level of the costs of reproduction. This theory does not improve earlier classical analysis.[28] Walras did not say how the costs of reproduction are formed. The connection

[27] Walras, *Eléments*, p. 129.
[28] *Ibid.*, pp. 12-13.

of the Walrasian theory of imputation with the marginal utility theory is very loose.

Menger based his theory of imputation entirely on utility and not on costs. He rejected the classical cost theory, but he still had to explain the value of the factors of production, for otherwise an empty spot remained in his system. He filled the gap with a new version of Galiani's and Condillac's cost theory. Not the value of the cost goods determines the value of the finished goods, but the opposite is true; the value of the consumer goods or, in Menger's terminology, the value of the goods of lower order determines the value of the factors of production or goods of higher order.[29] Menger introduced an interesting refinement into Condillac's statement: not the actual marginal utility of the consumer good but the presumed future value determines the value of capital, labor, and land. Menger, in a theory of production and distribution, emphasized the time element much more strongly than Galiani and even Gossen.

Menger understood quite well that the transfer of value creates a new problem, because factors of production are complementary. They work together in the production of consumer goods. Menger, like Gossen, tried to find a key with which the marginal value of consumer goods can be distributed on each factor inside the factor combination; in this Gossen was more skeptical and cautious than Menger. The latter believed indeed that the problem can be solved and that he had already done so. His interpretation contains ideas which Gossen had already mentioned, and some new suggestions which his student Boehm-Bawerk had refined. Menger's and Boehm-Bawerk's theorem will be discussed together. What Menger thought about this problem is not as important as the fact that he started a discussion in the Austrian camp which is still going on.

[29] Menger, *Grundsätze*, p. 124.

Neither Menger nor Walras improved essentially the older analysis of imputation or value accounting, but other parts of the value system were changed considerably. To gauge the progress we have to distinguish between repetitious rediscoveries, improvement of older theories, and the creation of new thoughts. Jevons' and Walras' equalization of marginal utility is a rediscovery of Gossen's second law, but Gossen is improved; the marginal utilities are now equalized for each participant in the exchange. Menger does not add anything to Gossen's analysis of imputation. Walras' system of equations is an original contribution to economic analysis, but his work does not increase the understanding of the marginal utility concept; it is an essential application of consumer value to price theory. Only Carl Menger gave marginal utility a new meaning through the combination of marginal utility and value. In our special field of investigation he did more than Jevons and Walras. But this grading of achievements is completely alien to the way in which the men themselves judged their work. They rightfully assumed that they had broken new ground, because only a small part of earlier efforts was known to them before they published their findings for the first time.

CHAPTER VII

LITERARY SOURCES AND NEW IDEAS

MENGER'S SO-CALLED PLAGIARISM

THE new ideas of Menger, Jevons, and Walras were not grafted on the work already done by the early marginalists. The three discoverers were stimulated by some minor writers whom the historians of economic thought usually neglect. Some authors are suspicious of this overflow of discoveries and declare positively that at least Menger must have committed plagiarism.

Maffeo Pantaleoni and Otto Weinberger believed that Menger had read at least Gossen and Mangoldt before he published his discoveries and had concealed this knowledge from his readers.[1] In the Hitotsubashi library, new facts have been discovered which make it unlikely that Menger had copied either author. Menger, indeed, had studied Julius (Gyula) Kautz, who is the earliest author who mentions Gossen (1858),[2] and Menger underlined the two Gossen quotations.[3] But it is still very doubtful

---

[1] Maffeo Pantaleoni, *Principii di Economia Pura* (Florence: G. Barbara, 1889), p. 121: "Carl Menger has perpetrated the most impudent plagiarism on Cournot, Gossen, Jennings and Jevons. Not even Bastiat has dared to exploit Carey in such a manner" (my translation). In fairness to Pantaleoni it must be stated that later editions do not contain this remark. Ottone Weinberger "Economia matematica," *Societa Reale di Napoli, Atti della Reale Accadimia Pontaniana Di Scienze Morali e Politiche*, LIX (1938), 92.

[2] Julius Kautz, *Die Nationalökonomie als Wissenschaft* (Wien, 1858); Kautz, *Die Geschichtliche Entwicklung der Nationalökonomie* (Wien, 1860).

[3] Kautz, *Die Nationalökonomie*, p. 9; *Die Geschichtliche Entwicklung*, p. 704.

that Menger had read Gossen before he finished his *Principles*. Menger had bought his copy of Gossen on May 8, 1886.[4] The pages are marked in many places, and Menger always did this when he studied an author for the first time. Menger did not approve of Gossen, rejecting his purely hedonistic approach, his emphasis on labor, and the application of mathematics in the realm of psychology.[5] It is not very probable, to say the least, that a writer would copy another author whose methods and findings he does not consider acceptable.

There is also reason to believe that Menger was unaware of Mangoldt's condensed version of the marginal utility theory. He read Mangoldt; so far Weinberger is correct. In Menger's copy of Mangoldt pages 1-8 are rather heavily marked. No remark or pencil stroke can be found in the chapter of Mangoldt which deals with marginal utility. Mangoldt's value theory is hidden away in his mathematical section. Apparently, Menger disliked reading mathematical economics. He owned the works of Cournot, Jevons, and Walras, but most of the pages are not even

[4] Note on the title page of Menger's copy of Gossen.

[5] Here are Menger's remarks from the inside of the front cover of his Gossen copy (edition 1854). Where I had to complete words, completions are indicated by square brackets. Some words remain illegible: "Gossen fehlt: Für ihn hat Arbeit [technische] eine ganz exceptionelle Stellung. Alle Mängel der mathem[atischen] Methode in psychol[ogischen] Dingen. Nur Genuss-nicht Wichtigkeit für Leben und Wohlfahrt [Höchster Genuss des ganzen Lebens] Arbeit und Genuss ähnlich wie bei Bastiat (?) [the last two words cannot be deciphered]." "It is Gossen's error that technical labor has a completely exceptional position. He reveals all the errors of the mathematical method in psychological matters. He is only interested in enjoyment and not in the importance for life and welfare. (High enjoyment for the whole life.) Labor and enjoyment have a similar role as in Bastiat's work." See also Menger's remarks to Gossen, p. 38: "Gossen schreibt dem Genuss zu hohe Bed [eutung] zu Wichtigk[eit] für Erhaltung des Lebens etc. übersieht er." "The significance which Gossen attributes to enjoyment is too high. He overlooks the importance for the preservation of life, etc."

cut. He read Auspitz' and Lieben's mathematical price theory, but with great misgivings.[6] He did not approve of the method on which mathematical economics is based.

MENGER'S REAL FORERUNNERS

Before he wrote his *Principles*, Menger knew neither Gossen nor Mangoldt nor the greatest part of the older marginalist literature. Most works which he perused for the publication of his *Principles* are quoted in two lengthy footnotes which read like a history of the value-in-use theories from Aristotle to Albert Schäffle.[7] He examined, but not too carefully, Montanari, Galiani, Turgot, and Condillac.[8] He dismissed the achievements of the earlier French and Italian writers with the remark that the German economists offer a more profound treatment of the subject.[9] Besides Aristotle, the German economists of the first half of the nineteenth century were his main teachers. He was attracted by their criticism of Smith's utility concept and the intrinsic value.[10] Menger shared the conviction of the earlier German economists that the source of value is man's judgment and that labor had no power to create value. Menger became especially interested in Eberhard Friedländer's (1799-1869) interpretation of value. According to Friedländer, the concrete unit of needs (die konkrete Bedürfniseinheit), that means the ability of a specific commodity to satisfy a concrete need, determines the value-in-use. However, Friedländer's concrete unit is

---

[6] Auspitz und Lieben, *Zur Theorie des Preises* (Leipzic, 1887).

[7] Menger, *Grundsätze*, pp. 78-80, 108-13.

[8] *Ibid.*, pp. 108ff.   [9] *Ibid.*

[10] "Aber der Werth selbst ist keine den Dingen anhaftende Eigenschaft, sondern hängt von unserem Urtheil ab. Er hat also keine andere Quelle als die Vorstellung. . . ." Heinrich Storch, *Handbuch der Nationalwirtschaftslehre*, ed. Dr. Karl Rau (Carl Menger Library). The quotation is underlined by Carl Menger. "But the value is dependent on our judgment and not on the quality of things" (my translation).

not a marginal but an average unit.[11] Friedländer lost his way, and by substituting the average with the marginal need, Menger corrected him.

In Menger's library I found one author whom Menger forgot to mention in his footnotes. He is Joseph, Ritter von Kudler (1786-1853).[12] Not Menger but Kudler started the value discussion at the University of Vienna, and Kudler's textbook was Menger's primer in economics.[13] Menger's copy is well worn and dilapidated, and as a university student Menger underlined vigorously Kudler's theory of comparative value (der verglichene Werth). Kudler taught that man compares the different purposes for which commodities can be used. The higher the intensity of a specific need, the higher is the rank of the commodity which satisfies this need.[14] Kudler conceived a scale of needs which Menger improved later on. Menger avoided Kudler's error to pair off concrete goods with their respective needs. From his study of Friedländer Menger knew that only one need determines value. Obviously, Kudler plus Friedländer does not equal Menger, for it was the stroke of a genius to introduce the dependent or marginal utility. Old records and

[11] Eberhard Friedländer, *Die Theorie des Wertes*, Zur Jubelfeier der Kaiserlichen Universität Dorpat, 12. und 13. Dezember, 1852. (Book in the library of Columbia University.) See especially p. 67. Eberhard Friedländer was born in 1799 in Königsberg, East Prussia, and died in 1869 in Heidelberg, Germany. For a long time he was professor at Dorpat. See *Russkii Biograficheskii Slovar* (St. Petersburg, 1901), Vol. 21, p. 231. For a critical analysis of Friedländer's work see Johann Komorzynski, "Ist auf Grundlage der bisherigen wissenschaftlichen Forschung die Bestimmung der natürlichen Höhe der Güterpreise möglich?" *Zeitschrift für die gesamte Staatswissenschaft* (Tübingen, 1869), Vol. 25, p. 230.

[12] Joseph, Ritter von Kudler (1786-1853) was from 1821 professor of political science and law at the University of Vienna. See W. Lustkandl, *Sonnenfels und Kudler* [Wien, 1891] (Menger Library).

[13] Dr. Joseph Kudler, *Die Grundlehren der Volkswirthschaft*, Erster oder theoretischer Theil (Wien: Braumüller und Seidel, 1846) (Menger Library).

[14] *Ibid.*, part I, pp. 54 and 55ff.

worn out books allow us to reconstruct Menger's development, and ample material is also available to trace Jevons' and Walras' literary genealogy.

JEVONS, WALRAS, AND THE EARLIER LITERATURE

William Stanley Jevons had more contact with earlier literature on marginal utility than Menger. He was thoroughly acquainted with Bentham, whose *felicific* calculation of pain and pleasure he adopted. In his survey of older literature he mentioned earlier followers of the value-in-use theory, Jean Baptiste Say, Nassau-Senior, Banfield, and Richard Jennings.[15] From Bentham to Jevons is a much shorter distance than from Kudler and Friedländer to Menger. Jevons refined Bentham's theory, he added the mathematical explanation, he found the connection between household planning and exchange economy, and last but not least, he was a better psychologist than Bentham. However, he was not as original as Menger.

Léon Walras did not rediscover marginal utility. He inherited this concept from his father, Auguste Walras, who wrote in 1831 that value is derived from scarcity.[16] His son later studied Cournot and Dupuit,[17] and surpassed his teachers and even Jevons.[18] Walras' eminent place in the

[15] In the first edition of 1871, p. 2, he mentioned these forerunners. To his great annoyance he had in later editions to enlarge the list of forerunners.

[16] Auguste Walras, *De la Nature de la Richesse et de l'Origine de la Valeur* (Evreux: Ancelle Fils, 1831), pp. 41ff.

[17] Léon Walras, *Études d'économie politique appliquée* (Lausanne, Paris, 1898), p. 467. Marcel Boson, *Léon Walras. Fondateur de la Politique Économique Scientific* (Lausanne, Paris, 1951), pp. 28ff., 36. According to Bompaire, Walras studied Cournot from 1853 on and published in 1863 a paper about Cournot in *L'Independence Belge de la Moselle*. François Bompaire, *Du Principe de Liberté Économique* (Lausanne, Paris, 1938), p. 238.

[18] Jevons did not claim to be a mathematician. "In short, I do not write for mathematicians, nor as a mathematician, but as an economist wishing to convince other economists that their science can only be satisfactorily treated on a mathematical basis." Jevons, *Theory*, 4th ed.; pp. xiii and xiv.

history of economics is not secured by his modest contributions to the marginal utility theory but by his mathematical work. Even his opponent, Hans Mayer, admired him as "l'inventeur de l'equilibre économique." "There is no other achievement in the whole history of economic theory which allows close comparison with Walras' greatness and consistency of the general outline. In an almost playful manner, he combines the rigidity of his logical deductions with the economic elements."[19]

Early Stages of Their Discoveries

With a flair for dramatic presentation, Walras described the origin and the early development of his ideas. As early as 1860, in a book written against Jean Pierre Proudhon, Walras repeated his father's principle: value is an increasing function of utility and a decreasing function of quantity. Walras admitted that he suffered a defeat in the discussion of his book on Proudhon with the Saint-Simonist, Lambert Bey (1861).[20] Leaving the apartment of his victorious opponent, Walras decided on the spur of the moment to construct a mathematical system based on the intensity of the last satisfied desire. He wanted to prove that only under free competition can the maximum of utility be reached. His father warned him that utility cannot be measured, but the son's intentions could not be changed.[21]

Jevons made his essential discovery a short time before Walras. In a letter of June 1, 1860, Jevons first explained the law of diminishing utility to his brother Herbert.[22] Two

---

[19] Hans Mayer, *Der Erkenntniswert . . . ,* p. 195.

[20] Léon Walras, *L'économie politique et la Justice, examen critique et réfutation des doctrines économiques de J. P. Proudhon* (Paris, 1860).

[21] Léon Walras, *Études d'économie* (Lausanne, Paris, 1898), pp. 411-12.

[22] "One of the most important axioms is, that as the quantity of any commodity, for instance plain food, which a member has to consume, increases, so the utility or benefit derived from the

years later, his studies were so far advanced that he could present his findings before the Association for the Advancement of Science.[23]

Both Jevons and Walras made their main contributions between the ages of twenty-five and twenty-seven. According to the Austrian tradition Menger came across the great discovery of his life at the same age. In 1869 when the young Menger prepared the market reports for the official *Wiener Zeitung*, he became acquainted with price problems which he could not solve with the tools of the classical theory.[24] He found a more plausible explanation.

Menger himself had indicated the year 1869 as the date of his discovery. According to Menger's notes at the Hitotsubashi University, he had reached in 1867 a half-way house between the German classical tradition and his own formulation in the *Principles*. In a copy of Karl Heinrich Rau's *Grundsätze der Volkswirtschaftslehre* (Leipsic, 1863), the young Menger wrote a rather coherent text which I consider *the first draft* of his *Principles*. The young Menger marked the time of this composition as September-October, 1867. Here is a catalogue of Menger's thoughts on value from this first draft:

First: The labor value is discarded. *Second*: He calls his own doctrine the law of quantity (Das Quantitätsgesetz);

---

last portion decreases in degree. The decrease of enjoyment between the beginning and the end of a meal may be taken as an example. . . ." W. St. Jevons, *Letters and Journals* (London, 1886), p. 151.

[23] W. Stanley Jevons, "Notice of a General Mathematical Theory of Political Economy," Report of the 32nd meeting of the British Association for the Advancement of Science, held at Cambridge, October, 1862, London, 1863. Report of sections, p. 158.

[24] I heard about this explanation of Menger's intellectual development from Ewald Schams (1932) and from Richard Schüller (1957). See also Hayek, "Carl Menger," Henry William Spiegel (ed.), *The Development of Economic Thought* (New York, 1952), pp. 531-32.

he means utility *and* quantity determine the value. *Third*: Value is a personal judgment. *Fourth*: Value cannot be measured; however, it is possible to relate one value to another, but this comparison is rather inexact. *Fifth*: The imputation theory is already completed. "The value unifies consumer-and-producer goods into one group." The value of the producer goods is determined by the value of the finished products, and the value of the finished products is based on the value judgment of the consumer. The classical sequence—labor sacrifice, cost of production, value of finished product—is turned upside down as had been done by Galiani and Condillac. This sequence, which was later accepted by the whole Viennese school, turns up already in the draft of 1867! In the same draft Menger presented the formula by which the value of complementary producer goods is distributed among the individual factors of production. "In the production the lack of one element can reduce or even destroy the value of the other elements." The difference between the draft of 1867 and the *Principles* of 1871 is in the field of imputation and is a matter of emphasis. In 1871 Menger wrote that the complete loss of value is an exception; in most cases the value will only be reduced. *Sixth*: The draft does not contain the identification of value and marginal utility. This core position of his value system might have been discovered in 1869. In 1867 Menger still pursued an abortive line of thought. He had a vague notion of some collective value, a public value (öffentlicher Wert) which is determined by the market. Further investigations in this direction have not been pursued.

Between 1870 and 1874, Menger, Walras, and Jevons published their fully developed theories. None of them added in later life anything of consequence to their value theories. Jevons' development was cut short by a premature death. Walras became more and more involved in his mathematical analysis and in problems of applied economy. Menger increased his scientific reputation with his book on the methods of the social sciences. His later work on money did not reach the high level of his two earlier publications. After 1900 he started a major project. He wanted to add a psychological foundation to his system; therefore, he studied Wilhelm Wundt and the Austrian psychologists Franz Brentano, Christian von Ehrenfels, and Oskar Kraus.[25] He collected a great number of travelogues and books on foreign customs and mores to show that consumer behavior everywhere and in all times follows the immutable laws of value. But his grand design came to nought; he wrote and rewrote a new edition of his *Principles* without reaching a satisfactory conclusion.[26] The posthumous edition prepared by his son Karl Menger and Richard Schüller is inferior to the first. This failure cannot be explained by the lack of original ideas; the old Menger provided many ideas whose elaboration he left to his followers. But new ideas were not sufficient to complete a project of such scope, and there is a note of disillusionment in the life and work of this great man.[27]

---

[25] According to my interview with Carl Menger's son, his father had studied Wilhelm Wundt. Menger owned the works of the Austrian psychologists and has made some marginal notes.

[26] I owe these facts to Karl Menger, the son of the economist. In the second volume of the catalogue of the Menger Library the items about traveling, geography and anthropology fill the columns 826 until 948.

[27] While the printing of this manuscript was in progress, Professor Richard Schüller, one of the few surviving members of the Menger seminar, wrote me: "Menger worked in his old age on the philosophical foundation of theory, which due to the paradoxes of metaphysics became a failure" (letter of February 2, 1964). As far as I can remember, Ewald Schams told me already in 1932 that old Menger studied Hegel unsuccessfully. Karl Menger, Jr., denied emphatically that his father was interested in metaphysics or in Hegel. Despite this démenti Schüller and Schams sound very plausible. Their observations can explain Menger's long silence. But as long as more material cannot be discovered, I must refrain from taking a definite stand.

CHAPTER VIII

DIFFERENCES IN PHILOSOPHY AND METHOD

IT was the greatest disappointment in Menger's life that Jevons and Walras were not his comrades in marginalism. At first Menger was not aware of the differences. When he studied the work of his French colleague, he discovered that a breach existed.[1] Menger was annoyed by the mathematical treatment of economic problems. In a letter to Walras of February 1884, Menger exploded: "The mathematical method is wrong. . . ."[2] He rejected Gossen's mathematical psychology and Auspitz-Lieben's price theory. This animosity was not due to lack of mathematical understanding—the students of a "Gymnasium" in old Austria had a thorough training in mathematics; it was Menger's conviction, shared by his followers, that equations and curves had no place in economic theory. In his last years his opposition to mathematics grew somewhat weaker. In 1911 he wrote in a letter addressed to Ismar Feilbogen that he was interested in Cournot and in mathematics.[3] This letter is a puzzle, as Menger owned all the economic works of Cournot and never read them. No trace of the French economist can be found in Menger's published or unpublished work, and I have found only very few and simple mathematical equations in his manuscripts and books. Whatever the reasons for the strange letter, in

---

[1] Etienne Antonelli "Léon Walras et Carl Menger à travers leur correspondance," *Economie appliquée*, VI (Paris, April-September, 1953).

[2] Antonelli, *Economie appliquée*, p. 282.

[3] Letter from June 26, 1911. See *Freedom and Economic Theory*, p. 70.

his creative period Menger was a fanatical opponent of mathematical analysis and had written a methodology free from mathematics. How antagonistic this theory was to Walras' and Jevons' views can be indicated by the following table.

Walras, Jevons	*Menger*
Science has a pragmatic character. It is the purpose of science to increase happiness.	Science is a value in itself. It is not bound to moral and political goals.
The search for pleasure conflicts with moral goals.	A conflict between moral and utilitarian values exists, but a solution of the problem is not given. Menger's thinking is inconclusive.
Mathematics is especially suitable for solving economic problems, because it describes the relation of interdependent factors.	Economic theory does not investigate the interdependence of economic phenomena but rather the *essence* of value, rent, profit, division of labor, bimetallism, etc.
The laws of exchange can be expressed in mathematical equations.	Equations can lead only to arbitrary statements, not to exact laws. The description of an equilibrium can be only the end, not the beginning of an analysis. The theorist has first to trace the chain of cause and effect before he describes the equilibrium. The genetic-causal method is more important than functionalism.

The four reasons for dissension have to be explained in detail.

Science: at the very end of his work on methods Menger wrote that the dignity of a science is based on the importance, the depth, the originality of its achievements.[4] For Menger pure science has only one purpose: the acquisition of knowledge. Theoretical understanding has no moral or political purpose.

The separation of ethics and social science is much more strongly emphasized in his handwritten notes than in his publications. In his notes to his *Principles*, Menger demanded that economic analysis ought to be purified from ethical additions. Theory deals with the existing facts and not with right or wrong. Menger knew that he was not the earliest defender of value neutrality. He followed Cairnes, who separated politics from scientific economy.[5]

Jevons and Walras drew economic science and morals much tighter together than Menger. ". . . the object of economics is to maximize happiness by purchasing pleasure, as it were, at the lowest cost of pain."[6] Jevons like Gossen considered the theory of marginal utility a device for maximizing pleasure. For Walras, marginal utility also makes a contact with the Saint-Simonists;[7] under the influence of Etienne Vacherot, he formed an eclectic world view.

---

[4] Carl Menger, *Untersuchungen über die Methode der Sozialwissenschaften und der politischen Oekonomie insbesondere* (Leipzic, 1883).

[5] J. E. Cairnes, *Essays in Political Economy. Theoretical and Applied* (London, 1873), pp. 253, 260.

[6] Jevons, *Theory*, 4th ed., p. 23.

[7] Boninsegni discovered the influence of Saint-Simon on Walras. *Discours de j. Le Dr. Boninsegni, Jubilée du Professeur V. Pareto, 1917* (Lausanne, 1920), pp. 9-10. Already in 1860, Auguste Walras warned his son against too close a contact with the Saint-Simonists. See Léon Walras, *Études d'économie sociale* (Paris, 1896); Walras, *Études d'économie politique appliquée* (Paris, 1898), p. 467; Marcel Boson, *Léon Walras. Fondateur de la Politique Économique Scientifique* (Lausanne, 1951), pp. 28ff., 36.

For Walras it is the destiny of man to perfect himself, to improve his knowledge, freedom, and personality. Science is one of the ways to perfection.[8] This idealism, typical for the French Laicist of the nineteenth century, found some echo in Jevons' way of thinking. Jevons wavered between Hedonism and religious idealism. Bentham was his guide in economic psychology, but in spite of some agnostic leanings, the British economist remained a Unitarian due to sentiment and family tradition.[9] Unitarianism in Jevons' time was a strictly monotheistic denomination. The conflict between Bentham's felicific calculus and Christian morality is reflected in the social function which Jevons assigns to marginal utility.

Moral Decisions and Marginal Utility: the conflict between the morally right and the useful action is a fundamental ethical problem, and it has its special significance for the theory of marginal utility. If man strives for pleasure and avoids pain, so Jevons and Walras thought, he cannot do his duty; he cannot act charitably or justly, because the fulfillment of one's duty requires one to disregard the pleasure reward and the pain penalty. For Walras and Jevons it is difficult to imagine a marginal utility of one's moral conscience. Bentham and Gossen, however, denied that a conflict exists. Bentham believed that every man is charitable by nature, and Gossen resolved the conflict by claiming that even the monk and the martyr act as they do to increase their pleasure. Jevons and Walras did not explain away this collision. Both authors came from different philosophies to the same problem, how to reconcile the pleasure calculus with moral decisions? Jevons offered a solution with an aristocratic bias by separating the social world into two parts, the masses and the leaders.

[8] Bompaire, *Liberté économique*, pp. 484-86.
[9] Jevons, *Letters and Journals*, pp. 65, 431ff.; Jevons, *The Theory of Political Economy*, pp. 23-25.

Economic actions are mainly motivated by pain and pleasure, and the masses are guided by economic considerations. Where no higher moral issue is at stake the economic calculus ought to prevail. But the ruling of the body social must be entrusted to the people committed to ideals and not to those who seek for the maximum of utility. The higher duties, honor and uprightness, "the safety of a nation, the welfare of great populations" shall have a greater weight than pain and pleasure. The responsible leaders, especially "the soldier and the statesman," ought to take care of the moral obligations.[10] Jevons' economic mechanism based on pleasure and pain works only inside an idealistic framework.

Walras hoped that the rift between moral and economic forces would be closed in future times. Until that moment is reached, he felt, this antagonism will rend the social fabric. Industry and mathematical economy are separated from mores and morals; industry produces utilities, and mathematical economy shows how the maximum of utility can be reached. Mores are the practical source of justice, and morals analyze justice. As justice cannot exist without utility, both forces have to be united.[11] Free men enlightened by social sciences will eventually bridge the gap between Hedonism and morals,[12] but how this can be achieved, Walras did not predict. His solution, if it is one, remains at best a pious hope.

Clearly the conflict between moral obligations and the pleasure drive has had its impact on the writing of economics. Jevons and Walras had to tear the social fabric

[10] Jevons, *The Theory of Political Economy*, 1st ed., pp. 25-27.

[11] Walras, *Économie appliquée*, p. 458; Bompaire, *Liberté économique*, p. 488.

[12] Walras, *Études d'économie social*, p. vi, ". . . et la science social apparait comme étant, en partie du moins, la mécanique des forces morales . . ."; Walras, *Études d'économie politique appliquée*, p. 461; Bompaire, *Liberté économique*, p. 484.

apart in order to construct a uniform economic system inside of one sector. In the economic sector man calculates pleasure and pain and balances on an imaginary scale the marginal utilities of his last pennies. In the world of government the moral values of honor, duty, and justice, reign without the interference of Gossen's first law.

In Menger's printed publications this conflict played a minor role; this social antagonism was rooted in specifically Western ideas of state, society, and economics which were mostly alien to the Austrian intellectual climate. Hedonism, Unitarian ethics, and French Laicism did not form a part of Menger's thinking, which, like that of many other Austrian intellectuals of the second half of the nineteenth century, was still influenced by Aristotle.[13] Menger's welfare scale is an application of Nicomachean ethics to economics somewhat conditioned by Austrian life of about 1870. For Aristotle the good life is the end and the self-sufficient goal for all forms of human activity.[14] The good life becomes Menger's economic welfare.

As Aristotle started his ethics with a hierarchy of human aims, so Menger also constructed a scale of welfare gains and goals. A conflict between the region of pleasure and the realm of morals is not mentioned in his published work. Yet the notes of the Menger library reveal that Menger knew about the moral limitations of his economic value theory. One of the first notes added in his copy of his *Principles* contains his conviction that life is not the highest goal for everybody.[15] More openly than in his publications,

---

[13] R. Mühlherr, "Ontologie und Monadologie in der österreichischen Literatur des XIX Jahrhunderts," *Festschrift der österreichischen Nationalbibliothek* (Wien, 1948); Emil Kauder, "Intellectual and Political Roots of the Older Austrian School," *Zeitschrift für Nationalökonomie*, XVII.4. (Vienna, Austria), pp. 411ff.

[14] Aristotle, *Nicomachean Ethics*, 1 book .7. 1097b 7-30.

[15] Menger's note in his copy of his *Principles*: "Das Leben ist nicht höchstes Ziel für alle. . . ."

Menger separated here his theory from outspoken hedonism. Most likely he drew nearer to Aristotle, although Aristotle's attitude to hedonism is controversial. In his author's copy, Menger rejected pain and pleasure as the only driving forces of human action, and this decision led to an incomplete reappraisal of human goods. Without reaching a definite answer he asked himself several times in his handwritten notes to his *Principles* whether or not man himself, love, friendship, God are economic goods. Man is a purpose in himself and cannot be means to an end. The discussion of God is later crossed out, for Menger became an agnostic, perhaps an atheist. Love and friendship are non-transferable goods of indefinite duration; their availability (Verfügbarkeit) is restricted, and while they are goods, they are not economic commodities.[16] Menger came to the tentative conclusion that non-economic needs (*res extra commercium*) exist, but he did not go further. He did not ask himself whether this insight might lead to a restriction of marginal utility. If love and friendship are not economic goods, then it is at least doubtful whether the law of diminishing utility can be applied and whether friendship and love can be chopped off into particles like bread or wine. Menger's inconclusive thinking went into the direction of separating virtues from economic goods, but he did not take a firm stand as the French and the English economists had.

This difference of opinion played no role in the Walras-Menger correspondence. Menger and Walras did not discuss morals but the meaning of science and the function of mathematics. First, with amazement and later with growing annoyance, the Austrian economist found out that his approach was not accepted by Walras.

---

[16] Emil Kauder (ed.), *Carl Menger's Zusätze zu Grundsätze der Volkswirtschaftslehre* (Hitotsubashi University, Tokyo, 1961), pp. 29, 35, 43, 59.

Interrelation of Factors and Essences: Jevons wrote: "I contend that all economic writers must be mathematical so far as they are scientific at all, because they treat of economic quantities, and the relation of such quantities, and all quantities and all relations of quantities come within the scope of mathematics."[17] Walras agreed with him.[18] He reduced the appearances of economic life by abstraction and by isolation to ideal types.[19] In opposition to them Menger claimed that the subjects of science are not the constructions of our mind but are rather the social essences. Essence means the reality underlying a phenomenon. An economist like Menger who seeks for the hidden reality has to trace the eternal pattern of social events and structures. The belief in essences is a principle of philosophical realism; Aristotle is the greatest author of this school. Werner Jäger, eminent Aristotelian scholar, had described Aristotle's theory of understanding as follows: "Any real knowledge presupposes a subject which is outside the mind and which is touched, copied, reflected by the mind."[20] The mind, so taught the great Greek philosopher, has to grasp what belongs to the being of a thing, what it is and nothing else.[21] In the same vein Menger defines the essence of economic life: "We understand the phenomenon, if we have recognized the reason for its existence (the reason for its being and its so being)."[22] Menger's theory deals with the Aristotelian essences, with exact types, and typical relations, and these theoretical

---

[17] Jevons, *Theory*, 4th ed., p. xxxi.

[18] Walras, *Elements*, p. 29.

[19] *Ibid.*

[20] Werner Jaeger, *Aristotle* (Oxford, 1962), p. 215.

[21] B. A. G. Fuller, *History of Greek Philosophy*, vol. 3: *Aristotle* (1931), p. 43.

[22] ". . . wir verstehen dieselbe [the phenomenon], wenn wir den Grund ihrer Existenz und ihrer eigentümlichen Beschaffenheit (den Grund ihres *Seins* und ihres *So-Seins*) erkannt haben." C. Menger, *Untersuchungen*, p. 14. The italics are Menger's.

types provide knowledge which transcends the immediate information. Menger's theoretical analysis produces laws and concepts valid for all times and places. He combined an up-to-date theory with a philosophy which in 1883, the year in which he published his methodology of social sciences, was already more than two thousand years old. Like his Greek master, Menger searched for a reality hidden behind the observable surface of things. This X-ray technique of investigation is far removed from the way in which Walras, Jevons, and their followers worked. But in the Viennese school this search for the essences is still lingering on.

Equations and Genetic Causality: the description of the eternal pattern of economics does not necessarily interfere with the usage of mathematics, and the combination of essences can be expressed in mathematical language. The great dissension is due to the antagonism between interdependence and genetic causality. For Walras and for Jevons marginal utility, income, price influence each other. This interdependence—as I have said before—can be analyzed with the help of equations. The Aristotelian Menger rejected interdependence, equilibrium, equations, and functional relations. Genetic causality chains together the parts of Menger's system. The future needs of a consumer determine the value of the goods of higher order, labor, capital, and land.[23] The sequence of economic actions starts with the rational planning of the consumer, and this causal principle is strictly at variance with the mathematical method.[24] Menger's attitude is clearly expressed in his marginal notes to John Stuart Mill's *Principles*. Mill wrote that in the long run, the market price is identical with the natural price. Mill compared the market

[23] Menger, *Grundsätze*, pp. 128-29.
[24] See Menger's annotations to Auspitz & Lieben, *Zur Theorie des Preises* (1887), p. 25 (Menger Library).

price with the waves of the ocean and the natural price with the smooth surface of the sea, which can be observed in the long run. Menger remarked that Mill had not given any reason for both phenomena, neither for the smooth surface nor for the natural price; according to Menger the cause in the first case is gravity, and in the second case it is consumer valuation.[25] "Finally the buying consumer is the *conditio sine qua non* of the value of the factors of production," Menger wrote on the margin of Mill's *Principles*.

Not Menger himself, but his follower Eugen von Boehm-Bawerk emphasized the affinity of genetical causality with Aristotelian logic. For Menger and for Boehm-Bawerk the wants of the consumer are the beginning and the end of the causal nexus. The needs of the consumers are the purpose of producing; they are also the cause for the value of all goods. The purpose and the cause of economic action are identical. There is no difference between causality and teleology, claimed Boehm-Bawerk,[26] and he knew the Aristotelian origin of his argument.[27]

[25] John Stuart Mill, *Grundsätze der politischen Oekonomie*, Adolf Soetbeer translation (Hamburg: Perthes-Besser und Mauke, 1864). Menger's handwritten notes. "Was ist nun aber der Grund hievon. Anziehung des Erdmittelpunktes (So auch beim Wert)." See also Mill, Book I, ch. v., no. 9, Menger's remark: "Der konsumtive Käufer am Schlusse ist die conditio qua non des *Wertes des Elementes. . . .*" Element is used by Menger in the sense of factors of production. (The text contains the translation of Menger's note.)

[26] E. von Boehm-Bawerk, *Positive Theorie des Kapitales* (2nd vol., Excurse, Jena, 1921), pp. 177ff. For a modern version of this argument see M. N. Rothbard, "Toward a Reconstruction of Utility and Welfare Economics," in M. Sennholz (ed.), *On Freedom and Free Enterprise. Essays in honor of Ludwig von Mises* (New York, 1956), p. 236.

[27] F. Paulsen, *Introduction to Philosophy*, tr. Thilly, 2nd American edition, translated from the third German edition, p. 219. See also L. Robin, *Aristote* (Paris, 1944), p. 129. A similar identification of causality and teleology can also be found in Leibnitz,

It was Menger's conviction that the Aristotelian logic, ontology, and morals form the proper foundation for a philosophy of the social sciences. It was Walras' conviction that the economist has to use the mathematical method of the natural sciences. When during the 1880's the French and the Austrian economists explained their viewpoints to each other, they soon found out that their differences were of a methodological nature. The duel between Menger and Walras has a greater bearing on modern theory than Menger's attack on the historical school. In his correspondence with Walras, Menger tried at least to be more polite than in his rough encounter with the head of the historical school. He made every effort to win Walras over to his side. Walras, politely but in a somewhat irritated mood, refused to change his opinion.[28] At the end of this exchange of less and less conciliatory letters, Menger's patience gave way: "A conformity does not exist between us. There is an analogy of concepts in a few points but not in the decisive questions."[29] These bitter words overstated the rift. It has been stated before that much later Menger became aware of the fact that his attack against Walras and the mathematical economy went too far. Essential elements of thought remain common to both groups, as the following chapters will show.

---

see R. Eisler, *Wörterbuch der philosophischen Begriffe* (4th ed.; Berlin, 1927), Vol. 1, p. 815.

[28] Etienne Antonelli, "Léon Walras et Carl Menger à travers leur correspondance." Walras did not like Menger's dominating attitude. In the first draft of Walras' letter to Menger (February 2, 1887), Walras intended to ask Menger to write a condensed version of the Austrian theory of value. In a later draft this invitation was crossed out. Antonelli, p. 286.

[29] Étienne Antonelli, "Léon Walras et Carl Menger à travers leur correspondance," p. 284.

PART III

THE DEVELOPMENT OF
MARGINAL UTILITY THEORY
BETWEEN 1880 AND 1947:
CONSOLIDATION AND REFORM

CHAPTER IX:

THE DOMINANT POSITION
OF THE AUSTRIAN SCHOOL

THE FORMATION OF SCHOOLS

HISTORY was kind to Menger, Jevons, and Walras. In a few decades they were accepted by the majority of economists, and their works are still studied. But the following generations showed preferences. Jevons could not establish a school; he had, however, some followers. Walras established the school of Lausanne, and he still has a great influence. But his lasting fame is not built on his value theory. His successor to the chair of economics at the University of Lausanne, Vilfredo Pareto, was more influenced by F. Y. Edgeworth's indifference curves than by Walras' theory of rarity.[1]

Only the Austrian school established by Menger persists to this day. It formed a continuity of thought because one generation after another studied the marginal utility theory. Alan Sweezy, an outspoken opponent of the Austrian school, wrote: ". . . The Austrians have gone into the role of interpretation more seriously than writers elsewhere."[2] Many contributed to this coherence, and the most important factors are the structure of Menger's work, his ability as a teacher and mentor, and the scientific qualifications of the men who came after him.

[1] F. Y. Edgeworth, *Mathematical Psychics* (London, 1881). No. 10 in a series of reprints of scarce tracts in economics and political science.

[2] Alan Sweezy, "The Interpretation of Subjective Value Theory in the Writings of the Austrian Economists," *The Review of Economic Studies*, Vol. 1, No. 3 (June, 1934), p. 177.

Menger's Influence

Menger's students inherited a field of study and the out-lines of a system. But their master had not answered every question, nor had he marked every detail, nor did he explain the character of his utility numbers. He denied that these figures could be used for measuring as do meters or grams, but what the real function of these numbers are, he did not say. He gave only some hints about the possibilities of applying his budget plan to reality. He discovered marginal utility and individual value but did not analyze the total value of a group of goods for one individual. Enough empty spots were left to be filled by his students, and they did not hold their master's word as sacred and unchangeable. They rewrote the value theory and produced several new versions of the imputation principle. Only an impressive personality and a great teacher could attract students who would fulfill such tasks, and Menger was both.

His students loved the tall, elegant man who could be very courteous.[3] They admired the teacher who spent all his time for their improvement, so that he had no leisure to finish his own literary production. He taught the members of his seminar everything from correct breathing to the right organization of their papers; some essays had to be rewritten eight times before Menger was satisfied.[4] His library was always open to his students; he bought books for those who worked on special projects. His students were even permitted to make free use of ideas and plans which he did not publish during his lifetime.[5] After so many years, a complete list of these suggestions cannot be given, yet it is quite likely that Menger's critical re-

[3] Interview with Richard Schüller.
[4] Richard Schüller told me that this happened to him.
[5] Interview with Richard Schüller.

marks about classicism, mathematical economy, Marxism, freedom, teleology, and causality somehow found their way into the writings of his students.

Menger was exacting even with his best students. He did not believe in Boehm's originality, and in the discussions between Boehm-Bawerk and Wieser, the master took Wieser's side.[6] Menger did not endorse every publication of his students, but no shred of evidence exists that he had no hope for the continuation of his work, as Othmar Spann has claimed.[7]

Why should Menger have felt desperate about the further development of his work? Between the year 1870, when his *Principles* were published, and the year of his death, his school and his personal reputation had grown considerably. Long before his death, other leaders had taken over, and even today the school has representatives. The history of Menger's school can be divided into four periods: *1870*: discovery of marginal value—Menger; *about 1880-1927*: systematization and consolidation— Eugen von Boehm-Bawerk, Friedrich von Wieser; *about 1920-1947*: Neo-Marginalism—Hans Mayer, Ludwig von

---

[6] See Menger's handwritten notes to Eugen von Boehm-Bawerk, "Grundzüge der Theorie des wirtschaftlichen Güterwerts" (Jena, 1886). Menger did not accept Boehm's concept of an objective value in exchange, pp. 4, 5, 477. To judge by his handwritten remarks, Menger apparently liked Wieser's work.

[7] According to Othmar Spann, Menger had no hope for the continuation of his system. Othmar Spann, *Die Haupttheorien der Volkswirtschaftslehre* (22nd ed.; Leipzic, 1932), p. 162. Karl Menger, junior, and Richard Schüller most vehemently denied this. No trace of Menger's desperation can be found in Menger's library.

Richard Schüller told me that Spann's surmise was based on misunderstanding: Menger did not write much after 1900. He may have been dissatisfied with his own later achievements, but not with the progress of the Viennese school. Menger dedicated the last twenty years of his life to the rewriting of his *Principles* and teaching his students, as I mentioned before.

Mises, Paul Rosenstein-Rodan, Leo Schönfeld-Illy; *1943—*: three schools dealing with preference and indifference, the French blending of sociology and economics, Mises' philosophical anthropology, von Neumann and Morgenstern's theory of games.

The Austrian School

During the second era the two greatest leaders after Menger—Eugen von Boehm-Bawerk and Friedrich von Wieser—systematically investigated many aspects of the value theory: total and marginal utility, indirect and direct utility, the equilibrization of marginal utilities, costs, and imputation. Boehm-Bawerk published his *Theory of Capital* in his younger years (1888). In this ponderous treatise, he combined capital and interest theory with a detailed explanation of value. In later years, his duties as civil servant and Minister of Public Finance did not give him enough leisure to reorganize his book. In the later editions, he attached to the text a number of critical commentaries (Exkurse) in which he tried to persuade his many critics, in the manner of a benign father, to give up their errors and to follow him; but his courteous remarks are not always convincing. One of his main opponents was his own brother-in-law, Wieser.[8]

Friedrich von Wieser developed his ideas gradually. During his later life, he corrected his earlier views; even his posthumous sociological treatise, *The Law of Power* (1927), contained new ideas. Wieser was a historian, an economist, a sociologist, and a statesman. In his mature economic work, *The Theory of Social Economics* (1914), he blended historical illustrations and sociological thoughts with economic theory. This subtle thinker had a longer

[8] Wieser did not discuss economic problems with Boehm-Bawerk personally. Correspondence with Wesley C. Mitchell-Friedrich von Hayek. Hayek's letter of December 15, 1923, Columbia Library.

lasting influence on the following generations than Boehm, and his most important student was Hans Mayer.

In the year 1922, Hans Mayer enumerated four elementary conditions of economic theory: a plurality of given purposes; a quantitative insufficiency of given means for the achievement of all given purposes; the organization of all given purposes according to rank; the connection of all the purposes which ought to be reached by the same means.[9]

This program sounds like a condensation of all previous thoughts. But Hans Mayer has changed the emphasis. The "plurality of given purposes" now forms the center of scientific interest. Hans Mayer and his circle of friends and followers investigated first of all the consumer's strategy.[10] This change of focus led to a reappraisal of pivotal concepts. The fourth point of Hans Mayer's manifesto dealt with the technical complementary nature of needs. This is not new, but in earlier literature it was not emphasized so strongly as in Mayer's four points. In 1924, Schönfeld-Illy applied complementarity to the psychology of needs.[11] The main source of inspiration for Schönfeld

[9] Hans Mayer, "Untersuchung zu dem Grundgesetz der wirtschaftlichen Wertrechnung," *Zeitschrift für Volkswirtschaft und Socialpolitik.* N.F. I (Wien, 1921), 431ff. N.F. Bd. II (1922), pp. 1ff. This quotation is from Bd. II, 4-5.

[10] Hans Mayer, "Der Erkenntniswert der funktionellen Preistheorien," *Die Wirtschaftstheorie der Gegenwart* (Vienna, 1932), II, 147ff.; Hans Mayer, "Zurechnung," *Handwörterbuch der Staatswissenschaften* (4th ed.; Jena, 1928), VIII, 1206ff.; Rosenstein-Rodan, "La Complementarita prima delle tre etappe del progresso della Teoria Economica Pura," *La Riforma Sociale,* XLIV (Torino, 1933), 257; Rosenstein-Rodan, "La funzione del tempo nella teoria economica," *Annali di Statistica e di Economia,* IV (Genoa, 1933), 3ff.; Rosenstein-Rodan, "Grenznutzen," *Handwörterbuch der Staatswissenschaften* (4th ed.; IV, 1190ff.); Leon Schönfeld-Illy, *Grenznutzen und Wirtschaftsrechnung* (Wien, 1924); Leon Schönfeld-Illy, *Das Gesetz des Grenznutzens* (Wien, 1948).

[11] "Celle-ci [the new school] énonce qu'il existe entre tous les biens à la disposition du sujet *une complémentarité générale de*

was a paper written by Menger's colleague at the University of Vienna, Johann Komorzynski.[12] In connection with the complementary concept, the law of diminishing utility was changed to the law of marginal substitution, and the household plans were reformed to include the *future* needs of the consumer. All these new ideas were demonstrated in literary language with little or no use of mathematics. Hans Mayer renewed the traditional taboo against curves and equations. Only Schumpeter dared to integrate Austrian and mathematical methods. About 1940 the time was ripe for a new evaluation of the connection between mathematics and economics. In 1943 John von Neumann and Oskar Morgenstern found a connection between both methods.

The Austrian economists had always claimed that the consumer plans his consumption without knowing the exact utility of future enjoyment. The household leader deals with an *estimated* future utility (*der veranschlagte Nutzen*). For instance, it is probable but not certain that I will enjoy my next meal. The consumer organizes his household in a realm of uncertainty. Neumann and Morgenstern claimed that the consumer's strategy can be calculated with the help of probability mathematics, and the two authors applied their new method in many fields of economics. They created a new interpretation of imputation based on Boehm's price theory and even tackled

---

caractère psychique" (Perroux italics). François Perroux, *La Valeur* (Paris, 1943), p. 182. "It [the new school] proclaims that between all the goods which a person owns a general psychological complementarity exists" (my translation).

[12] Dr. Johann Komorzynski, "Ist auf Grundlage der bisherigen wissenschaftlichen Forschung die Bestimmung der natürlichen Höhe der Güterpreise möglich?" *Zeitschrift für die gesamten Staatswissenschaften*, Vol. 25 (Tübingen, 1869), p. 236. "Is it possible to determine the natural price of commodities on the basis of the past research?" (my translation).

the most difficult problem of marginal utility, the measuring of value. It is a proof of the vitality of the Austrian school that seventy-three years after Menger, two authors imbued with the Austrian tradition could produce so many new ideas.

It is understandable that such a vigorous movement both attracted many economists and repelled others. Especially between 1880 and 1927, during the golden period of the Viennese school, students of many nations flocked to the seminars at the University of Vienna. The influence of Menger and his followers was considerable, but the Austrian ideas never completely dominated international opinion. In the United States Jevons' version was studied before 1890 and after that date the Austrian interpretation received attention.

THE MARGINAL UTILITY THEORY IN THE U.S.A.

An early student of the value problem was the astronomer and mathematician Simon Newcomb.[13] Around 1872 he became interested in Jevons and Cournot. His university, Johns Hopkins, became the nucleus of studies in marginal utility. David I. Green, who received a doctorate from Johns Hopkins in 1893, defended the Austrian value theory against the persistent classicist Mac Vane. Sherwood, W. G. Langworthy Taylor, J. B. Clark, Davenport, and others, were on Green's side.

In 1927 the older Fetter described in the *Wieser Festschrift* the situation in the U.S.A., where the Austrian theories gained acceptance in spite of classical and institutional opposition.[14] The American friends of the Viennese

[13] The American development is well described in Joseph Dorfman, *The Economic Mind in American Civilization* (New York, 1949), Vol. 3, pp. 83, 243.

[14] Frank A. Fetter, "Amerika," *Die Wirtschaftstheorie der Gegenwart*, Vol. 1, *Gesamtbild der Forschung in den einzelnen Ländern* (Wien, 1927), p. 31.

school accepted Wieser's opportunity costs, discussed the relation between total and marginal value, and investigated the social element in the value complex.[15] Davenport accepted some Austrian ideas but complained about the Benthamite "flavor" of the Austrian explanations. "It must be admitted that in all fields of investigation, other than jurisprudence and economics, Utilitarianism stands as a point of view discredited and outworn."[16]

GERMAN RESISTANCE

Those countries where the Austrian school gained only a small foothold were the exception. In Great Britain Marshall's authority prevented a strong movement in favor of the Austrian school. Northern Germany remained the domain of the historical school; the few theorists (Adolph Wagner, Franz Oppenheimer, Ladislaus Bortkiewicz) taught a mixture of Ricardo, Marx, and Rodbertus. It is quite possible that Menger's rude treatment of Schmoller created resentment in Northern Germany. But even German economists were not immune to Viennese influence. Eugen von Philippovich's standard handbook and Wieser's *Theory of Social Economy* acquainted German students with the main ideas of the Viennese school. There were

[15] Besides Fetter the following publications were read: Mac Vane, "Marginal Utility and Value," *Quarterly Journal of Economics* (April, 1893); H. J. Davenport, "The Formula of Sacrifice," *Journal of Political Economy*, Vol. 2, p. 561; David I. Green, "Pain Cost and Opportunity Costs," *The Quarterly Journal of Economics*, Vol. 8, pp. 218ff.; H. J. Davenport, "Proposed Modifications in Austrian Theory and Terminology," *Quarterly Journal of Political Economy*, Vol. 16 (Boston, 1902), pp. 355ff.; Benjamin M. Anderson, *Social Value* (Cambridge, Mass., 1911); Charles E. Persons, "Marginal Utility and Marginal Disutility as Ultimate Standards of Value," *Quarterly Journal of Economics* (August, 1913), pp. 548ff.; A. F. McGoun, "Higher and Lower Desires," *Quarterly Journal of Economics*, Vol. 37 (Cambridge, Mass., 1923), pp. 291ff.

[16] Davenport, "Proposed Modifications," p. 355.

some defenders of marginalism in Northern Germany such as Wilhelm Vleugels. He refined Wieser's Theory of Imputation, and played an essential role at the meeting which the German economists arranged for discussion of the value problem at Dresden in 1932.[17]

The meeting revealed the strength and weakness of the Austrian school and of all German economic studies. At that time the Austrian school had existed for sixty-two years, but of the ten essays which were prepared by the participants of this meeting, only three were consistently in favor of the Austrian value theory— those of Oskar Morgenstern, Ludwig Mises, and Wilhelm Vleugels.[17a] Furlan was a follower of Pareto. Wilhelm Kromphard and Robert Liefmann recommended some modification of Neo-classicism, and Liefmann was not so far away from the Austrian school as he claimed to be.[17b] The most implacable opponents of the Austrian value theory were Gottl-Otlilienfeld, Franz Oppenheimer, Zeisl,

[17] *Probleme der Wertlehre*, ed. Ludwig Mises and Arthur Spiethoff, Schriften des Vereins für Sozialpolitik (München, 1931), Vol. 183, II (München 1933), contains the discussion.

[17a] Oskar Morgenstern, "Die drei Grundtypen der Theorie des subjektiven Wertes" (the three elementary forms of the subjective value), pp. 1ff.; Ludwig Mises, "Vom Weg der subjektivistischen Wertlehre" (The method of the subjective value), p. 73; Morgenstern, "Die psychologischen Wurzeln des Widerstandes gegen die nationalökonomische Theorie" (The psychological motivations of the resistance against economic theory), pp. 275ff.; Wilhelm Vleugels, "Zur Verteidigung der Wertlehre" (In defense of the value theory); pp. 251ff. All papers in *Probleme der Wertlehre*, Vol. 183, I.

[17b] V. Furlan, "Die Lehre vom wirtschaftlichen Gleichgewicht" (The theory of the economic equilibrium), pp. 43ff.; Wilhelm Kromphardt, "Cassels Gründe der Ablehnung der Wertlehre" (Cassel's criticism of value theory), pp. 95ff.; Robert Liefmann, "Von der Wert- and Grenzertrags lehre" (About value and marginal productivity), pp. 109ff. All papers in *Probleme der Wertlehre*, Vol. 183, I.

and Othmar Spann.[17c] Only with reluctance do I criticize Franz Oppenheimer, the last knight of undiluted Ricardianism. His was a charming personality; he had a friendly sense of humor and, even at the age of 70, an elegant appearance. Due to his sharp and concise way of thinking, he was a fearsome debater. But he never understood marginal value, and, although he was refuted time and again, especially by Vleugels, he stormed against Boehm-Bawerk and defended Ricardo's inconsistent labor value theory.

Hans Zeisl treated marginal utility theory with more respect than did Oppenheimer; he tried to integrate the Austrian doctrine into the Marxian system. It is easy to find the leading idea in Oppenheimer's and Zeisl's papers, but it is difficult to make sense out of Gottl's and Othmar Spann's contributions. Apparently Gottl's economic dimension (*die wirtschaftliche Dimension*) is some kind of substitute for the value. Whoever wants to know more about Gottl ought to read Gottfried von Haberler's penetrating analysis and devastating criticism.[18] It is still more difficult to understand Othmar Spann. He could not tear himself away from the Austrian tradition, but at the same time he built his own system with a mystical pomp of sonorous phrases. The value discussion of 1932 revealed the inner weakness of German theory at that time, for eccentric systems were built by economists who coined their own

[17c] Friedrich Gottl-Ottlilienfeld, "Meine Ablehnung der Wertlehre" (My refutation of the value theory), pp. 133ff. Hans Zeisl, "Marxismus und subjektive Theorie" (Marxism and subjective theory), pp. 177ff.; Franz Oppenheimer, "Die ökonomische Theorie des Wertes" (The economic theory of value), pp. 147ff.; Othmar Spann, "Hauptpunkte der universalistischen Wert- und Preistheorie" (Main points of the universalistic value-and-price theory), pp. 201ff. All papers in *Probleme der Wertlehre*, Vol. 183, I.

[18] Gottfried Haberler. "Kritische Bemerkungen zu Gottl's Methodologischen Schriften," *Zeitschrift für Nationalökonomie* (May, 1929).

idioms and concepts. German economics lacked tradition; the trend of classical analysis was interrupted by Romanticism and the historical school. When the power of the historical school was on the wane and the need for theorizing arose, no root in the past existed; every writer, from the instructor to the full professor, thought he was at least a future Ricardo and could rely on himself. In Austria, as we have mentioned before, there was a tradition; the enlightened mercantilism of Sonnenfels was followed by Kudler, the classicist, and Kudler's classical value theory found an echo in Menger's discovery. To understand the scientific situation existing thirty years ago, one has to know that the Austrian school was forming a unity in spite of diversities, and one has to compare this group with the chaos and confusion outside. The Viennese movement could be a rallying point for serious theorists, but the school no longer had its former power.

THE DECLINE

With the death of Wieser the decline of the Austrian school began, and since that time the space reserved for value discussions in textbooks and journals has shrunk. New generations have grown up knowing very little about total and marginal utility and the eternal arguments about imputation. The reasons for this change have to be explained later.

The extension of this decline cannot be gauged exactly, for some strongholds remain. Inside and outside of Vienna, in Italy and France, the Austrian tradition is still full of vitality. The French economists (François Perroux, Jean Marchal) have combined the marginal utility theory with sociological and empirical material. Sociological questions are also integrated in Mises' standard work, *Human Action*.[19] The subtitle of this book, *A Treatise on Economics*,

[19] Ludwig von Mises, *Human Action* (New Haven, 1949).

is too narrow because Mises has written, in his own words, "the science of every kind of human action."[20] His so-called praxeology is a philosophical anthropology with the main thesis that man is a selecting animal who chooses rationally between material and ideal issues. This keynote appears time and again in his discussion of many different human situations. Although imbued with the Austrian tradition, he preserves a certain independence, for he gives his own interpretation of rationality and value, and he rejects the search for imputation. But he is in conformity with his predecessors when he categorically rejects the application of mathematics to economics.

However, the mathematical wing has shown some new life amidst the stagnation. The usual theory of indifference has remained in the form which Pareto and Eugen Slutzky have given, and indifference curves are still used in American and English analysis without paying attention to the increasing choir of opponents (Hans Mayer, Oskar Morgenstern, etc.). New impetus came into the whole value discussion through the theory of games which Neumann and Morgenstern have created. It is difficult to find the bridge between this new way of economic thinking and the older forms of value theories. The founders of this new method claim that the market behavior is a form of gambling; the gambler as well as the man in business deals with the uncertain future, and the theory of probability calculates the chances of the gambler. Because Daniel Bernoulli had described the value of chances in the so-called St. Petersburg game, the great Swiss mathematician is considered the forerunner of this new movement. This is correct, but the Austrian tradition is the other formative element of the new analysis. Neumann and Morgenstern have used the new tools forged by probability mathematics to solve problems which appear time and again in the

[20] *Ibid.*, p. 3.

value discussion, for instance imputation and measuring of value. It is quite true that Neumann and Morgenstern's *Theory of Games* does not resemble any other work written by the value theorists, but this can also be said of every work produced by the Austrian and the mathematical wing of the marginal utility theory. All these systems from the time of Menger, Jevons, and Walras until this moment have differed in style, structure, method, and content. What all these books have in common are certain problems.

THE SEVEN ASPECTS OF THE MARGINAL UTILITY THEORY

Seven problems appear time and again in the value discussions: the rational character of consumer's action; the nature of utility; the law of diminishing utility; total and marginal utility; budget planning and strategy; imputation; measuring of utility. These seven topics will be discussed in the following chapters.

CHAPTER X

RATIONALITY AND MARGINAL UTILITY[1]

THE ECONOMIC MAN

IN spite of many disagreements, Menger, Jevons, and Walras claimed that only the economic man evaluates goods and services according to marginal utility. This fictitious man, an heritage of early classicism, had no clear-cut profile. As an ideal type he was sometimes identified as a materialist utilitarian, and then again as a bookkeeper who balances thoroughly cost and utility. Some writers purified this model from all "idealistic" contamination and some did not see any difference between material and ideal motivations. A need existed for gaining clarity out of this confusion, and with the outside help of philosophy the generations after 1870 redefined the economic man. They were interested in three aspects: the form of action (rationality), the understanding of action (introspection and behaviorism), and the goal of action (maximum of utility). We start with the revision of rationality.

THE MEANING OF RATIONAL ACTION

During the last sixty years the meaning of rationality and its connection with marginal valuation has been discussed off and on. Interest in these problems has been shown throughout these years, around 1900 by Benedetto Croce and Vilfredo Pareto, about 1908 by Max Weber, after

[1] I thank Professor Ludwig von Mises and Dr. Murray S. Rothbard for the suggestions which are integrated in this chapter.

1940 by French economists and psychologists and Ludwig von Mises. Lack of cooperation between most of these writers did not prevent them from agreeing on some definitions. In many publications rationality became identical with planning for the future.

In 1901 Benedetto Croce in his controversy with Vilfredo Pareto defined rational action as long-term planning.[2] Max Weber identified rationality with the control of action by the accounting principle.[3] Thirty-eight years later P. Reynaud, who had a considerable influence on the new French economy, especially on Jean Marchal,[4] enumerated the following elements of rational action: first, a logical combination of means and ends; second, the means sufficient for reaching this end; third, a person's having reasoned out this conduct. All this is only an elaborate specification of planning.

Three famous authors, separated by decades and by linguistic differences, agree more or less on the definition of rationality. The exception is the non-conformist Ludwig von Mises; he accepts neither the definition nor the consequences drawn from it. Because human activity is an ultimate datum, Mises claims it cannot be traced back to its causes.[5] Following Menger's philosophy of science, rational action becomes an irreducible element of society, and Mises declares that human action is always rational. He claims

[2] See the controversy: Benedetto Croce-Vilfredo Pareto, *Giornale degli Economisti*, 1900 and 1901, English translation entitled "On the Economic Principle. A Correspondence between B. Croce and V. Pareto," *International Economic Papers* (London, 1953), No. 3, especially p. 201; see also Gabriele de Rosa (ed.), *Vilfredo Pareto. Lettere a Maffeo Pantaleoni* (Rome, 1960), Vol. 2, pp. 351, *et passim*.

[3] Max Weber, "Die Grenznutzlehre und das 'psychophysische Grundgesetz,'" in *Gesammelte Aufsätze zur Wissenschaftslehre* (2nd ed.; Tübingen, 1951), p. 394.

[4] P. Reynaud, *Économie Politique et Psychologie Expérimentale* (Paris, 1946).

[5] Mises, *Human Action*, p. 18.

that rationality and action have the same meaning, and that the words rationality and ratio are superfluous.[6] Irrational considerations do not exist. Mises is against these philosophies of his forerunners, Menger, Boehm-Bawerk, Jevons, who relegate the sacrifices of life, health, or wealth for the attainment of "higher" goods—for instance religious, political, and philosophical convictions—into the realm of the irrational. The striving for higher goals is as much a matter of choice as the selection of food and shelter. Therefore it is arbitrary, Mises concludes, to consider the satisfaction of bodily needs alone as rational and everything else as artificial and therefore irrational. It is easy to rest the case here and to capitulate before Ludwig von Mises' elegant logic. But, I believe, it would be a capitulation and not a conviction. The suspicion lingers that far-reaching differences between human activities exist although they are not registered in Mises' praxeology.

If decision-making is the essence of human activity, then Mises is right. But Benedetto Croce and Jean Marchal found another dividing line between rational and irrational action, *the time element*. Long-run planning is rational and sudden changes of the plan are irrational. Croce, arguing with Vilfredo Pareto, gives an illustration of this verdict. A person likes Rhenish wine; he is not very rich, nor does he wish to "indulge in gluttony," having devoted his money to other and preferable purposes. But in spite of this planning, he yields to the temptation of the moment, buys and drinks Rhenish wine. This person has put himself "in contradiction" with himself "and the sensual pleasure will be followed by a judgement of a disapproval, by a legitimate and fitting *economic remorse*."[7]

The French economists after 1940 refined Croce's ideas, eliminating the Hegelian formulation, and going

[6] *Ibid.*, p. 18.
[7] Correspondence Croce-Pareto, p. 201.

beyond Croce's verdict. Jean Marchal, together with his friends (Gaétan Pirou, François Perroux, André Marchal, etc.), revived French economics which for a long time had been in the doldrums. In the *Essays in Honor of Hans Mayer* he confronted rational and irrational action in a vein similar to Croce.[8] Jean Marchal told with great charm the story of the two students who planned to buy a scientific book which was important for their studies and their careers. The one buys the book although he has to go without satisfying other wants. The other student is seduced by a window display and the pretty face of the saleslady to buy a tie instead of the book. The first student follows a long-range plan; he acts rationally. The second student upsets his long-range plan; he acts irrationally. So far Jean Marchal reiterated only Benedetto Croce. The progress beyond Croce consisted in Perroux's clear understanding of the connection between rationalism and marginal utility. Marchal's two students represent two kinds of people:[9] the rationally acting man, or "l'homme de Descartes," and the person who reacts to stimuli, or "l'homme Pavlov." Jean Marchal's Cartesian man could come straight out of a textbook on marginal utility. This economic man wants to reach the maximum of utility. Before he buys anything, he balances the anticipated satisfaction derived from the new commodity with the sacrifices caused by this acquisition. Jean Marchal's Pavlov man does not act, but he reacts; he does not fulfill

[8] Jean Marchal, "Essay de révision de la Théorie des prix à la lumière des progrès de la Psychologie moderne," in *Neue Beiträge zur Wirtschaftstheorie. Festschrift anlässlich des 70. Geburtstages von Hans Mayer* (Wien, 1949); André Marchal, *Méthode scientifique et Science Economique* (2 vols.; Paris s.d. [1951?]); Marchal, *La Pensée Economique en France depuis 1945* (Paris, 1953); Jean Marchal, *Cours d'Economie politique* (Paris, s.d. [1955?]).

[9] Jean Marchal, "Essai de revision . . . ," pp. 127, 129; J. Marchal, *Cours d'Economie Politique . . . ,* pp. 374ff.

premeditated purposes, but he is swayed by the induce-
ments furnished by his social surroundings. Both types
are extreme cases. In real life one finds strict balancing
of advantages and disadvantages in business organizations,
while the consumer rarely follows the code of pure rationality. However, if the household manager does not balance
the advantages and disadvantages, then one should wonder
about the application of marginal utility. Jean Marchal
does not share this pessimistic mood. He believes that
each man is a medley of rationality and irrationality; therefore marginal utility still can explain a part of consumers'
actions.

Even the validity of this restricted explanation is not
self-evident. One condition must be fulfilled: the scholar
ought to blend two activities, the spontaneous creation
of scientific concepts and the reproduction of reality.[10] The
value theorist ought to understand the actions of the house-
wife in the supermarket, and at the same time he has to
fit these market observations into scientific concepts.
The economists are convinced that they can accomplish
this double task because they can use two different
methods for the understanding of social reality, introspection and behaviorism.

INTROSPECTION AND INTUITION

Introspection is the ability of the observer to reconstruct
events which go on in the mind of another person with the
help of self-observation.[10a] This form of comprehension
may be just guesswork or intuition or the result of long-
lasting experience. A number of philosophers, historians,
and economists, among them Dilthey and A. Schütz, be-

[10] A classical analysis of the relation between scientific concepts
and reality can be found in Ernst Cassirer, *Substance and Function*, English translation (New York, 1953), pp. 223, *et passim*.

[10a] Maurice Duverger, *An Introduction to the Social Sciences*,
tr. Malcolm Anderson (New York, 1964), p. 216.

lieved that this kind of understanding is possible.[11] If the mind of the other person works on similar lines as my own, I can transfer the pattern of thinking which I have found in my own mind, to the other person. If introspection is possible, the theory of value has not individual, but general, character.

Most members of the Austrian school have used some kind of introspection. Menger had worked in this direction. As I have mentioned before, he shared with Walras and Jevons the conviction that man in economics acts rationally. But he was not satisfied with rationality alone, although he did not take a definite stand. Apparently he believed that marginal utility is only a key to the understanding of man's behavior if human needs are similar.

Organizing his chart of needs, Menger followed the Aristotelian pattern. This public hierarchy of desires starts with the preservation of life on its lowest level; then the conservation of health, comfort, and luxury follow. The more we reach into the upper strata of this value table, the more the desires are colored by the whims and fancies of the cultivated man-about-town in the Vienna of 1870.[12] The hunting lodge, the reception room, and the game room reflect Menger's taste and the Viennese outlook on life in the year 1870. Menger was not aware of this environmental influence; therefore he overstressed the public character of his chart. The differences between private and public, and between general and historical valuations, are not clearly drawn. Although Menger studied Wilhelm Wundt and the Austrian school of psychology, he left his thoughts on the chart of needs in a fragmentary stage. Wieser explored this field anew.

[11] About the history of this method see Werner Sombart, *Die drei Nationalökonomien* (München, 1930), pp. 155ff.
[12] See also Menger's inventory of his belongings made by himself when he moved (about 1882), Hitotsubashi Library.

Wieser's main concern was with introspection. Unfortunately Wieser identified psychology with introspection, and so an unnecessary confusion was created. The "psychological" school which Wieser defended against the pragmatic approach of the young Schumpeter is really the "introspective" school.[13] Wieser believed that insight into oneself gives the value deductions a general and inevitable character. The inner experience of the theorizing economist is identical with the observations of the layman.[14] The lectures and the written word of the scholar help everybody to remember his own observations. Wieser's students had to grasp economic value principles in a similar way as Plato's disciples had to understand ideas by remembrance. Even the members of the Austrian school found that Wieser had gone too far. In a song written for the Mises' "kreis" the young philosopher Felix Kaufmann held Wieser's dogma up to ridicule: "so handle ich und das ist jedermann." (So I act and that means everybody.)[15] It is understandable that shortly after Wieser's death Schütz's more cautious interpretation of introspection prevailed.

About 1932 Mises and his friends studied the new book *The Meaningful Structure of the Social World*, by Alfred Schütz.[16] Schütz described how we reconstruct with the help of our own experiences the meaning of the other person's (alter ego) action. One gains an understanding of a third person by comparing the external signs of his body with one's own expression. From these observations one

[13] Wieser, *Gesammelte Abhandlunger*, p. 26.

[14] Wieser, *Der natürliche Werth* (Wien, 1889), p. 4.

[15] *Miseslieder*. Fritz Machlup, of Princeton, was kind enough to send me a mimeographed copy of the songs. These songs were used for seminar celebrations. The libretti are new; the scores come from old Austrian and Viennese folksongs. Their artistic value is not as high as their documentary importance.

[16] See *Miseslieder*. Alfred Schütz, *Der sinnhafte Auflau der sozialer Welt* (Wien, 1932). I used the unchanged second edition of 1960.

can build up with the help of his imagination the trend of consciousness which goes on in the other man's mind. The progress beyond Wieser consisted in Schütz's insight that experience and imagination provide only an incomplete and often inaccurate comprehension of another person's mind.[17]

Ludwig von Mises accepted Schütz's analysis: "It is beyond doubt that the practice of considering fellow men as beings who think and act as I, the Ego, do has turned out well. . . ."[18] Introspection is a necessary assumption for whose validity only "incomplete evidence" can be provided. The behaviorists claim they can provide more complete evidence for their own philosophy.

BEHAVIORISM

Fritz Machlup described behaviorism as a movement which tried to confine "social sciences to the establishment of regularities in the physical behavior of man under strictly controlled conditions."[19] The behaviorist rejects introspection; his social insight is based entirely on experiment and controlled observation. It is very interesting to know whether a general plan of consumer behavior can be built exclusively on induction, and whether marginal utility calculation would be the outcome. John R. Hicks is a defender of this method. He denies that the econometrist can see inside the heads of the individuals.[20]

Apart from the fact that John R. Hicks misunderstood the introspectionists, neither Schütz nor Mises claimed

[17] Schütz, *Der soziale Aufbau*, pp. 126-28.
[18] Mises, *Human Nature*, p. 24.
[19] Fritz Machlup, "The Inferiority Complex of the Social Sciences," *On Freedom and Free Enterprise* (Mises *Festschrift*), ed. Mary Sennholz (Princeton, 1956), p. 168; see also Fritz Sander, "Der Behaviorismus," *Zeitschrift für Nationalökonomie*, Vol. 3 (Wien, 1932), p. 704.
[20] John R. Hicks, *A Revision of Demand Theory* (Oxford, 1956), p. 6.

to have such magical powers. Hicks is also a strange behaviorist who does not even use his own method. He
describes a man who reacts to the smallest advantages
and disadvantages in his choices. Hicks did not distill
this ideal of economic virtues from experiences; he constructed a model. That Hicks failed is not sufficient proof
of the uselessness of behaviorism in our field, for behaviorism has not been seriously tried.

It is my impression that behaviorism can only be correctly judged if the old antagonism of behaviorism contra
introspection is eliminated. A theory cannot be constructed without figuring out how a rational person
will act. But a theory remains an hypothesis unless it can
be verified by empirical observations. It seems to me that
introspection and behaviorism belong together. Yet we have
not reached this goal; we are long on thought and short on
observation. Von Neumann and Morgenstern have complained about this situation of our science, and the achievements of these two authors have been praised by the
majority of the theorists. Yet the authors themselves have
remained rather skeptical; they fear that "mathematical
treatment a priori appear hopeless. . . ."[21] One of the reasons is the inadequate empirical background. The relevant
facts of economics are less well known than those of
natural science at the time when "the mathematization of
that subject was achieved."[22] This complaint did not prevent the two authors from redefining the goal of rational
action as the maximum of satisfaction.

THE MAXIMUM OF UTILITY

Since Gossen, most economists have considered the *maximum of utility* to be the goal of rational action. This
maximum was a catch-all concept which contained many

---

[21] Von Neumann and Morgenstern, *Theory of Games*, p. 4.
[22] *Ibid*.

shades of meaning. It could be the maximum of satisfaction for all individuals inside a market economy or the maximum of utility for one isolated person. Menger's Robinson Crusoe can reach by a wise application of his resources the maximum of satisfaction for himself as an isolated person. Menger's followers accepted his viewpoint, but they were not so sure that each individual participating in the exchange can reach this situation. Boehm-Bawerk claimed that in an exchange between two persons who deal with two goods no definite price can be calculated. If the price cannot be determined then it seems possible that the participants in this exchange cannot reach their maxima.[23]

Thus the Austrians did not offer a clear solution, but by no means would they accept Alfred Marshall's simplified theory. Alfred Marshall wrote that under condition of free competition "every position of equilibrium of demand and supply may fairly be regarded as a position of maximum satisfaction."[24] Vilfredo Pareto investigates with his indifference curves Boehm-Bawerk's situation of two individuals with two commodities. The Italian economist, more explicit than Boehm-Bawerk, declared that the two dealers cannot reach at the same time their individual maxima of utility.[25]

From Menger to Pareto the concept of maximum satisfaction became less and less meaningful. The value-theorists hesitated to say how Robinson Crusoe's perspective can be changed into the attitude of a participant in a market. Von Neumann and Morgenstern went even fur-

[23] Eugen von Boehm-Bawerk, *Kapital und Kapitalzins. Positive Theorie des Kapitales*, 4th ed.; Vol. 1, pp. 269ff. See also Hans Mayer, "Der Erkenntniswert," p. 184.

[24] See Alfred Marshall, *Principles of Economics* (London, 1930), p. 470.

[25] Vilfredo Pareto, *Manuel d'Economie Politique* (Paris, 1927), pp. 198-200.

ther; they even cut the bridge leading from Robinson Crusoe to the market economy. Robinson Crusoe is a textbook case for marginal utility, but von Neumann and Morgenstern claimed that its relation to modern reality is rather precarious.[26] More forcefully than their forerunners did, von Neumann and Morgenstern emphasized that the Robinson novel "is not fit for the behavior in a social exchange economy."[27] A maximum can be reached only if the economic man has at his disposition all the factors, but in a market economy each consumer controls only a segment of all the circumstances. Each individual integrated in a social economy tries to reach an optimum position; therefore situations of conflicting maxima arise. Von Neumann and Morgenstern presented several cases which they explained with the Theory of Games. Their discovery of conflicting optima created new problems. The two authors came out with the most startling declaration: "It is not clear at all, however, what significance it [marginal utility] has in determining the behavior of a participant in a social exchange economy."[28] They are of the opinion that the principles of rational behavior under market conditions need a new formulation,[29] and that this additional work is lacking.

[26] Von Neumann and Morgenstern, *Theory of Games*, p. 30.
[27] *Ibid.*, p. 21.
[28] *Ibid.*, p. 31.
[29] *Ibid.*

CHAPTER XI

THE MEANING OF UTILITY

THE TREND OF DISCUSSION

ACCORDING to Max Weber, the consumer satisfying his needs follows a rational pattern. The goal of this planned selection is the acquisition of useful goods and services. Rationality is the method, and the reaching of highest utility is the goal. The expressions "useful" and "utility" have been discussed since the days of Plato. The old controversies between Stoics and Epicureans, between utilitarians and ethical idealists, are reflected in the discussion of the economists. In contrast to the philosophers, the value theorists very rarely took a consistent stand; perhaps Bentham is the only value theorist who was a consistent utilitarian. Jevons and Walras borrowed freely from various philosophical sources, and they used the pain and pleasure balances for the bread and butter needs, but not for the final moral goals. As we have mentioned already, after the publication of the *Principles*, Menger became aware of the inconsistencies inherent in his welfare system. The majority of the following generations eliminated the philosophical discussion; they purified utility from all utilitarian and idealistic suggestions and the result was the neutral or formal utility. A minority had rather cogent reasons to oppose this new definition. Even Boehm-Bawerk, who was most likely the creator of neutral utility, was in his later years no longer certain that such a rigid restriction of utility discussion helped the understanding of economic value.

NEUTRAL UTILITY

In the year 1884 the young Boehm-Bawerk wrote in his early paper, *Principles of Commodity Value* (*Grundzüge der Theorie des wirtschaftlichen Güterwerts*): "It seems almost unnecessary to say that I give here the word 'welfare aims' (Wohlfahrtszwecke) the most general meaning which does not only include the egotistical goals of a person but also everything which seems worth striving for."[1] This cleansing of utility from egotistical, altruistic, ethical, and non-ethical motives was favored by economists inside and outside the Austrian camp. Irving Fisher and the Russian economist Eugen Slutsky, and later Rosenstein-Rodan and Ludwig von Mises, supported this neutral utility.[2] The majority favored this definition, because under the banner of neutrality the economists could write theory without being involved in philosophy and psychology. But not everybody was satisfied. Alan Sweezy discovered a vicious circle. If utility is what people consider useful, then utility is explained by utility.[3] Murray N. Rothbard answered Sweezy: ". . . desires exist by virtue of the concept of human action, and of the existence of action."[4] Rothbard's conclusion eliminates the restrictions of formal utility. If the economist infers from real actions specific desires, then different kinds of utility can be distinguished and their influence on preference and

[1] *Jahrbücher für Nationalökonomie und Statistiks* (n.f., Vol. 13, 1886), pp. 13ff.

[2] Eugen Slutsky, "Sulla Teoria del Bilancio del Consummatore," *Giornale degli Economisti*, Vol. 51 (July, 1915), pp. 1, 2, 24; Rosenstein-Rodan's article, "Grenznutzen," pp. 1195-96; Ludwig von Mises, *Human Action*, pp. 94ff.

[3] Alan Sweezy, "The Interpretation of Subjective Value Theory in the Writings of the Austrian Economists," *The Review of Economic Studies*, Vol. 1, No. 3 (June, 1934), p. 179.

[4] Murray N. Rothbard, "Toward a Reconstruction of Utility and Welfare Economics," Mises *Festschrift*, p. 226.

rejection has to be investigated. A minority of value-theorists proceeded on just those lines.

DUALISM OF GOALS

Eugen von Boehm-Bawerk did not remain faithful to his early proclamation of neutralism. Davenport and others found the "Benthamite flavor" of Boehm's value theory in the *Positive Theory of Capital* and criticized it.

Boehm answered his critics with arguments taken from the Austrian philosophy of value and from Jevons. Boehm learned from Franz Brentano that love and hate are the very roots of human preferences and rejections.[5] He admitted that these roots may also have a non-materialistic and non-egotistical character. Like Jevons, Boehm drew a demarcation line between the realm of morals and the world of pleasure; he abandoned his earlier opinion that the goals of human action have no bearing on economic theory. He wrote that marginal utility is not at home in the higher and highest regions of human endeavor, but exists in those comparatively low districts where marginal calculation creates value. These lower regions are dominated by the trite and trivial needs, whose values depend on degrees of lust and pleasure.[6]

With the acceptance of Jevons' dichotomy, Boehm-Bawerk repudiated his earlier defense of neutral utility. In Boehm's realm of marginal calculation, utility means pleasure; the hedonist meaning is stressed. This is perplexing because Boehm started out to prove that he was not a hedonist. He created some confusion in the minds of his readers, so that in 1928 Eugen Slutsky came to the conclusion that at least two value theories are interwoven

[5] Eugen von Boehm-Bawerk, *Kapital und Kapitalzins*, 2nd section, *Positive Theorie des Kapitales* (Jena, 1921), Vol. 1, p. 236; Howard O. Eaton, *Philosophy of Values* (Norman, Oklahoma, 1930), pp. 45-46.
[6] Boehm, *Positive Theorie*, Vol. 1, p. 238.

in the *Positive Theory*: one which is entirely based on pain and pleasure, and the other which acknowledges autonomous values as honor and duty. The second value system exists only in fragments.[7] The subtle Russian thinker had put his finger on a sore spot in the whole utility analysis. In spite of these immanent inconsistencies, Vilfredo Pareto also developed a dichotomy of utilities. His thesis rather resembles the viewpoint of Menger, who distinguished between the pleasure of the fleeting moment and the long-lasting welfare gain. In Pareto's terminology the label utility (*utilité*) is given to the complex of objectives which enhance personal or social welfare; ophelimity (*ophelimité*) means pleasure. "Morphine is not useful in the ordinary sense of the word, for it is dangerous to the drug addict; but from an economic point of view, it is useful because it satisfies the needs of a drug addict although it is unhealthy."[8] Pareto can easily be misunderstood. He did not imply that the social scientist ought to be interested in ophelimities alone. Man's actions are also determined by aims of cultural or social value.[9]

The Social Value

American economists tried to eliminate the distinction between social and pleasure values. They gave all human goals a social character. John Bates Clark wrote that it is not the individual but society which attaches value and

---

[7] Eugen Slutsky, "Zur Kritik des Boehm-Bawerkschen Wertbegriffs und seiner Lehre von der Meszbarkeit des Wertes," Schmoller, *Jahrbuch*, Vol. 51 (1927), pp. 545ff. Besides Jevons, Bentham also may have increased Boehm-Bawerk's confusion. Bentham became known to the Austrians, especially to Boehm-Bawerk, after 1900, when Oskar Kraus published his study on Bentham. Hayek's letter to Wesley Mitchell of December 15, 1923, Wesley Mitchell papers (Columbia Library).

[8] Vilfredo Pareto, *Manuel d'Économie Politique* (Paris, 1927), p. 157.

[9] *Ibid.*, pp. 41ff.

utility to commodities and services. Society is an "organic whole"; it measures value according to the social services derived from the goods. Value is social utility.[10] Similar ideas were expressed by other American writers.[11]

THE AUTONOMOUS NEEDS

American authors went back to the older tradition of the schoolmen and the mercantilists. The strong dependence on old ideas seems to have slowed down progress in this field. All the theories and explanations presented here, with the exception of neutral or formal utility, can be found in the writings of earlier writers. Menger, Wieser, and Boehm-Bawerk read the works of the Austrian school of psychology, but only seldom did they apply what they had learned; more often than not, they neglected the discoveries of the psychologists. Most Austrians believed that they cultivated a field which was left fallow by the other disciplines.

Only one, Oskar Engländer, improved his value theory considerably by his studies of the Austrian psychologists. His teacher was Alexius von Meinong, who advanced beyond the stage reached by Jevons. Meinong said that usefulness must not necessarily cause pleasure: ". . . in the case of the usefulness of the art of handwriting to the little child in school who is under the necessity of learning it with such difficulty, there is no pleasure as the immediate result of the valuable object."[12] Things which immediately bring pleasure are pleasant or agreeable; things which are useful produce pleasure indirectly or any other welfare goal. Engländer claimed that selection is not

[10] John B. Clark, *The Philosophy of Wealth* (Boston, 1886), pp. 81-83.

[11] Benjamin M. Anderson, *Social Value* (Cambridge, Mass., 1911); A. F. McGoun, "Higher and Lower Desires," *Quarterly Journal of Economics*, Vol. 37 (Cambridge, 1937), pp. 291ff.

[12] Eaton, *The Austrian Philosophy of Value*, p. 94.

a reflex of pleasure, but an autonomous and original element of psychology which cannot be reduced to other psychological factors. Man is able to select goods regardless of their utility intensity. Engländer's illustration has some similarity with the Meinong example quoted above: "I prefer studying a chapter in a textbook to the reading of a work of fiction, although in the moment I register no utility feeling in favor of the scientific value but a great desire for the novel."[13] Modern psychology does not add much to Engländer's statement of the year 1929.

Abraham Maslow's ideas in his book *Motivation and Personality*[14] remind us of Engländer, although the psychologist from New York did not know the economist from Prague. In Maslow's psychology, man is "a wanting animal."[15] Wants are motivated by autonomous but interrelated drives. His catalogue of wants is rather detailed; it consists of hunger and thirst (the physiological needs), the needs of safety, of love, of esteem, and of self-actualization, the desire to know and to understand. These wants are autonomous, for a common denominator of these drives does not exist; for instance, all these drives can be reduced neither to hunger, nor to sex, nor to the lust for power. At the same time all these motivations are interrelated. Engländer envisaged conflicts; Maslow did not consider this possibility, for his integration of needs consists of a sequence of wants. As soon as one desire is satisfied another one comes into the foreground. The needs of the stomach have priority before the cultural drives: "The basic human needs are organized into a hierarchy of

[13] Oskar Engländer, *Theorie der Volkswirtschaft*, Erster Teil (Preisbildung und Preisaufbau: Wien, 1929), pp. iv, 2.

[14] New York, Harper, 1954, especially pp. 67ff. I owe this and other information in this chapter to the good services of Frank Holmes, Ph.D., Professor of Psychology, Illinois Wesleyan University.

[15] *Ibid.*, p. 69.

relative prepotency." Non-integrated responses also exist. Maslow claims that the individual can deal with "unimportant or with familiar or with easily conquered problems" in isolation.

Maslow's study is proof of the waste of intellectual power due to the lack of cooperation between the faculties. This psychologist is at the same time *behind* and *ahead of* the economists. His hierarchy of prepotency is just on the level of Galiani. Maslow is not aware of the Austrian discoveries; he deals only with utilities in the abstract sense and not with concrete desires. His scale of satiation does not include the possibility of partial satisfaction. On the other hand, he is ahead of some economists for he knows that hunger, sex, power, are labels of different motivations. If a common denominator is missing, then it is difficult to use the equilibrium-principle. A balance between the ambition to become a senator, the wish to marry a beautiful woman, the plan to hire the best chef in town, is not very meaningful. At best, the word "equilibrium" has here only an allegoric meaning. These thoughts were known to Jevons, Boehm-Bawerk, and Engländer, but the majority of value theorists did not use these insights. Theirs is still the attempt to combine neutral utility with a diluted version of Bentham's pain and pleasure balancing. The felicific balance has no more than a precarious hold on the value theory; even Mises, who admired the grandeur of Epicurean eudaemonism, has to concede that pain and pleasure have only a formal character and are neither of material nor carnal nature.[16] But this means only that the consumer prefers or rejects. Mises' thesis remains remote from the philosophy of Epicurus, Helvetius, or Bentham. It is unfair, however, to focus our critical attention alone on the negative aspects of Mises' utility analysis, for it is his great merit to have stressed the

[16] Mises, *Human Action*, p. 21.

importance of hedonist philosophy for the utility concept. It is not clear to me whether a valid analysis of consumer valuation can be given without some reference to Bentham.

Bentham's solution offers a consistent answer which the later writers did not present. If there is no difference between pushpin and poetry, as Bentham assures us, then all preferences and rejections can be calculated in pain and pleasure. Then it is possible to balance utility with disutility and to find the goal of consumers' strategy in the maximum of pleasure and in the equalization of marginal utilities. Bentham's consistent theory is acceptable only if the satisfaction of our needs brings pleasure and if all pleasures are of the same kind. But these two conditions are challenged. Iris Murdoch describes the hedonist world "in which people play cricket, cook cakes, make simple decisions, remember a childhood, and go to the circus." But, she continues, this is not the world in which "men commit sins, fall in love, say prayers, or join the Communist Party."[17]

Meinong, Engländer, and others have understood the insufficiency of hedonism; neutral utility has not solved but rather only shelved a question whose answer is important for limiting the field in which marginal calculations are valid. It seems unlikely that the situation can be clarified without studying the relevant parts of psychology. The role of psychology for our whole field can be easily underrated, and the discussion of the law of diminishing utility would have been barren without the advice of the psychologists.

[17] Walter Kaufmann, *Critique of Religion and Philosophy* (New York, 1961), p. 37.

CHAPTER XII

THE LAW OF DIMINISHING
UTILITY

HISTORICAL SURVEY

A CHOICE presupposes an order of the available goods. Highest, medium, lowest utility, and any shade between them, can be distinguished only if bundles of commodities are arranged in a certain sequence. We believe that a falling sequence exists, for the enjoyment decreases with increasing saturation. During the last ninety years this law of satiety, also called Gossen's first law, had acquired different meanings. It was threatened by extinction, was replaced by another theorem, and was reinstated, but only with caution and suspicion.[1]

THE PRINCIPLE OF PSYCHOPHYSICS

Until the time of Menger, economists considered the law of diminishing utility to be a general expression for everyday experience; it was a self-evident truth. The situation changed with the development of psychophysics.[2]

Ernst Heinrich Weber (1846) and Gustav Theodor Fechner (1860) discovered a basic relation between physical quantities and psychological reactions.[3] The so-

[1] Article "Nutzen," *Handwörterbuch der Sozialwissenschaften* (Tübingen, 1961), 38 Lieferung, p. 8.

[2] R. S. Howey, *The Rise of the Marginal-Utility School 1870-1889* (Lawrence, Kansas, 1960), pp. 96ff., gives ample material about the development of the Weber-Fechner law.

[3] Ernst Heinrich Weber, *Tastsinn und Gemeingefühl* (Leipzic, 1905); Gustav Theodor Fechner, *Elemente der Psychophysik* (2 vols., Leipzic, 1860).

called Weber-Fechner law describes diminishing psychic returns caused by external stimuli. Weber watched the nerve reaction created by increased weights. As the number of ounces increases, each following ounce has less influence on the ability of the observer to judge relative weights. If the same effect should be repeated, the doses of stimulation have to be increased.

Lujo Brentano, Philipp H. Wicksteed, and others found the evidence for diminishing utility in this psychophysical law.[4] "The size of well-being which is created by one and the same enjoyment does not rise parallel with the increase of those unities of enjoyment which are employed."[5] The stimuli become the units of enjoyment and the degree of well-being will be identified with the reaction of the nerves.

This argument is only valid if the proof is more than an analogy. In 1908 Max Weber in his essay on marginal utility showed that there is not even an analogy.[6] He wrote that the psychophysical principle starts with a physical stimulus; the marginal utility begins with a psychological phenomenon. The want (Bedürfnis) is a complex of sensations, tensions, situations of disutility, and expectations. These highly complicated qualities are connected with images of memory and goals; they are burdened with contradicting motives of different kinds. Max Weber's second argument deals with the relation of outside phenomena and inner experience. In the Weber-Fechner law, a causal line is drawn from the outside world to the reaction of the

[4] Lujo Brentano, "Versuch einer Theorie der Bedürfnisse," *Sitzungsberichte der Königlich Bayerischen Akademie der Wissenschaften*, Philosophisch-Philologische und historische Klasse (Jahrgang, 1908), 10. Abhandlung (München, 1908), pp. 43ff.; Philipp H. Wicksteed, *The Alphabet of Economic Science* (New York, 1955), pp. 52-53.

[5] *Ibid.*

[6] Max Weber, "Die Grenznutzlehre," p. 364.

mind. According to Max Weber, the law of diminishing utility is based on the opposite approach. Weber and Fechner described how external stimuli create sensations. The economist dealing with diminishing utility told how a certain experience of the mind (feeling of a want) leads to a human action in the outside world (buying of a commodity). Max Weber concluded that two different disciplines are involved: physiology and common observation. According to him, physiology has no place in economics. The justification of value theory cannot be derived from other sciences; the point of departure for this law, as for so many other economic theories, is everyday experience (*Alltagserfahrung*).[7] Other writers were not satisfied with the justification by everyday experience; they went further than Max Weber. They wanted to restrict or even to abolish the law of diminishing utility.

CRITICISM OF THE LAW

Theoretical and empirical, sociological and historical reasons were used to challenge the law. In 1903 Pigou stated that diminishing utility is not an accurate statement because social class, place, or time have a great influence on the slope of the utility curve.[8] Yet Pigou did not contest a general trend of falling utility, but Graziadei went further and denied even this. The Italian economist found that the law of diminishing utility is not compatible with the psychology of Wundt, Lindworsky, and de Sanctis.[9] Sensations can be measured, but sentiments cannot. Furthermore, Wundt draws a pleasure curve which is com-

[7] *Ibid.*, p. 369.

[8] A. C. Pigou, "Some Remarks on Utility," *Economic Journal*, Vol. 13 (London, 1903), pp. 58ff.

[9] Antonio Graziadei, *Le Teorie sull'Utilità Marginale e la Lotta contro il Marxismo* (Milano, 1943), pp. 208ff.

pletely at variance with the line drawn by the marginalists, especially Marshall. If we irritate the nerve system of a per-

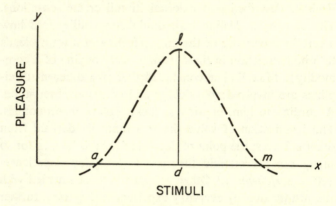

FIGURE 1. Wundt's Pleasure Curve[10]

son with an increasing quantity of stimuli, then pleasure will first rise till it reaches a climax; then it becomes negative and is pain. In Figure 1 the doses of stimuli are marked on the *x* axis and the height of pleasure on the *y* axis. The bell-shaped curve *a l m* symbolizes the sudden rise and fall of the pleasure feeling. The Marshallian curve (see Figure 2) which also indicated the stimuli on the *x* axis and the pleasure on the *y* axis presents the falling trend described by the marginalists. Graziadei doubts that the psychological and economic theories can be reconciled.[11]

The tax experts agree with the psychologists. For a long time marginal utility together with the law of diminishing utility justified progressive taxation. People with higher income can pay a higher percentage of their revenues as income tax because the last dollar of the rich man has a lower marginal utility than the last dollar of the poor

[10] Simplified figure after Graziadei, p. 216.
[11] *Ibid.*, pp. 222-23.

man. The validity of this argument is in doubt. Since 1920 writers in the field of public finance have criticized Gossen's first law.[12] These economists do not level their attack

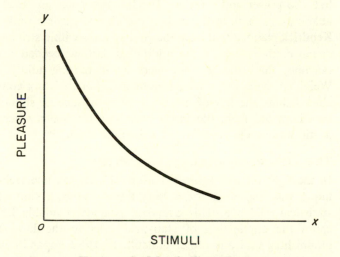

FIGURE 2. Marshallian Curve

against "the principle of diminishing utility as a law relating to the consumption of homogeneous commodities and services. . . ," but against its applications "to increase in the rate of money income."[13] Of all the reasons aimed against the law of diminishing utility of money, only two can be mentioned here. Fagan claims that this "static postulate is often contrary to the facts of life."[14] It is a common experience that people who have obtained a slight increase of income enjoy life now quite out of proportion

---

[12] Elmer D. Fagan, "Recent and Contemporary Theories of Progressive Taxation," *Journal of Political Economy*, Vol. 46, No. 4 (August, 1938), p. 457. This paper contains also a very detailed survey of literature; M. Slade Kendrick, "Ability-to-Pay Theory of Taxation," *The American Economic Review*, Vol. 29 (Evanston, 1939), pp. 92ff.

[13] *Ibid.*, p. 461.   [14] *Ibid.*, p. 463.

to the added revenue. In connection with this criticism M. Slade Kendrick raised a second point. The things which money can buy are not only food and furniture but also power and prestige. The last two goals are available only to those in the higher and highest income ranks. Kendrick claimed that once the goal appears within striking distance, the value of the additional fortune needed for reaching this goal is controlled by increasing utility.[15] Weighing these and similar arguments, Werner Marx concluded that "the law of marginal utility of income should be eliminated from the many economic textbooks where it still enjoys the standing of axiomatic truth."[16]

THE TESTING OF DIMINISHING UTILITY

In the fight for and against the law of satiation one technique was neglected for a long time—the collection of statistical evidence. This oversight is understandable because the application of statistical tests to the law of diminishing utility is rather difficult. In 1952 Papandreou and Kenneth O. May found out how hard the task is.[17] Papandreou considered the results of his studies "merely suggestive — not conclusive."[18] He is very cautious because he could offer only artificial choices. He set up a somewhat complicated machinery which can only be sketched here. Eighteen students had to select tickets for recreational events; the events and tickets were fictitious and were invented only for this testing. Five of these

[15] *Ibid.*, pp. 94-95.

[16] Werner Marx, "The Law of Diminishing Marginal Utility of Income," *Kyklos*, Vol. 3 (Basel, 1949), pp. 254ff.

[17] A. G. Papandreou, "An Experimental Test of an Axiom in the Theory of Choice," University of Minnesota, December, 1952 (a mimeographed paper); Kenneth O. May, "The Intransitivity of Individual Preferences," summary and notes presented at a joint session of the Econometric Society and the Institute of Mathematical Statistics, December 28, 1952 (a mimeographed paper).

[18] A. G. Papandreou, "An Experimental Test . . . ," p. 14.

tickets had a cultural and five an athletic character. The admission tickets were so bundled together that several selections by the students revealed whether they preferred definitely aesthetic or athletic entertainments.

Kenneth O. May shows how diminishing utility can be translated into a mathematical statistical sequence. If the law of satiety exists, then events A B C can be ordered into a transitive sequence $A > B > C$ and $A > C$. If a cyclical sequence prevails it will be $A > B > C$, but $C > A$. A cyclical order contradicts transition. May claimed that the cyclical order can be found very often in reality, and he gives several illustrations. A battleship sinks a destroyer, a destroyer sinks a submarine, but a submarine sinks a battleship. A mongoose kills a cobra, a cobra kills a cat, but a cat kills a mongoose. The events are excellently selected to show the circular sequence, but the relation with diminishing utility is rather remote. We have to observe the utility effect of an increasing number of equal goods in reality. But May speaks about battleships, destroyers, mongooses, and cats. Because he is not careful in the selection of his observations, his verdict that the law of diminishing utility ought to be abandoned does not sound convincing.[19]

The cautious Papandreou is of the opposite opinion; he believes that as a result of his tests the transitive sequence prevails and that an empirical trend may therefore exist which corresponds to the law of diminishing utility. Papandreou was apparently not satisfied with his experiment. A second time he used a test which was still more complicated and had the same result. He found that most likely "the universe of the bundles of commodities from which choices may be made is completely ordered."[20]

[19] May, "Individual Preferences," p. 1.
[20] A. G. Papandreou, "A Test of a Stochastic Theory of Choice," *Publication Economics*, Vol. 16 (University of California Press, Berkeley, 1957).

This is a thorough testing of transitivity, but not of the law of diminishing utility. Papandreou found an order in real life but did not investigate the cause of this order. That the law of satiation is the true explanation for this sequence has been denied again and again. Some critics have offered a substitute for the suspected law of diminishing utility.

CHAPTER XIII

DIMINISHING UTILITY
AND MARGINAL SUBSTITUTION

THE INDIFFERENCE CURVE

MARGINAL substitution is considered a replacement or a refinement of the law of diminishing utility. The theory of marginal substitution was propounded outside the Austrian camp. This reformulation of the old law is also known under its earlier name as the theory of *indifference curves*. Edgeworth presented the indifference relation in the form of an equation as early as 1881. Eleven years later Irving Fisher, in his doctoral thesis, added a system of geometrical curves.[1] The method of curve representation gained wider publicity when Vilfredo Pareto presented his famous graphs (see Figure 1). These curves are a result of balancing the utilities of different goods, e.g., an individual owns one pound of bread and one pint of wine. These two quantities together give him a certain general satisfaction. He will experience the same total enjoyment if he has a little less bread and a little more wine. The following table shows the quantities which give the same total satisfaction:

TABLE 1

Bread, amount in pounds					
1.6	1.4	1.2	1.0	0.8	0.6
Wine, amount in pints					
0.7	0.8	0.9	1.0	1.4	1.8

[1] F. Y. Edgeworth, *Mathematical Psychics* (London, 1881), No. 10 in a series of reprints of scarce tracts in economic and political science; Irving Fisher, "Mathematical Investigations in the Theory of Value and Price," *Transactions of the Connecticut Academy*, Vol. 9 (July, 1892), pp. 70, 121.

If the person has 1.6 bread and 0.7 wine, he has the same satisfaction as if he had 0.6 bread and 1.8 wine.

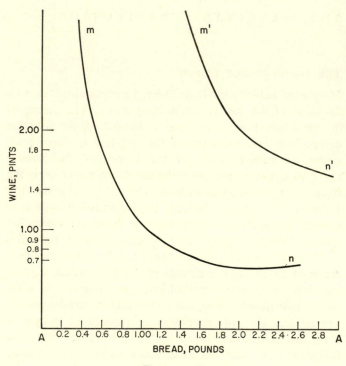

FIGURE 1[2]

Indifference Curve (Pareto)

The person is indifferent to the choices indicated in this table. These numbers can be easily translated into curves. The ordinate *O A* represents the quantities of bread, the abscissa *O B* measures the pints of wine, the line *m n* is the geometrical location of all those points which provide the same satisfaction. All the combinations of wine

[2] Vilfredo Pareto, *Manuel d'Economie Politique*, pp. 168-69.

and bread indicated by that line are indifferent to each other. The line *m' n'* indicates more bread and more wine, e.g., 2 pounds of bread and 2 pints of wine; therefore the satisfaction on *m' n'* is higher than the enjoyment indicated by *m n*. All points on *m' n'* are indifferent to each other.[3]

THE LAW OF MARGINAL SUBSTITUTION

In 1915 Eugen Slutsky recommended the indifference method as a substitute for the law of saturation.[4] During World War I no one became interested in this proposition. The first who worked along similar lines as Slutsky was Leo Schönfeld-Illy in 1924. Another fifteen years elapsed before John R. Hicks in his *Value and Capital* published the first treatment in English.[5] The new approach was adopted because the old theory had investigated consumer strategy under conditions contrary to elementary facts. Before Slutsky the economists had demonstrated diminishing utility by feeding a man too much cake or lavishing on him a second and a third motorcar. In reality, this man, unless he increases his income, can indulge in more cake if he eats less cheese, and he can have a fleet of cars only if he lives in a one-room apartment. A nation can build missiles if it spends less on motorcars. Consumer planning is a two or many-sided balancing problem. Under static conditions one can enlarge consumption in one field and reduce the intensity of utility, whereas consumption is reduced in one or more other fields where utility will be increased. Schönfeld-Illy used the literary

[3] *Ibid.*
[4] Eugen Slutsky, "Sulla Teoria . . ."; Schönfeld-Illy, *Grenznutzen und Wirtschaftsrechnung* (Wien, 1924). Professor Rosenstein-Rodan was kind enough to explain to me this connection between Slutsky and Schönfeld-Illy.
[5] John R. Hicks, *Value and Capital.* I assume that Hicks created the name for this theory.

form to describe this balancing effect. In his model household, the manager has one group of equal goods (*Teilmengen*).[6] The consumer uses these goods for one series of usages (*Verwendungsreihe*) called *A*. In *A* each additional piece creates less and less utility. The decrease of utility is indicated in Table 2.

TABLE 2

Series of Usages A

Units	Utilities
I	4
II	3
III	2
IV	1

Table 2 only illustrates the old law of Gossen. But now Schönfeld-Illy changed the order of experiment. If four units are used in *A*, they have to be taken from somewhere; suppose they are taken from Series *B*. The fewer units the consumer uses in *B*, the greater will be the utility of each piece in Series *B*. (See Table 3 and Figure 2.)

TABLE 3

Series of Usages B

Units	Utilities
IV	.3
III	1.0
II	2.9
I	5.0

Under these circumstances the consumer will direct two units into *A* and two other units into *B*. The second unit in *A* creates a utility of 3 and the second commodity in *B* produces a utility of 2.9. Any other distribution would be a less profitable one. Schönfeld-Illy proves that consumer strategy is based on two directions: the consumer

[6] Schönfeld-Illy, *Grenznutzen und Wirtschaftsrechnung*, 48/49, pp. 81ff., 135.

can expect from an additional unit only a smaller utility than from those goods which he already has, and furthermore he will dispatch the new unit to that usage where it

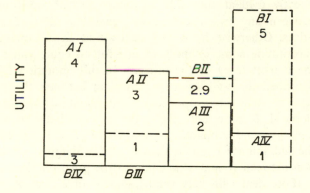

UNITS OF GOODS

FIGURE 2

Series of Usages

brings the highest utility. By trial and error the household manager has to shuffle his marginal units until the desired result is reached. This balancing of usages is called the principle of marginal substitution. Schönfeld-Illy's directives do not lose their significance if the Austrian calculation in units of goods is replaced by the usual calculation in utilities of small money pieces or in weighted utilities.

It has already been mentioned that Schönfeld-Illy's theory has some resemblance to Pareto's indifference curves. If Schönfeld-Illy's household manager balances his utilities, he comes near a point on an indifference curve. John R. Hicks expresses the connection between marginal substitution and indifference curves more forcefully than does Schönfeld-Illy. Hicks places the consumer on the market place and introduces the price calculation. Price and market are more or less neglected in Schönfeld-Illy's theory: "If an individual is to be in equilibrium with respect to a system of market prices, it is directly evident that this marginal rate of substitution between any two goods must equal the ratio of their prices. Otherwise he would clearly find an advantage in substituting some quantity of one for an equal value (at the market rate) of the other."[7] In this quotation Hicks described the well-known equilibrium between the price relation and the proportion of marginal utility. If the slope *A B* represents the price relation between commodity *X* and commodity *Y* and if at *P*, *A B* is tangent to the indifference curve *I*, then at *P* the marginal substitution between *X* and *Y* is equal to the price relation.

If we deal with very small amounts of *X* and *Y*, then gains and losses must be equal. The gain of *Y* × marginal utility of *Y* is equal to the loss of *X* × marginal utility of *X*.[8] This equation can be expressed in the following proportion:

$$\frac{\text{amount of } Y \text{ gained}}{\text{amount of } X \text{ lost}} = \frac{\text{marginal utility of } X}{\text{marginal utility of } Y}$$

FIGURE 3

THE RELATION BETWEEN DIMINISHING UTILITY AND THE LAW OF MARGINAL SUBSTITUTION

The application of marginal substitution to prices is Hicks' improvement on Schönfeld-Illy's analysis. Yet Schönfeld-Illy has a better understanding of the relation between marginal substitution and the law of saturation. Schönfeld-Illy knows that marginal substitution is a consequence of diminishing utility.[9] In his *Value and Capital* Hicks con-

[7] Hicks, *Value and Capital*, p. 20.
[8] *Ibid.*, p. 14.
[9] Schönfeld-Illy, *Grenznutzen*, p. 137.

sidered marginal substitution a replacement for Gossen's law. We have only to know that the indifference curve must be convex to O, the crossing point of the Y and the X axis.[10] But is not the shape of Pareto's curve only a mathematical expression of the decreasing utility? In his revision of the demand theory, Hicks corrected his earlier statement. Marginal substitution becomes a generalized "law of Diminishing Marginal Valuation."[11]

This revision erases a main difference between Schönfeld-Illy and Hicks. The two writers together with their forerunner Slutsky have considerably improved Gossen's first law. This progress was achieved without close cooperation between Schönfeld-Illy and Hicks. Hicks studied Slutsky rather thoroughly, but he may not have more than a hazy knowledge of Schönfeld-Illy's work.[12] Schönfeld-Illy was not aware of the strong affinity between his work and that of his English colleague. Both writers are at home in different schools. Hicks is trained in Marshallian and Paretian economy, while Schönfeld-Illy was a member of the Austrian school. Hicks' discovery dovetailed with the Paretian curves, while Schönfeld-Illy continued Wieser's work on costs. But *Marginal Utility and Economic Calculation* is more than a continuation of Austrian tradition. Schönfeld-Illy blended marginal substitution with a reinterpretation of marginal and total utility. His was the merit to have given a new direction to the Austrian value discussion.

[10] Hicks, *Value and Capital*, p. 20.

[11] John R. Hicks, *A Revision of Demand Theory* (Oxford, 1956), p. 153.

[12] Hicks mentioned Schönfeld-Illy once in his "A Reconsideration of the Theory of Value," *Economica* (February, 1934, New Series), pp. 52ff.

CHAPTER XIV

TOTAL AND MARGINAL VALUE

VALUE theorists have discussed composite values for a
long time; it was the merit of the Neo-Marginalists to put
this concept into the center of their studies. A precise definition of aggregate values cannot be given. For a first
orientation two related concepts will be described here:
the value of the series, and the welfare of the individual.
The value of the series is a summation of values attached
to individual goods of equal quality, quantity, and form.
The total well-being of a person is the effect of all the
goods and services which he enjoys. The search for such
greater value units was considered important to gain a
better understanding of consumer action. Planning his
household, the consumer deals rarely with small pieces;
he calculates mostly with bulky units which contain many
different intensities of utility. It was the goal of the value
theorists to reduce these aggregates to marginal utility.
Wieser and Boehm-Bawerk applied this reduction process
to the easier problem, the value of the series. Later, the
Neo-Marginalists investigated the more complex question of the individual welfare.

THE VALUE OF THE SERIES

Somewhat suspiciously Menger paid more attention to
Boehm-Bawerk's achievements than to those of his other
followers. Boehm had not strictly followed the words of his
master; rather he developed a more subtle interpretation of
value. Like Menger he assumed that the value of one good
in a series of equal goods is determined by marginal utility.[1]

[1] Eugen von Boehm-Bawerk, *Positive Theorie*, Vol. 1, p. 189.

So far his proof does not deviate essentially from the one given by Menger. But Boehm's deduction does not end here. What will happen if the consumer has to estimate a greater amount of goods, e.g., five loaves of bread instead of one? In this case the value of the goods is out of proportion to marginal utility.[2] On each loaf of bread, except the last, depends a higher utility than the marginal one. Boehm-Bawerk calculates the value of a stock by adding the different utilities from the lowest to the highest which are created by the available supply.

Wieser takes exception to Boehm's calculation.[3] He concurs with Boehm that value is marginal utility, but from this assumption he draws a different conclusion: the entire stock of available goods can only have the total value of the number of goods multiplied with marginal utility. Total utility is not identical with total value; it is higher than total value. If a pioneer on virgin land has a supply of 5 bags of wheat for his subsistence until the next harvest and if the utility of the 5 bags can be marked with 5 4 3 2 1, then, according to Boehm, the value of the series is $5+4+3+2+1$, and according to Wieser, 5×1.[4] Wieser readily concedes an exception to his rule. If a great supply of goods will be offered in one package, then the buyer is forced to evaluate the stock as the sum of all the concrete utilities. However, in this monopolistic situation the buyer pays for all the utilities created by the stock. Wieser's concession does not obliterate the principal difference. Both value calculations lead to absurd consequences. Schönfeld-Illy has proven that Boehm's thesis revives Adam Smith's value paradoxon, "the crux maxima of value theorists."[5]

If we use Boehm's calculation, Schönfeld-Illy argues, the

[2] *Ibid.*, pp. 190-91.

[3] Friedrich von Wieser, *Der natürliche Werth*, pp. 23ff.

[4] Boehm-Bawerk, *Positive Theorie*, p. 190. Apparently Wieser is nearer to Menger's original opinion than Boehm-Bawerk.

[5] Leo Schönfeld-Illy, *Das Gesetz des Grenznutzens*, p. 103.

total utility of all diamonds is low and the total utility of all bread is very high, yet the market relationship between these two goods is just the opposite. What Schönfeld-Illy means can be clarified by an illustration. The first slice of bread which prevents starvation has an infinite utility, even though the utilities of the next slices are rapidly falling off. The total utility is infinite because $\infty + 2 + 1 + \ldots$ is still infinite. The first diamond which a young man buys for his girl may have a high value but supposedly not as high as the first slice of bread. Whatever the utility of the first diamond is, the total value of all the diamonds in the possession of one person is lower than the total value of bread.

Wieser's calculation of the value of the series leads him into consequences of doubtful validity. A consumer has one unit of a commodity, Wieser calculates, and the utility of this good is 10; now the consumer acquires successively 10 units of the same kind, and the marginal utility of these newly bought pieces falls continuously to zero.[6]

Number of Goods	Marginal Utility
1	10
2	9
3	8
4	7
5	6
6	5
7	4
8	3
9	2
10	1
11	0

Using Wieser's formula, the following values of the series can be calculated:

Series with . . . goods	Value of the series
1	10
2	18

[6] Wieser, *Der natürliche Werth*, p. 27.

3	24
4	28
5	30
6	30
7	28
8	24
9	18
10	10
11	0

Smith's paradoxon is avoided but another absurdity appears. The total value rises until the consumer has acquired 5 or 6 units, then falls until it reaches zero at 11 units. It seems to be an obvious consequence of Wieser's calculation that in the long run accumulation of wealth must end. He tries to avoid this consequence. He did not live in the time of the "affluent" society and therefore he could justly assume that human economy generally moves within the rising branch of valuation, in his example between 1 and 6 goods. According to him, only accidentally a very good harvest, the discovery of new raw material, a sudden increase of production, even errors of the producers may, at least for a short time, push production into the declining sector of this value curve. Under such extraordinary circumstances alone the amount of goods and enjoyment, wealth and welfare, increases, but the value of goods decreases.[7] This contradiction between value and welfare does not exist in reality. Wieser constructs a long-range development under inadequate premises. Such a forecast ought to include dynamical changes. But he used only static assumptions. Wieser's two branches of utility exist only if the quality and form of the goods remain constant. The progress of society involves changes of goods and wants, so that the trend of total value cannot be forecast for any longer time intervals.

Here arises a fundamental question which concerns

[7] *Ibid.*, p. 31.

both Wieser and Boehm-Bawerk. Is it justifiable to add the values of the series? It seems difficult to understand how the different utilities of equal goods can be added. If the first bag of wheat protects the farmer on the virgin land from starvation and the last bag is used for feeding the chickens, the preservation of life and the anticipated enjoyment of future chicken dinners can be lumped together only when the utilities can be measured like length and weight. Under these circumstances a sum of utilities is meaningful. But when utilities are only comparable, when we only can say that preservation of life is more important than chicken dinners, then we cannot add the enjoyments, for we cannot add the first, the second, the third, etc. The whole difficulty of adding utilities can be only touched here. A more detailed explanation will be given in the chapter on measuring. The members of the Austrian school who were drawn into the Wieser—Boehm-Bawerk controversy avoided this thorny question. They focused their interest on the relation between marginal utility and the value of intramarginal goods. Oskar Kraus, Hans Mayer, and Schönfeld-Illy agree with Boehm-Bawerk and not with Wieser; each piece in a series can have only *alternatingly* the value of the last piece.[8] Mayer and Schönfeld-Illy are so interested in the Wieser—Boehm discussion because it is a starting point for their own analysis of individual welfare.

---

[8] Hans Mayer, "Untersuchung zu dem Grundgesetz der wirtschaftlichen Wertrechnung," *Zeitschrift für Volkswirtschaft und Sozialpolitik*, N.F., I (Wien, 1921), pp. 431ff.; N.F., II (Wien, 1922), pp. 1ff. Wilhelm Vleugels, "Bemerkungen zu Friedrich Wieser's 'Grundgesetz der wirtschaftlichen Nutzkomputation' und zum Gesetz des Vorrats," *Zeitschrift für Volkswirtschaft* . . . , N.F., V (Wien, 1927), pp. 653ff.; Oskar Kraus, *Zur Theorie des Wertes* (Halle, 1902), p. 109; Schönfeld-Illy, *Das Gesetz des Grenznutzens*, p. 130.

The Welfare of the Individual

It has already been mentioned that Mayer and Schönfeld-Illy established the priority of total utility over the individual utilities and values. Mayer actualized a tendency latent in the whole history of marginalism. Most value theorists were aware of the fact that goods and needs are woven together into an intricate pattern. The complementarity of goods and needs was taught by various value theorists, by Menger and Wieser as well as by Marshall. Menger emphasized the welfare of the whole life. Johann Komorzynski was a direct forerunner of the Neo-Marginalists. As early as in 1869 this contemporary and colleague of Menger placed total welfare in the center of the value discussion.[9]

Mayer may have been stimulated by these earlier thoughts. It is very likely that he also was familiar with Gestalt psychology, but his construction is apparently the product of his own thinking. Total welfare, in the sense of Mayer, can embrace the whole life, a day, or any period. It is not a static position which the individual can preserve constantly. In Mayer's way of thinking a situation of constant satisfaction is a physiological and psychological impossibility. Mayer sees welfare as a stream of desirable psychological situations. This sequence of choices repeats itself periodically. An ideal succession is reached that is so arranged that each good produces the maximum of utility. Mayer, like the Gestalt psychologist Wertheimer, compares his concept with a melody which can only be understood as a harmony of sounds and not

---

[9] Johann Komorzynski, "Ist auf Grundlage der bisherigen wissenschaftlichen Forschung die Bestimmung der natürlichen Hohe der Güterpreise möglich?" *Zeitschrift für die gesammte Staatswissenschaft*, Vol. 25 (Tübingen, 1869), pp. 236-37.

by considering each chord separately.[10] According to Mayer, the consumer is primarily aware of his whole well-being. If he buys a clock, a ham, or a motorcar, he wants to know whether or not he will be better off after the acquisition of these things. The new car changes his comfort, his social status, and many other factors which contribute to his whole welfare. But the application of "total well-being" to economics, as with the operation of other Gestalt concepts in economics, is difficult. How can one explain the height of total well-being; how can one analyze the role of a single good within this totality?

The mathematical economists believed that they could overcome these difficulties. Knut Wicksell considered "the total satisfaction or well-being as a function of all the qualities of goods consumed *simultaneously* per unit of time, or during a certain consumption period, so that if these quantities are a, b, c, etc., the function can be symbolically represented by F (a, b, c, . . .)."[11] Schönfeld-Illy, who did not oppose the mathematical method on principle, rejected this formula, for it is not the quantity of goods alone which decides the enjoyment of the whole life. The way in which the goods are consumed and the purpose for which they are used are also constituent factors of well-being.[12] The Neo-Marginalists considered the verbal method more adequate than equations for dealing with the complications inherent in the total welfare of an individual. Two problems especially interested them: the influence of time, and the combination of marginal

[10] Mayer, *Der Erkenntniswert*, pp. 175-76; Schönfeld-Illy, *Grenznutzen und Wirtschaftsrechnung*, pp. 4-5; Max Wertheimer, "Ueber Gestalttheorie," special edition of the *Symposion*, Heft I (Erlangen, 1925), pp. 11ff.

[11] Knut Wicksell, *Lectures on Political Economy* (London, 1946), Vol. 1, p. 48.

[12] Schönfeld-Illy, *Grenznutzen und Wirtschaftsrechnung*, pp. 52-53, n. 1. See also p. 43, n. 1.

calculation with the total welfare gain. The next chapter is devoted to the role of the time element. Schönfeld-Illy's total calculation will be discussed in this chapter.

Schönfeld-Illy agreed with Hans Mayer and with Wieser that the consumer tries to reach the best welfare situation (*Gesamtwirtschaftsnutzen*). Schönfeld-Illy is sure that the manager of the household cannot reach this goal directly. He lacks the ability to express the total utility in quantities and therefore he is not able to calculate it; yet, he can compare one state of general well-being with another by using the marginal calculation. He will select that additional service or good which leads to the greatest total utility.[13] The additional utility, which the consumer definitely selects, reflects in a nutshell his whole welfare situation. The consumer grasps the utility *directly*. "If the consumer says, I expect from another pound of tea, from an additional shirt, from an additional pound of bread, this or that utility—then this letter I contains . . . the whole man, exactly with all his needs, means, attitudes and circumstances."[14] So far Schönfeld-Illy has given only a more elaborate description of what Wieser and Hans Mayer said before him.

However, this is only a part of Schönfeld-Illy's theory. The consumer does not compare *marginal utilities* but *marginal surpluses*. In the last chapter Schönfeld-Illy's marginal substitution has been explained. This theory is the key for the marginal surplus. When the consumer has the choice between different last units which could fit into his household plan, he will use that unit which creates a greater utility than any other; what the consumer really enjoys is not the whole utility of the last piece but only the difference between this marginal utility and the utility rejected. If piece *A* is expected to bring a utility of 4,

[13] *Ibid.*, pp. 54-55.
[14] Schönfeld-Illy, *Das Gesetz des Grenznutzens*, p. 139.

and unit *B* produces 3.5, then the consumer selects *A* and not *B,* and he receives a benefit of 0.5 and not of 4. Schönfeld-Illy follows Wieser's opportunity cost theory, which will be discussed later. Generally, all the consumer needs is this marginal calculation. Under common circumstances he does not need to rebuild his planning chart every so often from scratch. Due to the constancy of our habits and customs, this shortened approach does not falsify our budget calculation.[15] Already Boehm-Bawerk has mentioned that everyday calculations are mechanically reproduced by our memory which draws heavily on former reflections and experiences.[16] The consumer need not be a virtuoso who plays with utility scales, anticipated utility, etc., if he buys only a loaf of bread.

It seems that most of Schönfeld-Illy's ideas were known to his forerunners, e.g., abbreviated calculation, opportunity costs, total welfare, and marginal substitution. Schönfeld-Illy's achievement is the combination of all these categories. Also there are essential details in which he differs from other value theorists. While Menger and Boehm argued that real or imagined loss reveals the significance of marginal utility, Schönfeld-Illy considered loss an unusual occurrence contrary to common business experience. People are insured against loss. The consumer calculates on the margin by adding to one service and restricting another. The emphasis on a utility gain separates Schönfeld-Illy from Hicks. Schönfeld-Illy drafts a consumer strategy which includes marginal gains; Hicks develops an equilibrium theory where an indifference situation is reached without gains or losses. Hicks' work was internationally recognized while Schönfeld-Illy did not reap the

[15] Schönfeld-Illy, *Grenznutzen und Wirtschaftsrechnung*, pp. 44-45, 82-83.

[16] Boehm-Bawerk, *Positive Theorie*, p. 235; Boehm-Bawerk, "Grundzüge der Theorie des wirtschaftlichen Güterwerts," p. 75.

fame he deserved, although Hicks quoted him, François Perroux described his work, and Rosenstein-Rodan propagated his ideas, both in German and Italian.

One of the reasons for the weak echo of Schönfeld-Illy's work is the fact that the central thought is not completely developed. Social and psychological difficulties are not overcome. If the last unit of goods and services should reflect the whole well-being of an individual, then the final piece must be detachable so that the consumer can experience a separate marginal utility. But Schönfeld-Illy claimed that all the utilities experienced by one individual form an indivisible unity. Here is a contradiction. Either marginal utility can be isolated, indicating then the welfare level reached by the individual, or the utilities are linked together in one closed formation, in which case the well-being cannot be measured with the help of marginal utility because marginal utility as an autonomous datum does not exist. In a not very convincing manner, Rosenstein-Rodan tried to solve this dilemma: in the marginal layers of the household, the complementarity of utility is not strongly developed; therefore, the consumer can experience the last enjoyment as a quasi-isolated moment.

THE PROBLEM OF ATTENTION

Perhaps the whole difficulty lies in the crude confrontation of the indivisible whole and the marginal event. The consumer is not always aware of his total well-being. His attention can be directed at different times towards different goals, as some philosophers have demonstrated. Henri Bergson, Edmund Husserl, and Alfred Schütz investigated this problem of attention.[17] Husserl wrote: "One compares usually attention with an illuminating light. Ex-

---

[17] Edmund Husserl, *Ideen zu einer reinen Phänomenologie und phänomenologischen Philosophie* (Halle, 1922), p. 191; Alfred Schütz, *Der sinnhafte Aufbau der sozialen Welt* (Wien, 1960), p. 77.

periences in which we are specially interested are placed in the centre of a cone of light, which is more or less strong, but the same events may also be pushed back into partial or even full darkness." Schütz added to Husserl's finding that time and circumstances (*Jetzt und So*) change the direction of our attention. According to this, the consumer may be interested in one single good, in a complex of goods, or in his whole welfare situation. He may enjoy a piece of jewelry today, he likes or dislikes his meal tomorrow, and he thinks about the state of his affairs the third day. Innumerable variations of awareness can be imagined. The case in which the consumer experiences only his total welfare is one direction of attention, yet many others are possible. The authors who analyze total welfare ought to consider these findings of modern philosophy. If the theory of attention is applied to total and marginal valuation, the original marginal calculation can still be used. Bergson, Husserl, and Schütz explain how the changing direction of our mind can detach the marginal good and marginal utility from the aggregate. Schönfeld-Illy and his group put themselves into a tight corner in assuming that the ray of attention is invariably directed toward the whole well-being of the individual. From this extreme position, no plausible way leads to marginal calculation. The Neo-Marginalists were not successful in their analysis of total well-being. Their great achievements lie in the field of consumer strategy.

CHAPTER XV

HOUSEHOLD PLANNING

The Neo-Marginalists' work on consumer planning is their finest contribution to value theory; their findings were based on Wieser's spadework but are independent of the deductions of the Western value theorists, who even now have not advanced beyond the level of marginal contribution and the Paretian law of indifference. The Neo-Marginalists left these two landmarks behind.

WIESER'S UNEVEN PROGRESS OF SATURATION

Wieser criticized that traditional explanation of consumer's strategy, the equalization of marginal enjoyment. Wieser maintained that this law has only a restrictive and negative meaning. According to him, it indicates only that in all classes of needs man strives to enjoy the lowest desire which he can reach with his scarce means, without leaving higher desires unsatisfied.[1] The last satisfied desires do not represent a straight line of equal intensity but a "split level" line whose final points indicate different intensities of utility. A table drafted by Vleugels illustrates Wieser's intention.[2]

In class III, 56 symbolizes a much lower intensity of utility than the limit 82 in class II and 72 in class I. The satisfaction of 56 does not prevent the enjoyment of higher utilities. Wieser believed that this unequal progress of satiation corresponds to reality.

[1] Wieser, *Der natürliche Werth*, p. 14.
[2] Wilhelm Vleugels, "Ertragswert und Kostenwert," *Zeitschrift für Nationalökonomie* (Wien, 1932), III, 696.

I	II	III	IV
123	—	—	—
—	—	—	—
—	106	—	—
—	90	—	—
—	82	—	—
72	—	—	—
—	—	60	—
51	53	56	—
			Line of satisfaction
42	43	47	40
—	30	—	31
20	28	—	24
16	—	10	15

If we watch a person whose income has increased, he will not spend equally more in all branches of consumption. Specific expenditures will be enlarged; others will remain on the old standard. The line of advance towards the lower ranks of utility is so unequally pushed forward because the points of relaxation are reached on different heights of the scale.[3] The points of relaxation are those positions on the utility table where the urge for satisfaction stops. Like Galiani, Wieser claimed that man has to pursue the satisfaction of specific needs until he reaches the satisfaction of relaxation. Water, expressed in utility numbers, has a very high point of relaxation, and so has food. The uneven character of the satiation line will be reinforced by the discontinuous character of some needs. The unit of needs for living quarters is one room. The need for the first room is separated from the want for the second and the third room by wide distances in which the scale of needs does not register an urge for more housing. (See the empty spots in Vleugels' scale.)

[3] Friedrich von Wieser, *Die Gesellschaftliche Wirtschaft* (Tübingen, 1914), in *Grundriss der Sozialökonomik*, Vol. 1, p. 149.

The Time Element and Consumer Strategy: Mayer's and Rosenstein-Rodan's Solution

In his attack on Gossen's second law Hans Mayer is more radical than Wieser. Wieser reduced the significance of the leveling of utility, but he accepted at least a modified form. Mayer would like to eliminate this principle altogether. Mayer claimed that the equilibrization of marginal utilities contradicts the complementarity of goods and utilities. According to him, members of the Austrian school have always emphasized the interdependence of all welfare aims but they have not applied this principle to the consumer's strategy. The enjoyment or increase of welfare is dependent on diminishing utility as well as on the amount and sequence of the consumption of all other goods.[4] More important than this correction of traditional thinking is the integration of the time element. Mayer and Rosenstein-Rodan described the consumer who regulates his purchase of goods for certain periods. Hans Mayer grafted this periodization on Menger's table.[5] He stressed the periodical repetition of the same needs.[6]

Mayer's consumer watches two time intervals, the production and/or income period, and the consumption periods of which several are included in one income period. Every consumer strategy has to ration the supply so that it lasts until new goods with the help of all commodities become available. For instance, the income period lasts one month, during which thirty consumption periods exist. It is the task of the household manager to harmonize the satisfaction of daily recurrent needs within

[4] Hans Mayer, "Der Erkenntniswert der funktionellen Preistheorie," p. 175.

[5] Hans Mayer, "Untersuchungen . . . ," *Zeitschrift für Volkswirtschaft und Sozialpolitik*, N.F., II, pp. 1, 14, 15. An interesting interpretation of Mayer's analysis can be found in François Perroux, *La Valeur*, pp. 186ff.

[6] Hans Mayer, "Untersuchungen . . . ," p. 16.

the large income period. For each day of the production period the consumer operates with a Mengerian Chart. The chief of the household would act irresponsibly if he satisfied his needs in the first period of satisfaction to a very low level of intensity and did not provide for the highest utilities of the following days. A wise strategy will be differently directed. The sensible consumer will figure with his available means and spread them over each consumption period so that he satisfies the highest needs in each period and disregards wants of lesser intensity.

François Perroux illustrated Mayer's budget planning with two charts.[7] He operates with a production period of three days and with a satisfaction period of one day. A, B, C, are recurrent needs of different intensity. A, which may be food, has a higher utility than B, and B ranks before C. For the complete satisfaction of A, B, C, during

General planning at the time t	I (1st day)	II (2nd day)	III (3rd day)
	$A \begin{cases} a_1 \\ a_2 \\ a_3 \end{cases}$	$A \begin{cases} a_1 \\ a_2 \\ a_3 \end{cases}$	$A \begin{cases} a_1 \\ a_2 \\ a_3 \end{cases}$
	$B \begin{cases} b_1 \\ b_2 \\ b_3 \end{cases}$	$B \begin{cases} b_1 \\ b_2 \\ b_3 \end{cases}$	$B \begin{cases} b_1 \\ b_2 \\ b_3 \end{cases}$
	$C \begin{cases} c_1 \\ c_2 \\ c_3 \end{cases}$	$C \begin{cases} c_1 \\ c_2 \\ c_3 \end{cases}$	$C \begin{cases} c_1 \\ c_2 \\ c_3 \end{cases}$

CHART I, according to François Perroux

the three days, 27 bundles of goods (a_1, a_2, a_3, b_1, b_2, b_3,

[7] François Perroux, *La Valeur*, pp. 187ff.

etc.) are needed. These bundles are equal in quality and quantity; they can be substituted for one another. In modern economics, continuous replacement is an unrealistic assumption, but money which is easily divisible guarantees a certain continuity. The same money pieces can be used for buying different goods, so that commodities with the help of money become substitutable.

Consider the planner who can afford 9 bundles. For a diligent selection he will attach utility coefficients to the units a, b, c, in accordance with the utilities of A, B, C.

Pieces of goods	a_1	a_2	a_3	b_1	b_2	b_3	c_1	c_2	c_3
Utility coefficient	9	8	7	6	5	4	3	2	1

Under these circumstances the consumer will acquire for each day a_1, a_2, a_3, meaning the highest utilities 9, 8, 7.

Mayer had only in part created a budget which conforms to his criticism of the older methods. He intended to reject the levelling of utility, but Perroux's illustration made it quite clear that a straight line of marginal utility is reached in Mayer's plan (utility 7 at a_3). At least Mayer fulfilled one essential requirement in his program; he integrated the periodical recurrence of needs into his budgets.

Another aspect of the time element is investigated by Rosenstein-Rodan.[8] For a short period the consumer knows exactly what he needs. The further he projects his budget into the future, the more uncertainty blurs his decision. Rosenstein saw that, with the projection of the household budget into the uncertain future, the needs that can be earmarked for specific goods become less and less frequent. We work more and more with vague abstractions; our plans for the future have not coalesced. In September Mr. X already knows that next summer he will need a

---

[8] Paul N. Rosenstein-Rodan, "La funzione del tempo nella teoria economica," *Annali di Statistica e di Economia*, Anno III., Vol. 4 (Genoa, 1936), pp. 1ff.

vacation. But where he will go and how he will travel is not clear to him. Rosenstein-Rodan did not claim that a vagueness in our planning begins in all classes of needs at the same time. In some branches of consumption the exact calculation stops rather early, while in others the switch to vague abstractions starts much later. On January 1 Mr. X does not know whether he will buy two or three pounds of meat on February 1, but he is certain that he will pay $75 rent for the month of February. Rosenstein-Rodan compared this change from concrete calculation to a vague projection of future needs with a gradated or echelon procession.

Rosenstein-Rodan gives a subtle explanation of long-run budget planning. Between him and Hans Mayer a plausible analysis of the consumer's strategy has been presented.[9] But some unfinished business remains; it is not quite clear what the definite meaning of these charts is. Do they indicate what the consumer does or what he ought to do to reach the maximum of utility? If they are meant as a general description of reality, they should be confronted with the events of everyday life. Questionnaires have to be sent at random for verification. Advertising agencies have to be interviewed to give their version of consumer reaction. The comparison of theory and reality is only the first step in the evaluation of these patterns. If Mayer's and Rosenstein-Rodan's charts give indeed a plausible picture of consumer reaction, the influence of this consumer action on the whole economy must be investigated.

There is still the other possibility that these plans are intended to advise the consumer. In this case the language of the theorist has to be translated into the vernacular.

---

[9] Paul N. Rosenstein-Rodan, "La Complementarita prima della tre tappe del progresso della Teoria Economica Pura," *La Riforma Sociale*, Vol. 44 (Turin, 1933), pp. 257ff.

Schönfeld-Illy did publish a small accounting book which was meant to teach the consumer how to get the best from his income, but this book is not available.[10]

With this report on consumer strategy a dividing line in this study has been reached. We have shown how marginal utility can be applied to consumer action and to the value of consumer goods. The Austrian and the mathematical theorists considered this usage of their core concept only one sector of the whole system. They believed that production is governed by the same rules of valuation as consumption; therefore they searched for a new explanation of costs and for the "right" imputation.

[10] Schönfeld-Illy mentioned this book in *Das Gesetz*, p. 336. The Austrian government granted him a patent, but only a few people used his book.

CHAPTER XVI

COSTS AND MARGINAL UTILITY

CLASSICISM, REFORM, AND RECONCILIATION

ARE costs an effect of consumer valuation or are they independent and irreducible factors? This alternative had already interested the economists of the eighteenth century (see p. 27). Galiani and Condillac claimed that consumer value determines costs. A short time later Adam Smith, in his *Wealth of Nations*, taught that "value in exchange" is determined by costs. Between 1776 and 1871 the majority of economists accepted Smith's verdict. After the ascendency of marginal utility this cost principle was put on trial. The ensuing discussions were rather confusing, because there was not one dispute but rather several contradicting positions which became intermingled.

In 1885 Heinrich Dietzel began his splendid but somewhat reckless and erroneous attacks against the Austrian value theory.[1] Boehm-Bawerk answered them; Marshall's approach was to reconcile classicism with the new ideas. The Viennese school did not oppose classicism or the Marshallian synthesis with a common front; Boehm and Wieser differed. So, after 1885 at least four interpretations

[1] About the Dietzel controversy: Dietzel, review of Wieser's "Ursprung und Hauptgesetz," *Conrad's Jahrbücher*, neue Folge, Vol. 11 (1885), p. 161; Dietzel, "Die klassiche Werttheorie und die Theorie vom Grenznutzen," *Conrad's Jahrbücher*, N.F., Vol. 20 (1890), p. 563; Zuckerkandl's reply to "Die klassische Werttheorie und die Theorie vom Grenznutzen," *ibid.*, Vol. 21 (1890), p. 519; Boehm-Bawerk, "Ein Zwischenwort zur Werttheorie," *ibid.*, Vol. 21 (1890), p. 519; Dietzel, "Zur klassischen Wert und Preistheorie," *ibid.*, dritte Folge, Vol. 1 (1891), p. 685; Boehm-Bawerk, "Wert, Kosten und Grenznutzen," *ibid.*, Vol. 3 (1892), p. 321.

of the cost principle were developed; Dietzel, Marshall, Boehm-Bawerk, and Wieser created them.

DIETZEL AND BOEHM-BAWERK

The controversy of Dietzel against Boehm-Bawerk lasted for a long time, yet the result can be condensed into a few sentences. Dietzel at least in his last papers accepted the marginal utility theory. But he did not want to exclude costs from value calculation. Several cost factors exist, the most important of them being labor. Under the condition of free competition and constant costs (*Beliebig vermehrbare Güter*), the cost factors decide the price. The value of the consumer goods and of the producer goods determine each other. Strangely enough Boehm-Bawerk accepted all these points. However, costs cannot be the final cause of valuation; the Archimedian point of valuation is marginal utility. One who today reads this discussion, the length of which even Boehm-Bawerk compared with that of a sea serpent, finds its result rather negligible. Not the scientific gain but the historical meaning made this discussion important. Boehm-Bawerk himself saw the significance.[2] After 1880 Heinrich Dietzel in Germany, Achille Loria in Italy, and others began a controversy about value. Boehm claimed that the beginning and the fast extension of this argument was symptomatic; marginal utility gained recognition.

Critics of marginal utility were infrequent as long as the new doctrine was accepted by only a few economists. When more and more thinkers accepted the theory, the dominating position of classicism was threatened. Boehm-Bawerk saw in this controversy the decisive battle between the old and the new theory. He understood the mean-

---

[2] Boehm-Bawerk, "Zur neuesten Literatur über den Wert," *Conrad's Jahrbücher*, 3. F., Vol. 56.1.1891, p. 875. See also Boehm-Bawerk, "Wert, Kosten und Grenznutzen," p. 321.

ing of this fight, but he misjudged the outcome. Outside of the Viennese camp the battle did not end with the total victory of one group, but with a compromise.

MARSHALL'S TWO SCISSORS

Marshall opposed the Austrians as well as Jevons who had eliminated cost calculation. Marshall developed a synthesis of classicism and the new theory of cost and utility. In the chain of cause and effect, costs of production and marginal utility determine themselves mutually. It is not true that utility is prior to costs or vice versa, rather, both factors have the same rank in the chain of causality. Marshall explained his statement with the well-known illustration of the scissors. The quarrel about the priority of costs and utility is as senseless as asking whether the upper or the lower blade of the scissors cuts a piece of paper. Utility and costs are the last irreducible elements of value and price analysis.[3] Many economists outside the Viennese camp accepted this explanation. Vilfredo Pareto considered costs to be hindrances which obstruct the production of goods; they are not identical with the utility for the consumer.

BOEHM-BAWERK'S REVIVAL OF GALIANI'S POSITION

In dealing with Marshall's scissor theory Boehm-Bawerk[4] demonstrated his great ability as a debater. Far from denying the validity of the scissor argument, he even used it for the defense of his own position. Costs are determining the supply of goods and utility is indicating the intensity of demand. If scarcity and utility are the two elements of value, then the scissor theory combines them and does not separate them. Costs mean scarcity. The two blades of Marshall's pair of scissors are only the two parts of the

[3] Alfred Marshall, *Principles of Economics* (London, 1891), p. 544.

[4] Boehm-Bawerk, *Positive Theorie*, II, Excurse VIII, p. 182.

Austrian theory of value. But Boehm-Bawerk continues: Marshall's explanation is insufficient; he does not deal with the *value* of the cost goods, the value of labor, land, and capital. The source of these values is the consumer's estimation. Johannisberger wine is not expensive because the rent of the vineyard is expensive, but rather the rent is high because the wine is high in demand. This sentence contains the key to Boehm's position.[5]

BOEHM-BAWERK'S SOLUTION: MARGINAL COSTS EQUAL MARGINAL UTILITY

Boehm was proud of this discovery. He called it the Copernican revolution in the field of economic theory. The Austrian economist went further than his forerunners Galiani, Condillac, and Turgot. He knew that the simple formula, value determines costs, does not harmonize with reality. If the individual consumer would pay for each individual good as much as he estimates the good to be worth, then costs, individual value, and marginal utility are indeed identical. In reality the household manager pays much less than his marginal value. Marshall and his followers call this surplus of utility over costs the consumer rent. So it seems that after all costs are a factor independent of utility. The millionaire could easily pay $2 for his newspaper, but he really pays only the costs, perhaps 10¢. The classical theory seems vindicated. But Boehm-Bawerk considered this popular explanation incomplete. Even under the condition of a consumer rent,

[5] Boehm-Bawerk's defense of his position seems confusing. If production is the means for the end, which is consumption, and if consumer valuation determines the value of cost goods, then Boehm does not describe a causal chain but a teleological relation. Yet Boehm, the Aristotelian, did not see here a mixture of two different orders of phenomena in time. He followed closely Friedrich Paulsen, the philosopher and educator and interpreter of Aristotelian logic, who taught that in the human world causality and teleology are identical. *Ibid.*, p. 186 text and footnote.

Boehm argued, costs are not a *final* but only an intermediary cause (*Zwischenursache*) of value formation. The final cause is always marginal utility.[6]

The following illustration is used for the clarification of Boehm's position. The same mixture of labor, land, and capital, which we shall call X, is used for the production of three different consumer goods A, B, and C. The marginal utility of $A = 200$, of $B = 150$, and of $C = 100$. Then the value of the marginal product C determines the value of $X = 100$. Costs are determined by the value of the marginal product, but the "cost" value of A and B cannot be higher than 100; the value of the cost product reflects its value borrowed from C to A and B. The causality of valuation runs a tortuous course: marginal consumer good→factor combination→intramarginal consumer good. (See Figure 1.)[7]

In Vleugels' illustration of Boehm's theory the arrows indicate that the causal nexus starts with C and goes over X to A and B. The original values of A and B are given in parenthesis; under each parenthesis the reduced cost values are given.

WIESER'S OPPORTUNITY COSTS

Wieser did not reject Boehm's explanation, he only considered it incomplete.[8] Wieser argued that it did not pay

---

[6] *Ibid.*, I, p. 223. The term "Zwischenursache" is apparently Boehm's own invention. But the thought can be found already in Neo-Scholasticism, where a similar idea is expressed by the "causa instrumentalis." Rudolf Eisler, *Wörterbuch der Philosophischen Begriffe* (Berlin, 1930), Vol. 3, p. 339.

[7] Adapted from Wilhelm Vleugels, *Die Lösungen des wirtschaftlichen Zurechnungsproblems bei Boehm-Bawerk und Wieser*, Schriften der Königsberger Gelehrten Gesellschaft. 7.5. (Halle, 1930), p. 251.

[8] Wieser, *Der natürliche Werth*, pp. 166ff. It is not quite clear when Wieser had discovered opportunity costs. Telemachos Lamprinopoulos, "Unterschiede innerhalb der österreichischen

COMBINATION OF PRODUCTION FACTORS CALLED *X*

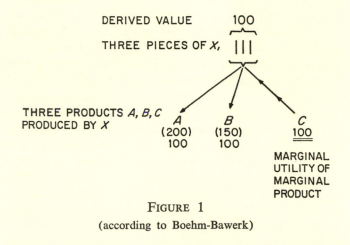

FIGURE 1

(according to Boehm-Bawerk)

Schule, Ein Vergleich zwischen Böhm-Bawerk und Wieser" (Doctoral thesis, Berlin, 1930), p. 40, claimed that Wieser already in an early work, *Über den Ursprung und die Hauptgesetze des wirtschaftlichen Werthes* (Wien, 1884), explained opportunity costs. In an interview with me, Rosenstein-Rodan expressed the same opinion. I am in doubt whether or not I can agree with the two authors. Wieser wrote: "Under normal conditions of economic procedure it is possible that missing specimens of those goods can be replaced which are dedicated to the most important services. The sacrifice for this replacement is identical with the sacrifice of those means of production which are needed under the most favorable circumstances; that really means a sacrifice of the lowest marginal utility derived from the same production." ("Ursprung," p. 153; my translation). This does not necessarily mean opportunity costs. It could also be an identification of costs with the lowest utility which *still* can be consumed. It seems to me that Wieser in 1884 described costs more or less as Boehm-Bawerk. It is very likely that Wieser did not formulate his law before 1889. In this year he had a rival in Robert Zuckerkandl (*Zur Theorie des Presies* [*Leipzic*, 1889], pp. 316ff.). But Zuckerkandl did not give a clear explanation. Sometimes he defined costs as leisure, sometimes as the sacrifice of the least utility, and sometimes in the sense of Wieser.

attention to the day-by-day usage of the word *cost*. Boehm's definition has nothing to do with the idiom of the business world. For Boehm, costs are the enjoyment derived from the consumer good produced on the margin, meaning the utility of 100 of our example. For the business world, costs mean a sacrifice, which only on rare occasions is pain, and more often than not is a loss of welfare gain. If we accept this definition, then costs are not identical with the marginal utility of the last finished product. Costs cannot be 100 in the example. Vleugels, Wieser's best interpreter, clarifies this point: 100 is a welfare gain and indicates the limit to which the sacrifice can reach. Even the last consumer will try to keep his sacrifice below this watermark so that he receives a surplus above costs. If costs reach 100, it does not pay to produce the commodity *C*. Vleugels' figure (Figure 2) indicates that costs are determined by the most valuable good which is *excluded* from production. With the help of the same elements *X* (factors of production) one can technically produce *A, B, C, D, E, F, G*. One *X* produces one consumer good. Three *X*'s are available; therefore *A, B, C*, will be produced. The utility of the excluded *D* is the sacrifice or costs.[9]

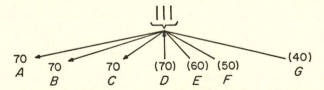

FIGURE 2. Combinations of Factors *X* according to Wieser

The difference between Boehm-Bawerk and Wieser is not as great as Vleugels' figure indicates. If we have *n* usages of *X* and infinitely small intervals between the produced

[9] Vleugels, "Ertragswert und Kostenwert," p. 695.

values, then the difference between Boehm's and Wieser's formulation becomes insignificant. Let the utility of the last available consumer good, $a_{(n-1)}$, be 101 and the utility of the first excluded or sacrificed good, $a_{(n)}$, be 100.99; then it does not matter very much whether we define costs according to Wieser or according to Boehm-Bawerk. But on the international scene Wieser's formulation has been accepted, not Boehm's cost concept.

OPPORTUNITY COSTS IN THE UNITED STATES

The development of the ideas about opportunity or sacrifice costs in the United States is very interesting. As this concept was discussed in American journals only after 1890, it seems obvious that Wieser was a source of the new American concept. David Green, the constant defender of Austrian ideas, recognized in Wieser the creator of this term.[10] He accepted Wieser's relegation of costs "to the region of the might-have-beens."

But Patton and Davenport were apparently not so strongly influenced by Wieser. Patton spoke about sacrifice of opportunities. Opportunities are the surpluses over the exertions.[11] This is not exactly Wieser's theory. Davenport would not like to use costs in this connection: "The term *cost* seems not quite satisfactory to cover the case. Perhaps *displacement* (Davenport's italics) or *foregoing* would be preferable."[12] In the historical chapters of his *Value and Distribution* he dealt with Wieser without men-

[10] David J. Green, "Pain Cost and Opportunity Cost," *The Quarterly Journal of Economics*, Vol. 8 (Boston, 1894), p. 255 n.

[11] Simon N. Patton, "Cost and Utility," *Annals of the American Academy*, Vol. 3 (Philadelphia, July 1892-June 1893), p. 412.

[12] Herbert Joseph Davenport, *The Economics of Enterprise* (New York, 1913), p. 61. In an earlier work he is somewhat confused about the term. He calls opportunity costs "personal-product-displacement costs." Davenport, *Value and Distribution* (Chicago, 1908), p. 6.

tioning opportunity costs.[13] All these omissions and deviations make it quite probable that in spite of the chronological coincidence Wieser is not the only source of inspiration. With the help of the well-known principle of substitution some American economists may have created cost theories which are similar to Wieser's principle.

The American school of marginal utility was never a blind imitation of Austrian teaching. Late classical elements and Jevons' economics were used for the interpretation of the thoughts which came from Vienna. The independence of American economists is nowhere better documented than in the field of imputation, where the different Austrian theories never could gain ground against the classical tradition and genuine American thought.

[13] *Ibid.*, pp. 326ff.

CHAPTER XVII

IMPUTATION—I

MENGER, BOEHM-BAWERK,

AND HANS MAYER

The Problem

THE curiosity of the theorist was not satisfied by calculating the bulk of the cost goods; he wants to know which part of the value can be attributed to each isolated element of the cost aggregate, to land, labor, capital and other factors separately. A key for this distribution had to be found. Wieser, who had the great ability to coin the right word, called this distribution doctrine *imputation* (*Zurechnung*). The German word comes from the legal language, where "Zurechnung" means the process by which in penal law the judge will distribute responsibility to each criminal who participated in the action. The word is Wieser's creation; the attempts to find the key are much older. Implicitly Aristotle and the scholastics dealt with this question when they asked that each worker who participated in production should receive his fair share.

Since that time almost every economist has had some vague notion about a principle of distribution, but no one before Jean Baptiste Say saw the problem clearly. He stated that each factor gets its share from the whole product according to its productive service. Say did not explain what the productive service is. About forty years later, John Stuart Mill and the historical school denied the existence of a general key, claiming that the specific scheme of distribution changes in history. This opinion has been forcefully defended quite recently. With the development of economic thinking during the last 100 years the principle of imputation has acquired very different shades of meaning. The object of imputation can be either the distribution of the national income or the splitting up of the single value inherent in one consumer good. The theory is either an application of price analysis on consumer valuation or of laws concerned with technical productivity.[1]

American and British economists explained the distribution of national income with the help of the Marshallian price equilibrium and marginal productivity. Their theory is widely accepted. The Austrians offered five different solutions not counting smaller variations. These five theories are with one exception special adaptations of marginal utility. Menger, Boehm, and Hans Mayer work with the categories of loss and substitution. Wieser, von Neumann, and Morgenstern use mathematical explanations. The latter two do not explain value but do analyze price distribution.

MENGER AND BOEHM-BAWERK

Boehm-Bawerk had provided a clear and systematic variation of Menger's imputation.[2] According to Perroux, Boehm asked himself, how will the entrepreneur use the factors of production if loss and substitution regulate his decisions.[3] Boehm presented five cases, of which three are sufficient to explain his way of reasoning.

[1] I have not read the whole literature on imputation. Besides the works of Menger, Boehm-Bawerk, Wieser, and Morgenstern, the following publications have been consulted: Hans Mayer, "Zurechnung," *Handwörterbuch der Staatswissenschaften* (4th ed., Jena, 1928), Vol. 8, pp. 1206ff. (hereafter quoted as Mayer, "Zurechnung"); Wilhelm Vleugels, *Die Lösungen des wirtschaftlichen Zurechnungsproblems, op. cit.*; Emil Lederer, *Aufriss der ökonomischen Theorie* (Tübingen, 1931); Eugen Haydt, *Die ökonomische Zurechnung, Wiener Staats und Rechtswissenschaftliche Studien* (Leipzic-Vienna, 1931), Vol. 19; François Perroux, *La Valeur.*

Case one: The factor combination is $a + b$. Neither a nor b, as isolated pieces, produces any value. None of the two goods can be replaced by something else. Only loss regulates valuation. If I lose a, or b, the other part of this group becomes valueless. The good, which is actually lost or which we have lost only in our imagination, has the value of the whole group. Consider $a + b = 100$; then $a = 100$ or zero, $b = 100$ or zero. Every factor can have the value of the whole group or no value *alternatively*.[4] A pair of gloves illustrates this case. If I lose one glove, the other has the value zero. Boehm-Bawerk indicated that this case does not occur very often, and in reality the second situation is more important.

Case two: The factor combination is $a + b + c$. Each factor can be used isolated outside the group with a low utility. Then, every piece has alternatively two values, a maximum and a minimum. The maximum is the value of the whole group minus the added values of the other factors in their isolated employment. The minimum is the value of the piece in a separated usage, $a + b + c = 100$. Isolated values for $a = 10$, $b = 20$, $c = 30$. Maximum value for $a = 100 - (20 + 30) = 50$. Minimum value $a = 10$. A variation of my glove example can be used for illustration. Assume that the remaining glove can be used for polishing silverware. Then the maximum is the value of the whole pair minus the use as polisher, and the minimum is the value as polisher.

Case three: This is the main case. Again $a + b + c = 100$. In this case two complementary goods can find employment outside the original combination. In addition to it, in this case the original combination can be preserved

[2] Menger, *Grundsätze*, p. 138; Boehm-Bawerk, *Positive Theorie*, I, p. 208.

[3] Perroux, *La Valeur*, p. 104.

[4] Vleugels, *Die Lösungen des wirtschaftlichen Zurechnungsproblems*, pp. 258ff.; Mayer, "Zurechnung," pp. 1212ff.

by replacing productive elements, which have been lost, with other factors. Consider an entrepreneur who owns three a's — a_1, a_2, a_3, — and a_1 is used in the original combination $a + b + c$. Apart from it three other usages of a are available which have the importance 50, 20 and 10. The existing stock of a permits only the satisfaction of the two productions with the utility of 50 and 20. The employment with the importance 10 remains uncovered. The situation is presented as follows:

$$a_1 + b + c = 100$$
$$a_2 = 50$$
$$a_3 = 20$$

Opportunity of production not used in the moment $(a_4) = (10)$. If a_1 is lost, a_3 will be transferred to the original combination $a_1 + b + c$; a has the maximal value of 20. In this case $b + c$ has the value of 80. Consider that b is irreplaceable and is no longer available; then the combination $a + b + c$ is broken up and the value of a is determined by the minimum usage $a_4 = 10$. Loss and substitution, breaking up and reforming of combinations, permit us to mark maximum and minimum. The value of a is between 20 and 10. Boehm illustrates his deduction with the planning of a contractor who builds a house. He needs a building lot, bricks, beams, and labor. If some bricks are lost or workers quit and take another job, the construction will not be interrupted, for new workers will be hired and another load of bricks will be ordered. If for some reason the house is not built, the ground, material, and men would be transferred to other productions.

Wilhelm Vleugels claimed that Boehm constructed these and other situations for the benefit of the entrepreneur.[5] He asserted that this theory of imputation is a *rule book example* showing the leader of the plant how

---

[5] Vleugels, *Lösungen*, p. 263.

he ought to evaluate his production factors in case he wants to expand a complementary group or to sacrifice some members of the productive aggregate. The whole procedure, he continued, does not contain directions for finding the "right" value but is rather for designing upper and lower limits between which the entrepreneur can place his valuations. Vleugels' ingenious defense did not diminish the ranks of opposition. So many objections had been raised against Boehm's doctrine that it is only possible to mention the strongest strictures. Boehm's doctrine does not contain the rule of distribution; he only postpones the solution of the problem.[6] The value of the substitutable goods is determined by their employment in another place (*die anderweitige Verwendung*). The higher limit of a is given by $a_3 = 20$. But we know the value of 20 only if we can split up the production combine of the substitution. In this process of separation we have to find another production and another one, ad infinitum. Another objection, also raised by Hans Mayer, is directed against Boehm's point of departure.[7] Boehm starts with an existing combination of factors and then tries to evaluate the value of each factor ex post. In reality the values will be formed *pari passu* with the construction of the whole combination, which cannot be planned without knowing the utility dependent on the different factors of production. Hans Mayer tries this genetic approach.

HANS MAYER AND THE VARIATION METHOD

Hans Mayer's model is an isolated economy without markets and without prices. The isolated individual knows his preference scale, and owns a limited stock of factors of

[6] Wieser, *Der natürliche Wert*, p. 84n.; Mayer, "Zurechnung," p. 1217.

[7] *Ibid.*, p. 1218.

production.[8] His goal is the optimal organization which he finds by varying the combination of his means of production, by adding or substracting small units of labor, land, or capital. The needed factors can be released from one production and can be attached to another production combination. A farmer can produce with many workers on a small plot of land or with relatively few workers on a large field. The losses and gains caused by this variation are indicators for the value accounting. It seems that Hans Mayer used the same reasoning on which John Bates Clark and Alfred Marshall based the theory of marginal productivity. This is only correct to a certain extent. Hans Mayer did not accept marginal productivity without far-reaching restrictions. The difference between him and the principal Anglo-American thinking can be illustrated with an example taken from François Perroux.[9]

A farmer has four units of land $(4\ L)$ and four units of labor $(4\ W)$. He employs these factors in four different combinations. The factors can be transferred from one combination to the other. P_1, P_2, P_3, P_4, are the homogeneous products, for instance bags of wheat. For simplifying the calculation let us assume that each bag of grain has the marginal utility of one.

$$4 \text{ Combinations} \begin{cases} (1) & 1\ L + 1\ W = P_1 \\ (2) & 1\ L + 1\ W = P_2 \\ (3) & 1\ L + 1\ W = P_3 \\ (4) & 1\ L + 1\ W = \dfrac{P_4}{P} \end{cases}$$

Perroux's Table

For providing an exact valuation of each factor, the farmer varies the factor combination. In combination 4, he leaves out $1\ L$; then he loses 30 bags of wheat or 30 times the marginal utility of one. This reduction of output is due to the unemployment of L *as well as* W. The unit

[8] *Ibid.*, pp. 1222ff.
[9] Perroux, *La Valeur*, p. 119.

W cannot be used any longer for want of 1 L. The sum $L + 1 W = 30$ bags of wheat. It is necessary to separate L from W. This can be done by absorbing the unemployed L into the other three combinations. Not counting number 4, the combinations 1, 2, 3, produce 10 bags more. The total loss of output due to the missing 1 $L = 30 - 10$ bags $= 20$ bags $= 20$ times marginal utility one. The same operation can be repeated for the factor W. The reduced loss may be 10 bags in the second case. The two loss figures 20 bags for L and 10 bags for W indicate the distribution of the whole product. If the reduction of production is 20 for L and 10 for W at the margin, the whole output will be split up in the proportion of 2:1. If the whole product of all four combinations is 120 bags, then L receives 80 and W 40 bags.

This illustration emphasizes Mayer's attempt to steer clear of Clark's and Marshall's over-simplification. The latter two authors relate different amounts of output to varying factors of production. Under free competition a small increase of one factor must lead to some addition to the finished product. In case of equilibrium the value or price of the additional finished good will become equal to the price of the factor of production. This is the well-known doctrine of marginal productivity. Mayer denies that his theory is identical with this Anglo-American solution of imputation. The main mistake of the American and English theorists is, Mayer wrote, that they base their calculation on absolute figures, on the additional product, and on the increase of one factor. Mayer denied that these absolute figures have this significance. He wrote that these data have been calculated under different conditions, meaning that the increase of each factor presupposes another set of stable factors. Therefore these numbers have only alternative significance and cannot be used simultaneously. But the business manager needs for his calculation figures which remain constant; that means, they do not change with every expansion or contraction of one factor. If he follows Mayer's theory, he can derive the desired data from the marginal contributions, but he must use figures of marginal return as indicators for the proportion of gains and losses. In the same proportion in which the increase or decrease of the last factor particles enlarge or diminish the total product, the whole value product will be divided by the different factors of production.[10]

This refinement did not make Mayer's theory immune to criticism. Perroux wrote that the losses and gains which his entrepreneur registers are of a technical nature and do not have much to do with economic valuation and with the market mechanism.[11] According to Perroux's illustration, labor receives 80 bags from 120. Under the conditions of unemployment, flexible wages, and free market, the workers may lose a part of this calculated share. Scarcity and utility may completely change the quotas which are calculated only on the basis of technical productivity. Apparently marginal productivity and marginal utility should not be separated. As early as 1889 Wieser had tried to combine the two forces which Mayer kept apart, the technical and the value element.

[10] Perroux, *La Valeur*, pp. 118ff.
[11] *Ibid.*, p. 122.

CHAPTER XVIII

IMPUTATION—II

WIESER, VON NEUMANN, AND

MORGENSTERN: THE

MATHEMATICAL SOLUTIONS

WIESER'S SIMULTANEOUS EQUATIONS

WIESER offers a system of simultaneous equations as his solution of the imputation problem. The preparation of his theory is more important than the final result.

Unlike Menger and Boehm-Bawerk he did not calculate the value of a factor under conditions of possible or actual loss.[1] Wieser's entrepreneur examines the value of a productive element under the condition of undisturbed possession and best usage. Wieser emphasized that imputation is not a *cost* accounting but a *value* calculation. Following his theory of opportunity costs (see p. 172), the total of all costs must be *lower*, and the sum of all values of the productive elements must be *equal* to the value of the finished consumer good. Like Jean Baptiste Say, he calls the values of these factors the productive contributions. For a correct calculation of these productive services Menger's marginal estimation has to be applied.[2] If the value of the consumer good is determined by its marginal utility, then the derived value of the factor has also to be based on the estimation of the consumer good. For a correct calculation of the productive services Wieser instructs the entrepreneur to find the layer of marginal values, and

[1] Wieser, *Der natürliche Werth*, p. 82.
[2] *Ibid.*, p. 96.

to prepare a survey of all the factor combinations employed in this region. After these preparations the manager of a plant can calculate the productive services with the help of simultaneous equations.[3] If there are n marginal combinations of n productive factors, and the marginal utility of the consumer goods is known, then the calculation of the n unknown is possible. Wieser illustrated his calculation with three productive factors x, y, z, and three equations:

$$x + y = 100$$
$$2x + 3z = 290$$
$$4y + 5z = 590$$

then $x = 40$, $y = 60$, $z = 70$.

Wieser's calculation is simple and clear; its results are not *alternatives* but *definite* figures. Vleugels had defended this solution, but other members of the Viennese camp disapproved.[4] Wieser, according to Otto Weinberger, figured with exceptional conditions. The formula operates with three equations for the unknown factors x, y, z. Why should there not be $3 + n$ equations? asked Weinberger.[5] According to Pantaleoni, a factor of production may have a different value in each combination in which it enters.[6] The third and perhaps the most important argument is taken from higher algebra: N equations with n unknown may have an infinite number of solutions.[7] Since

---

[3] *Ibid.*; Wieser, *Theorie der gesellschaftlichen Wirtschaft*, pp. 212-13; Otto Weinberger, "Alcuni Appunti sull'Economia Matematica in Austria," *Periodico di Matematiche*, Serie IV, Vol. 20, No. 2 (April, 1940), pp. 84-98.

[4] See Weinberger, *ibid.*, and Joseph Schumpeter, "Bemerkungen über das Zurechnungsproblem," *Zeitschrift für Volkswirtschaft, Sozialpolitik und Verwaltung*, Vol. 18 (Vienna, 1909), pp. 79ff.

[5] Weinberger, "Alcuni Appunti."

[6] Maffeo Pantaleoni, *Principii di Economia Pura* (Milan, 1931), p. 294.

[7] Weinberger, "Alcuni Appunti"; Maxime Bocher, *Introduction to Higher Algebra* (New York, 1915), p. 47.

all the solutions of the imputation problem have encountered strong and plausible criticism, it seems justified
to ask: is imputation really an application of marginal
utility? Ludwig von Mises, otherwise a staunch defender
of the Austrian school, did not see a direct connection between imputation and value. For him, imputation is a
price problem.[8] Mises acknowledges Menger's and Boehm-
Bawerk's causal principle: prices of production goods are
determined by the prices of consumer goods; these prices
are a reflection of "the subjective valuations of all members
of the market society."[9] The approval of this chain, Mises
continues, does not mean that imputation can be translated
into a value problem. The marginal utility of all the consumers has only a very indirect influence on the prices
of the factors of production. The owners of the productive
factors adapt their prices to changes of consumer prices,
so that the highest profit can be reached. Mises concludes
that imputation is not a value but rather a price problem.
von Neumann and Morgenstern came to a similar conclusion.

VON NEUMANN-MORGENSTERN, AND THE MULTIPLE SOLUTIONS

von Neumann and Morgenstern tried to solve the great
puzzle for a price-directed economy with the help of
mathematics. Although they changed the direction of the
investigation, their work is still connected with the Austrian
tradition. They deviated from their forerunners because
they analyzed the distribution of income under incomplete competition (olygopoly) and not the separation of
values in an isolated economy. They accepted, however,
the main aspects of Boehm's price theory as a basis for
further investigation. Boehm discovered that one buyer
and one seller on the market (case of the bilateral monop-

[8] Ludwig von Mises, *Human Action*, p. 330.   [9] *Ibid.*

oly) create a maximum and a minimum price; these two prices may be separated by a large gap called by von Neumann and Morgenstern "the zone of uncertainty." The actual price can be at any point between the price limits.

A house is for sale. The minimum price under which the seller A will not offer the house is $9,000. Above the maximum price of $22,000 the buyer C will not purchase the house. The zone of uncertainty is between $22,000 and $9,000. Any price for this house between these two limiting points can be paid. If a second buyer B with a price maximum of $17,000 is introduced into our model market, the price according to Boehm-Bawerk will lie between $17,000 and $22,000. Boehm's solution is at least incomplete.[10] He does not envisage the possibility of a coalition. Yet a coalition is possible if C pays a bribe to B. In this case, seller A may be forced to concede a price under $17,000 to C. Thus two solutions exist in our market. Boehm-Bawerk's solution: C pays to A a sum between 17 and 22 (the zeroes have been left out here and in the following illustrations) and pays B nothing. The new solution: C pays for the house a sum between 9 and 15 and pays B a bribe of 2. But these are not the only solutions. A number of others are possible.

These and many other solutions may be computed. The gains can be figured out by observing the following rules. In our table, A's gains may be computed by subtracting his price limit from the actual price paid; i.e., in solution #1 his price limit is 9, the actual price is 19, and his gain is 10 ($19 - 9 = 10$). The gain for C may be found by subtracting the sum of actual price plus bribery paid to B from his price limit. In solution #1, $22 - (19 + 0) = 3$. B's gain is either the bribery alone or the price limit he would offer, less the actual price.

[10] Von Neumann and Morgenstern, *Theory of Games*, pp. 36ff.

From all the five cases (and in reality many more cases can be computed) only cases 1, 2, and 5 can be enforced. In case #5, *A* is worse off than in case #1 and case #2, but he cannot force solution 1 or 2 on *B* and *C* because both buyers can block *A*'s action by a coalition.

Cases #1, #2, and #5 can be called the dominant imputations. An imputation is dominating if some of the participants have greater gains separately in it than in any other non-dominating imputation, and if the imputation can be enforced. The dominating imputations are indifferent to one another. There is no tendency to *move from one dominating imputation to the other*. A number of solutions is possible.

Assume that *A*, *B*, and *C* have dedicated factors to the production of one consumer good. It is then possible to divide their contribution to the final product in different ways. Several divisions will be dominant. Which of these

Table Illustrating Some Solutions: According to Marschak[11]

Number of Solutions	Price of the House	Actions of the Three Persons	Distribution of Gains A B C	Chance of Enforcing a Solution
1	19	*C* buys, *B* does not receive a bribe	10 0 3	Can be enforced
2	21	*C* buys, *B* does not receive a bribe	12 0 1	Can be enforced
3	11	*B* buys	2 6 0	Cannot be enforced
4	12	*C* buys, *B* gets 8 as a bribe	3 8 2	Cannot be enforced
5	12	*C* buys, *B* gets 2 as a bribe	3 2 8	Can be enforced

[11] See also J. Marschak, "Neumann's and Morgenstern's New Approach to Static Economics," *Journal of Political Economy*, Vol. 54 (1946), pp. 97-115.

many imputations will be materialized in reality is, according to von Neumann and Morgenstern, dependent on the established order of society or the "accepted standard of behavior."[12] The accepted standard of behavior is the totality of legal and moral codes which have developed in the history of society. The last statement violates an Austrian taboo, for imputation was considered a general problem which in its basic elements remains identical for all times and all societies. Von Neumann and Morgenstern's accepted standard of behavior is a concession to John Stuart Mill and the historical school. The analysis of imputation in terms of price and not in terms of value theory means also a break with traditional thinking. This twofold revolt led to an interesting explanation of income distribution. But the result is rather disturbing. If von Neumann and Morgenstern are right, then the economists have wasted time and effort in seeking a solution in the wrong direction. They meditated about utility, technical productivity, loss, etc., to find the only right answer, while there are many correct solutions. Furthermore, it is quite possible that an economist can no longer take a stand based on scientific conviction in a labor dispute, because both parties may offer a correct arrangement. These baffling consequences are partly due to the method used by von Neumann and Morgenstern. The same approach also produced interesting results in the field of the measuring of utility.

[12] Von Neumann and Morgenstern, *Theory of Games*, pp. 41ff.

CHAPTER XIX

THE MEASURING OF UTILITY:
DEVELOPMENT UNTIL 1934

SURVEY

SINCE the time of Bernoulli, marginalists have been interested in the measuring of utility. Today this question attracts more attention than all the other problems. A recent intensive study produced startling results which were not achieved in the preparatory period before 1870 nor in the following 70 years, when marginalism became dominant. From 1870 to about 1934 most Austrian as well as mathematical economists participated in a confusing discussion. The same economists are at one moment in favor of, and at the other against, measuring.[1] Defenders as well as opponents can be found in all the camps of marginalism. Confusion did not prevent some

[1] George Stigler and Rosenstein-Rodan drew up a tidy list confronting the supporters and the adversaries. George J. Stigler, "The Development of Utility Theory," *op. cit.*, p. 383; Rosenstein-Rodan, "Grenznutzen," *op. cit.*, p. 1193. But the opinions of most authors cannot be easily classified. Menger, as has been mentioned before, believed in an objective standard of values. Consistent with this conviction, he ought to be in favor of measuring. But in the Hitotsubashi papers he writes against it. Boehm-Bawerk believed in measuring, yet with certain restrictions. Boehm-Bawerk, *Positive Theorie*, II Excurse; "Exkurs X Betreffend die Messbarkeit von Gefühlsgrossen," Concerning the Intensity of Feelings, pp. 205ff. In his *Natural Value* Wieser supported measurability and in his *Theory of Social Economy* he was against it. Wieser, *Der natürliche Werth*, p. 56; Wieser, *Theorie der gesellschaftlichen Wirtschaft*, pp. 215-16. See also Mises, *Human Action*, p. 205. Pareto's development has some similarity with that of Wieser. Before 1900 he defended measuring and after 1900 he presents the most telling arguments against it.

progress. The discussion of seven decades had at least shown that neither conventional logic nor geometrical presentation provides useful tools for measuring. Obviously, this is a purely negative insight, but without the understanding that traditional approaches led into a dead end street, recent authors would not have been forced to seek new ways which promise positive results.

IRVING FISHER AND ALFRED MARSHALL

Obviously measuring is a mathematical technique. Therefore it is understandable that as early as the end of the nineteenth century the mathematical wing of the value theorists examined the possibility of constructing a yardstick. The most important defenders at that time were Irving Fisher and Alfred Marshall. Three possible cases formed Fisher's basic assumptions: *Equality of utility.* An individual has no desire for commodity A excluding commodity B. $A = B$; *inequality of utilities.* If A and B are commodities, then the utility of A is higher than that of B. $A > B$; *the utility of some commodity depends alone on the quantity of that commodity.* The utility of B has no influence on the utility of A. This independent utility is essential because the marginal independent utility can be measured with the utility increment of any other commodity.

With the help of these three cases, Irving Fisher proved that a ratio of two infinitesimal utilities is measured by the ratio of two infinitesimal increments of the same commodity.

Hisatake objected to the third case basic to Fisher's measuring the independent utility because it cannot be confirmed by direct experience.[2]

[2] Masao Hisatake, "A Reconsideration on the Concept of Utility," *The Annals of the Hitotsubashi Academy*, Vol. 10, No. 2 (December, 1959), pp. 171ff.; Irving Fisher, *Mathematical Investigations in the Theory of Value and Prices* (New Haven, 1892).

Marshall proposed another method of measuring: "The fact that he would just be induced to purchase one ton if the price were £10, proves that the total enjoyment or satisfaction which he derives from that ton is as great as that which he could obtain by spending £10 on other things. In other words, the satisfaction derived from, or the value in use to him of, a single ton a year, is economically measured by £10; and therefore his power of purchasing one ton of coals for £1 gives him a surplus satisfaction, of which the economic measure is £9; that is to say, it gives him a Consumers' Rent of £9."[3] This definition corresponds to the common sense understanding of marginal utility. The utility of the increment of a commodity is measured by the increment of money just equal to it. Marshall himself admitted that his measuring is only possible if the marginal utility of money itself remains constant. Hicks denied that the marginal utility of money is constant.[4] Marshall neglects the income effect caused by the change of price, although this event cannot be neglected, and therefore the Marshallian method should not be used in the general case.

Hisatake and Hicks criticized only some attempts at defining utility as a quantity; Pareto went much further, for he tried to prove that any attempt to measure is futile.

VILFREDO PARETO

It is noteworthy that Pareto himself was first in favor of measurement, but later changed his opinion; we are mainly interested in his later opinion. The table of curves, he wrote, has to be read like a contour map of physical geography. The geographical contour lines indicate equal

[3] This Marshall quotation is from the first edition of the *Principles*, p. 175; in the third edition changes were introduced which, however, did not change the meaning. Alfred Marshall, *Principles of Economics* (9th [Variorum] ed.; New York, 1961), Vol. 2, notes, p. 258.

[4] John Hicks, *Value and Capital* (Oxford, 1939), pp. 20-32.

heights above sea level. Similarly, the indifference curves
indicate equal intensities of utility. The bundle of indifference curves forms a slope of a hill. The higher the utility
the higher is the indifference curve. The basis of this
utility structure is formed by the ordinate and the
abscissa; a vertical axis measuring the elevation of the
indifference curve could easily be used for the measuring
of utility, but Pareto did not think so. The older Pareto,
who wrote the *Manual*, did not believe that his indifference
figure could be interpreted this way.[5] The slope of the
rising surface is arbitrary; every ascending slope can
represent the differences in utility between the indifference
curves.

Figure 1 represents a family of indifference curves; the
line *O A* cuts a profile through the utility surface.

The profile is indicated in Figure 2. The line *O B*
represents the slope of rising utilities. However, Pareto
claims that this line *O B* could be easily substituted by
the lines *O B'* or *O B''* or by any other slope, as long as
the distance between the indifference curves is indicated. The
absolute height of any point on *O B, O B',* or *O B''* is
partially arbitrary. ("Cette surface demeure en partie
arbitraire.")[6] Due to the arbitrariness of the yardstick it is
not possible to measure value.

Theoretical and practical attempts to measure went on
in spite of Pareto's arguments. Ragnar Frisch tried to
measure the concrete utilities in daily life, following Irving

[5] Vilfredo Pareto, *Manuel d'Économie Politique* (Paris, 1927),
pp. 275, 539ff.; Heinrich Stackelberg, "Die Entwicklungsstufen der
Werttheorie," *Schweizerische Zeitschrift für Volkswirtschaft und
Statistik*, 83rd year (February, 1947), p. 12; Knut Wicksell, "Vil-
fredo Pareto's *Manuel d'Économie Politique*," *Selected papers on
Economic Theory* (London, 1958), pp. 161ff. In my explanation I
follow the interpretation given to me by Dr. Aaron Gurwitsch,
Professor at the New School for Social Research.

[6] Pareto, *Manuel*, p. 543.

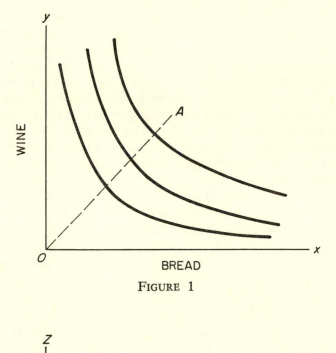

BREAD

FIGURE 1

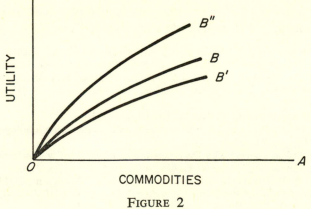

COMMODITIES

FIGURE 2

Fisher, who long before Pareto's verdict attempted to measure real events.[7] Both used sugar as an independent commodity. Ragnar Frisch measured the marginal utility of sugar in relation to income of Parisians from 1920 to 1922. When Pareto's manual was published, Wicksell vigorously attacked Pareto's refutation.[8] But also Pareto had his supporters, e.g., Luigi Amoroso and most of the Austrian economists whose opinions will be discussed later.[9] The fight reached a new climax in the year 1934. At that time Oskar Lange wrote: "From the assumption that the individual is able to know *whether* one increase of utility is greater than another increase of utility the possibility of saying *how many times* this increase is greater than another one follows necessarily."[10] Harro Bernardelli and Phelps Brown found the weak spot in Lange's argument.[11] They claimed that Lange gives to equality and inequality of utility a rather strange meaning. If, in the field of utility sensations, the commodity X creates the same utility sensation as the commodity Y, then $X = Y$, but this assumption does not justify the conclusion that $X + Y = 2X$; the consumer who doubles the amount of X or Y must not necessarily "have twice of anything that he has when he takes but one."[12]

[7] Irving Fisher, "Mathematical Investigations in the Theory of Value and Price," *Transactions of the Connecticut Academy*, Vol. 9 (July, 1892); Ragnar Frisch, "New Methods of Measuring Marginal Utility," *Beiträge zur ökonomischen Theorie*, No. 3 (Tübingen, 1932).

[8] Knut Wicksell, "Vilfredo Pareto's *Manuel*."

[9] Luigi Amoroso, *Lezioni di Economia Matematica* (Bologna, 1921), pp. 91, 92.

[10] Oskar Lange, "The Determinateness of the Utility Function," *The Review of Economic Studies*, Vol. 1 (1933-34), p. 220.

[11] E. H. Phelps Brown, Harro Bernardelli, "Notes on the Determinateness of the Utility Function," *The Review of Economic Studies*, Vol. 2, No. 1 (October, 1934), pp. 66ff.

[12] *Ibid.*

Čuhel contra Boehm-Bawerk

The Austrian school did not directly participate in the interpretation of the indifference curves, but they also were interested in measuring. Due to strong anti-mathematical bias, the Austrian discussion was interesting but not as penetrating as the debate outside the school. One high point of their investigation was the dialogue between Boehm-Bawerk and Čuhel.[13] Čuhel believed that the natural unit of measuring must be the goods of equal quantity, quality, and form. But this procedure does not create a yardstick. With every additional commodity the utility falls. Measuring becomes impossible if the common unit of measuring, the utility of the commodity, changes its size with every addition and subtraction. The law of diminishing utility prevents measurement of utility.

Boehm-Bawerk was not satisfied with the findings of his former student. According to Boehm, *exact* measuring is not possible but *approximate* measuring is. The distorting effect of Gossen's first law can be overcome by composing the yardstick from values out of different intensities, meaning that Boehm envisages a measuring stick whose divisions become smaller and smaller. This tool already exists, Boehm-Bawerk concludes, because it is an everyday accomplishment for the consumer to sum up different intensities of feeling (*Gefühlsintensitäten*).

Boehm-Bawerk compared the consumer with the officer on a shooting range who calls out the distances for the benefit of the practicing riflemen. The perspective prevents the officer, and the law of diminishing utility prevents the consumer, from measuring exactly, but they measure anyway.

[13] Franz Čuhel, *Zur Lehre von den Bedürfnissen* (Innsbruck, 1907), esp. pp. 187ff. Boehm-Bawerk answered Čuhel. Excurs X—Franz Čuhel, 1862-1914, member of Boehm-Bawerk's seminar. In service of the Chamber of Commerce, Prague, 1889-1903.

In spite of detailed explanations the two writers could not pinpoint their real difference. They saw difficulties: Boehm-Bawerk concluded that difficulties did not prevent measuring; Čuhel had the opposite opinion, but he was not consistent. He demanded a uniform utility thermometer. In spite of these inconsistencies Čuhel contributed considerably to the development of the analysis.

More important than Čuhel's inconsistent attack against measuring is his clear systematization of the controversial material. He distinguishes between comparison or scaling and measuring. He illustrates scaling with Mohs' scaling of hardness. Mohs' scale indicates the hardness of a mineral in comparison with other minerals. We cannot measure hardness but only weight, distances, and volumes. Measuring as well as scaling can be accomplished accurately or by estimation. Scaling or comparison works with ordinal and measuring with cardinal numbers. The utility of goods can be scaled and not measured. Only ordinal numbers can be attached to valuations. Čuhel's subtle distinctions are still used in recent discussion, but it is doubtful that modern writers have directly borrowed their terminology from Čuhel. Even the name of this author has been forgotten.

BILIMOVIČ AND PIGOU

Besides Čuhel, another member of the Austrian school, Alexander Bilimovič, has to be mentioned. Bilimovič claimed that only one person can compare his utilities, that the intensities of need of different individuals can be neither compared nor measured. Alexander Bilimovič only repeated a widespread opinion.[14] He published his verdict in 1932. Around this time all attempts to attach ordinal value coefficients to goods were of no avail, and

[14] Alexander Bilimovič, "Die Preis und Wertlehre," *Wieser Festschrift*, Vol. 2, p. 100.

yet this could not be the end of our story. If measuring and interpersonal comparisons are not possible, then the field for the application of marginalism is narrowed down considerably. It becomes difficult to lay the foundation of welfare economics and of public finance. Pigou did not share this opinion. He assured us that the theory of economic welfare can be written without measuring utilities but that interpersonal comparisons of utilities are necessary for his system.[15] How interpersonal comparisons are possible without measuring is not quite clear. Yet measuring as well as interpersonal comparison had been ruled out by the earlier authors. In public finance measuring becomes important for two reasons; it plays a role in the justification of progressive taxation and in the explanation of taxes as public prices. The defense of the income tax hinges upon the equal sacrifice of each taxpayer, who must give up the same amount of utility if the burden should be equally distributed. The allotment of equal tax loads is dependent on a uniform denominator. The explanation of taxes as a price for common utilities encounters similar difficulties. If the tax is a price, then the utility losses caused by taxes and the gains derived from common utilities must be figured in utility weights. If the critics are right, then computation is impossible. So welfare economy and public finance can be compared to houses built without foundations. Since 1943 strong efforts have been made to improve this situation.

[15] A. C. Pigou, "Some Aspects of Welfare Economics," *The American Economic Review*, Vol. 41, No. 3 (June, 1951), pp. 290-92.

CHAPTER XX

UNCERTAINTY AND MEASURING

THE GREAT CHANGE

WITHOUT a complete change of technique and goals the impasse described in the last chapter could not be overcome. Instead of the literary method used by the older Austrian school and the calculus applied by Pareto and his followers, probability mathematics became the new approach of von Neumann and Morgenstern, Friedman, Savage, and others.[1] This replacement of techniques involved a rethinking of the leading concepts. Since the whole reform is rather complex, I follow the advice of von Neumann and Morgenstern and divide the difficulties. Von Neumann and Morgenstern have redefined utility, the process of measuring, and the evaluation of events. The following paragraphs deal with these three steps of the reform.

THE DEFINITION OF UTILITY

Before 1943 the object of measuring was utility, which was defined as a bundle of pleasure feelings. Even at that time economists were not completely satisfied with this definition; they created a new concept which became very important for von Neumann and Morgenstern's reform: *neutral utility*. With this new notion the economists designed empty boxes cleansed of ethical, political, and hedonist contents. Von Neumann and Morgenstern adopted Irving Fisher's definition. He defined utility as a quan-

---

[1] I am indebted to many mathematicians for their help, for instance, Oskar Morgenstern, Karl Borch, Robert Meacham, Dudley South, Morton Davis, and especially Forrest Dristy. None of them, either mentioned or not, is responsible for the mistakes I have made. They are my own.

tity. Utility is nothing but an indicator of preferences.[2] These preferences can be numbered. Under certain circumstances, which will be discussed later, these separate utilities may be numbered in the order of the corresponding preferences.[3]

THE REFORM OF CARDINALISM

To explain the character of measuring, we start again with the period before 1943. Until that time economists hoped to find some instrument by which the strength of feeling in the marginal unit could be tested. This procedure was not successful and is a dead issue now.[4] The new measuring contains elements of prediction and free choice. In opposition to ordinal ordering, cardinalism predicts something about two events in combination. Baumol tells about the two pieces of cloth which ought to cover the table at home. If I know the length of the table, for instance, in yards, I do not have to take the two pieces of cloth home from the store to find out whether they fit. I can predict with the help of the length marked in yards that the two pieces will turn out to be too long, too short, or just right.

All cardinal measuring consists of adding units or indices. These units are yards, grams, gallons, etc. In mak-

[2] John von Neumann and Oskar Morgenstern, *Theory of Games and Economic Behavior* (Princeton, 1947), pp. 8-16. This is the edition which I used throughout the study. The first edition is from the year 1944. Luce-Raiffa were not completely satisfied with this definition of utility "because there have been so many past uses and misuses of various concepts called utility." R. Duncan Luce and Howard Raiffa, *Games and Decisions* (New York, 1958), p. 12. I think it not wise to break up tradition, because pleasure utility is the forerunner of neutral utility and neutral utility is a needed element of the von Neumann and Morgenstern calculation.

[3] Von Neumann and Morgenstern, *Theory of Games.*

[4] Robert H. Strotz, "Recent Development in Mathematical Economics and Econometrics. An Expository Session. Cardinal Utility," *The American Economic Review*, Vol. 43, p. 387. William J. Baumol, *Economic Theory and Operation Analysis* (Englewood Cliffs, New Jersey, 1961), p. 341.

ing our yardstick we have two kinds of freedom, says Baumol: we can freely assign the unit and the zero point. The measures are unique to linear transformation. Luce and Raiffa have explained the linear transformation as follows: "if a and b are any two constants such that $a > O$, then the function u', where $u'(L) = a.u(L) + b$ for any lottery L, is also a linear utility function. . . ."[5] Figures 1 and 2 show examples of utility functions u' which are linear transformations of a given utility function u. In all three figures, utility is marked on the y axis and the lottery cases ordered according to the amount of money spent for each lottery are on the x axis. In figure 3 the function u' is *not* a linear transformation of the function u because there are no numbers a and b for which $u'(L) = a u(L) + b$ is true for every lottery L.

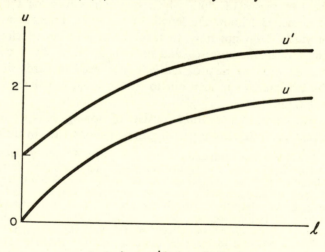

$$a = 1, \ b = 1, \ u'(L) = u(L) + 1$$

FIGURE 1

[5] The basis for this and following explanations is Luce-Raiffa, *Games and Decisions*, pp. 25-30. I owe this geometrical interpretation of linear transformation to F. Dristy.

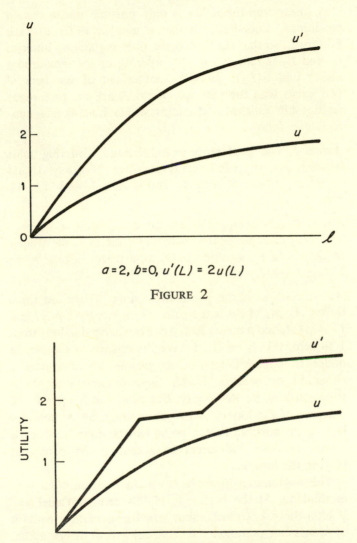

$a = 2, b = 0, u'(L) = 2u(L)$

FIGURE 2

FIGURE 3

A linear transformation is only possible under certain conditions: Luce-Raiffa assign a number $u(L)$ to each Lottery L, so that the preference ordering among lotteries L_1 and L_2 is reflected in the ordering of the magnitudes $u(L_1)$ and $u(L_2)$. Second, another set of numbers u' (L) exists with the same property. Third, the preference relationship satisfied six axioms which Luce-Raiffa enumerate as follows:

Axiom 1. The "preference or indifference" ordering holds between any two prizes and is transitive. "For any A_i and A_j either $A_i > A_j$ or $A_j > A_i$; and if $A_i > A_j$ and $A_j > A_k$, then $A_i > A_k$."

Axiom 2. Any complex lottery can be reduced to a simple one. (An example of the multi-stage lottery is the wheels of chance in Paris which have, as a prize, tickets in the National Lottery.)

Axiom 3. This is the continuity axiom. There are three tickets A_1, A_i, A_r, p is the prize. $A_1 > A_i > A_r$ if $p \, A_1$ and $(1-p) \, A_r$ and p is near to 1, p can be changed so long from 1 to zero, till $A_1 = A_r$. I have the chance to receive 1¢ under all circumstances or to gamble where I receive either $1 or nothing. Under these circumstances most people will prefer the lottery. But what will happen if the outcome of the lottery is 10¢ or nothing, 5¢ or nothing? It is quite possible that a point will be found, where a person becomes indifferent to accepting the penny or playing the lottery.

This assumption means a deviation from an older way of thinking. At the beginning of this century Čuhel and Boehm-Bawerk argued about whether a certain amount of prunes can guarantee the same enjoyment as one apple. This old debate has been abandoned. The new discussion compares a secure gain with an insecure gain, with a lottery chance. In this new case a point of indifference can be reached. This solution does not reflect on the old case.

Axiom 4. This axiom, which is connected with the third assumption, means that if two lottery tickets are of indifferent value, one can be substituted for the other. Carl Menger had already laid down a similar rule; he wrote about substitution between goods equal in quantity, quality, and form, but he did not mention lotteries.

Axiom 5. "Preference and indifference among lottery tickets are transitive relations."

Axiom 6. Monotonicity means that "between two lotteries involving only the most and least preferred alternatives one should select the one which renders the most preferred alternative more probable."

Luce and Raiffa know that the last axiom cannot always find its equivalent in real life. Man who follows the sixth axiom should generally prefer life to death. There are exceptions. A mountaineer while climbing may think otherwise. On his way to the top he actually prefers some lottery "of life and death to life itself."

Also to amalgamate the other five axioms with reality is no easy task. The two authors frankly admit that exceptions exist; but in spite of this drawback these six assumptions are indispensable for the new measuring, as the following pages indicate.

CERTAINTY AND MEASURING

The reformation of utility and of measuring is not enough. There still is Pareto's verdict that the utility surface is partly arbitrary. Only new information can challenge the validity of this declaration. Von Neumann and Morgenstern borrowed a leaf from Bernoulli's paper and introduced risk or gambling as a new factor.

Von Neumann and Morgenstern and their followers distinguish between two kinds of future enjoyments: the certain enjoyments and risky enjoyments. Either the businessman or the consumer is sure that the goods or services he needs are available, or he is in doubt as to whether the wanted utilities can be obtained at the right moment. In this second case the man faces a risky proposition; he will gamble if the probability of gain and the value of the event permit it.[6] In most cases of everyday

---

[6] Von Neumann and Morgenstern, *Theory of Games*. The following papers have been used: Milton Friedman and J. L. Savage, "The Utility Analysis of Choices Involving Risk," *The Journal of Political Economy*, Vol. 56, No. 4 (August, 1948), pp. 279ff.; Friedman and Savage, "The Expected Utility Hypothesis and the Measurability of Utility," *Journal of Political Economy*, Vol. 60, No. 6 (December, 1952), pp. 463ff.; Friedman and Savage, "What All is Utility?" *Economic Journal*, Vol. 65 (September, 1953), pp. 405ff.; Sir Dennis Robertson, *Utility and All That* (New York, 1952), pp. 13ff.; D. Robertson, "Utility and All What?" *Economic Journal*, Vol. 64 (December, 1954), pp. 665ff.; see also the papers by Tyszynski and Ellsberg in the same volume. Armen A. Alchian, "The Measuring of Utility Measurement," *American Economic Review*, Vol. 63 (March, 1953), pp. 26ff.; J. K. Mehta, "La Misurabilita dell' Utilita di un Nuovo Punto di Vista," *Rivista Internazionale di Scienze Economiche e Commerciali*, Anno III (1956), pp. 521ff.; Tapas Majundar, "Behavioral Cardinalism in Utility Theory," *Economica*, 38th year, New Series, Vol. 25, No. 97 (February, 1958), p. 27; Murray N. Rothbard, "Toward Reconstruction of Utility and Welfare Economics," *Essays in Honor of Ludwig von Mises*, pp. 224ff.; Masao Hisatake, "A Reconsideration of the Concept of Utility," *The Annals of the Hitotsubashi Academy* (Tokyo, Japan), Vol. 10, No. 2 (December, 1959), pp. 224ff.; C. E. Ferguson, "An Essay on Cardinal Utility," *The Southern Economic Journal*, Vol. 25, No. 1 (July, 1958), pp. 11ff.; Leonard J. Savage, *The Foundation of Statistics* (New York, 1954), see especially pp. 91ff.; Karl Borch, "Recent Developments in Economic Theory and their Application to Insurance," The Astin Colloquium, Juan-les-Pins, May 23-26, 1962 (mimeographed paper); F. J. Anscombe and R. J. Aumann, "A Definition of Subjective Probability," revised version of Research Memorandum No. 30 (Econometric Research Program, August 16, 1961), Princeton, July, 1962.

life the selecting consumer chooses commodities or services whose appearance on the market he takes for granted. In the case of certainty preferences *we have not advanced beyond Čuhel and the Mohs scale*. We still simply rank the events. *A* is preferred to *B*; *B* is preferred to *C*. Therefore *A* is preferred to *C*. Even this order is true only if transitivity exists. (See Axiom 1 and 5.) These ordinal numbers can be neither added nor subtracted nor multiplied nor divided.[7]

BERNOULLI AND RISK

F. P. Ramsey (1931)[8] and von Neumann and Morgenstern (1943) tried to advance the analysis introducing risk, meaning mixing chances with utility. The three authors had one great forerunner, Daniel Bernoulli, whose thoughts guided them in their new analysis. In the earlier chapters of this study only a part of Bernoulli's achievements have been discussed. Here is the rest of the story: Daniel Bernoulli's discovery of marginal utility was a by-product; his main goal was to describe the reaction of the gamblers while playing the Petersburg game.[9] Some details of this game have to be presented here.[10] The Petersburg game consists of throwing a coin. *A* flips a coin; if it is heads, then *B* receives from *A* one ducat, and the game is finished; if it is tails, the game continues. *A* flips the coin a second time; if it is heads, *B* receives from *A* two ducats and the game is finished; if it is tails, the game continues. At the third time, and under the same conditions, *B* can gain 4 ducats, etc. In general the gambler

[7] Luce-Raiffa, *Games and Decisions.*

[8] F. P. Ramsey, "Truth and Probability," *The Foundations of Mathematics and Other Logical Essays* (London, 1931).

[9] Daniel Bernoulli, "Specimen Theoriae Novae . . . ," p. 31.

[10] Karl Menger, "Das Unsicherheitsmoment in der Wertlehre," *Zeitschrift für Nationalökonomie*, Vol. 5 (Vienna, 1934), pp. 459-61.

receives 2^{n-1} ducats if the first head shows up on throw n. To find out how much B should pay for entering this game we have first to know B's expected gain. B receives 1 ducat with the probability one-half, 2 ducats with the probability one-fourth, 4 ducats with the probability one-eighth, so that B's expectation $= \frac{1}{2} + \frac{1}{2} + \frac{1}{2} \ldots$ which is not finite.

The equation means that the Petersburg game does not produce any finite number. The gambler B can pay any sum for entering the game. The probability calculation does not tell us how much he will give; it may be 1 ducat or it may be 10,000 ducats. Now it is most unlikely that a gambler will give his whole fortune for the right to participate in this game. The gambler will possibly offer a rather small sum.[11] This answer is only a conjecture based on some observation. Already Daniel Bernoulli calculates an accurate answer. His solution may no longer be accepted, but the way in which he reaches his answer is still important.

Bernoulli combines probability with utility value. This procedure is still acclaimed by mathematical economists, but his calculation has not been accepted.

Bernoulli suggested that not the probable *monetary* value but the probable *utility* value ought to be averaged.[12] Here Bernoulli integrated his marginal value, which has been described in the beginning of this study, into his deduction. In agreement with his value theory the utility value of money increases with the amount of money, but at a diminishing rate. A function having this property is the logarithm.[13] Therefore, if the utility of m dollars is $\log_{10} m$, then the right price would not be the probable

[11] *Ibid.*, p. 461.
[12] See here, Bernoulli, "Mensura Sortis," Sommer translation, p. 25; Luce-Raiffa, *Games and Decisions*, p. 20; Karl Menger, "Das Unsicherheitsmoment . . . ," p. 466.
[13] Luce-Raiffa, *Games and Decisions*, p. 20.

money value but the expected utility value of the money sum:

$$b = (\tfrac{1}{2}) \log_{10}2 + (\tfrac{1}{4}) \log_{10}4 + (\tfrac{1}{8}) \log_{10}8 + \ldots$$

In the limit this sum reaches the value b. In this case Bernoulli could offer a finite solution. He found the price b would pay for the privilege of participating. He even discovered more; in the case of the Petersburg game utility can be measured.

But the mathematical economists were not satisfied. Karl Menger, the son of the famous economist, published an essay in 1934 dealing with the Petersburg game which stated that an indefinite number of curves satisfy Bernoulli's conditions. Menger presents four of them; the first is Bernoulli's logarithmic curve.[14]

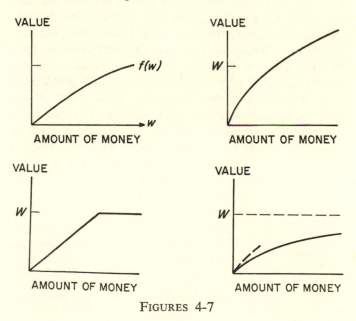

FIGURES 4-7

[14] K. Menger, "Das Unsicherheitsmoment . . . ," p. 470 n.

W. is the limiting value which cannot be overreached by the curve. Bernoulli's solution is correct only for the first of these curves. The association of values expressed in these curves may fit one person at a certain time, but not another person under different conditions. Therefore Bernoulli's calculation is not satisfying. However, his approach, the combination of probability and utility, is used two hundred years later.

GAMBLING AND UNCERTAINTY

In 1932 Oskar Morgenstern prepared a paper for the meeting at Dresden at which the value theory was discussed.[15] In his survey of value problems he also mentioned the measuring of utility. At that time Morgenstern was still undecided which way to go. He first repeated the traditional opinion: measuring is impossible because utilities are intensive qualities and not extensive quantities. A footnote reveals a somewhat different opinion. Here he remarked that the majority verdict against measuring can be accepted only as a preliminary and problematic solution, because it does "not correspond more entirely with mathematic analysis which alone can decide about the possibility of measuring. . . . A decision in favor of measuring would be advantageous."[16] In 1943 Morgenstern, together with von Neumann, decided in favor of measuring. They accepted Bernoulli's main propositions that the utility of gambling can be measured, that the "mix" of probability and utility gives the key for the calculation of measuring. For von Neumann and Morgenstern, Bernoulli's assumptions, but not his solution, are acceptable. A set of alternatives has to be found as a substitute for Bernoulli's logarithmic curve. These alterna-

[15] Oskar Morgenstern, "Die drei Grundtypen der Theorie des subjektiven Wertes," *Schriften des Vereins für Sozialpolitik*, Vol. 183, I (München, 1932).

[16] *Ibid.*, p. 14.

tives must cover all possible cases of gambling, not only the Petersburg game.

Here is a somewhat rough sketch of what von Neumann and Morgenstern have done. They found the weighted utility of a game—the weight is of course the probability. Weighted utility is utility times probability. Von Neumann and Morgenstern warn against identifying probability with estimation, because this interpretation excludes numerical expression. They define probability "as frequency in long runs."[17] This explanation is similar to Laplace's classical definition: "Probability is the ratio of the number of favorable cases to the total number of equally likely cases." Von Neumann and Morgenstern restrict their observation of events to *one time* periods to avoid complications. New problems arise if preferences between "events in different periods of the future"[18] are observed.

Probabilities in which favorable events are compared with unfavorable events occur in games of chance or lotteries where the gambler faces the alternative of gain or total loss. The simplest illustration is the casting of a die in which one gambler bets that he will throw a six; his probability of success is 1:5 or 1/6. The utility of the lottery has to be equalized with the utility of an event whose occurrence is certain. If the point of indifference between the utilities of the certain event and of the game has been reached, the utilities become measurable. (See *Axiom 3*.)

A more detailed explanation follows: consider that there are three events or future enjoyments, *A*, *B*, and *C*. The utilities of these events are transitively ordered, meaning $A > B > C$ implies $A > C$. (See *Axiom 1*.) In this form of

[17] Von Neumann and Morgenstern, *Theory of Games*, p. 19. Apparently Richard von Mises was not satisfied with this definition. Richard von Mises, *Probability, Statistics, and Truth* (London, 1957), p. 230.
[18] Von Neumann and Morgenstern, *op.cit.*

ordering, *B* is a certain event. *A* and *C* are prizes or lottery games. They are also alternatives; you get either *A* or *C*. In the first moment one would think that this sequence *A*, *B*, *C* has no connection with reality, but this is not true.

Consider a young man who has a chance to enter an export-import business. He may become a shipping clerk, stay a shipping clerk all his life, and make $80 a week; this is *B*, the certain option. Or he may enter an insurance company feared for its big turnover of employees but also known for its high salaries. In the insurance company he will either soon make $140 a week or be thrown out. Here are the alternatives: *A*, $140; and *C*, $0. Now the young man may select the alternative $140:0, or the certain gain of $80, or finally he may not know what to do, being indifferent to the three possibilities. This situation of indifference can also be artifically created by changing, in actuality or in the imagination of the clerk, the price tagged on case *B*. This position of balance, whether artifically created or already existent, is very important because now it is possible to measure utility.

Consider that *A* has the probability of p and that *C* has the probability of $1 - p$.[19] It is plausible that the nearer p comes to one, the more the gamble seems preferable to the certain case, and vice versa, the nearer p comes to 0 the more the certain case reaches priority. (See *Axiom 3*.) If our young man thinks that in the insurance company it is an eighty to twenty proposition whether he gains *A* or *C*, then we have $4/5A$ to $1/5C$. If we establish arbitrarily a utility of one for $140 and a utility of 0 for $0, then the man will gain a utility of 1, if he is employed for $140, and he will gain a utility of 0 if he is thrown out. The weighted average utility is

$$4/5 \cdot 1 + 1/5 \cdot 0 = 4/5$$

[19] Luce-Raiffa, *Games and Decisions*, p. 22; Robert H. Strotz, "Cardinal Utility," *American Economic Review*, Vol. 42 (Stanford, 1953), pp. 384ff.

This weighted average is Bernoulli's *moral expectation* or it may be called the *average utility*. The young man will be indifferent between this class of gambles and one special class of certainty. His strategy is explained in Figure 8. The *y* axis indicates utility. The *x* axis measures the amount of money. The distance *OA* is arbitrarily established as utility one. The point *B* indicates that $140 have utility one. Between *B* and *O* an infinite number of utility curves can be drawn. Only two curves U_1 and U_2 are

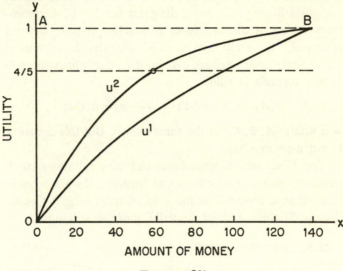

FIGURE 8[20]

presented here. If the young man operates on utility curve U_1, $100 are worth 4/5 utility. Under these circumstances the position as shipping clerk will not suit him, because he gets only $80, and he prefers the risky employment with the insurance company. Let us assume that our man is very much afraid of risks; then he may follow

[20] Figure 8 is patterned after Strotz, "Cardinal Utility," p. 389, figure 1, and p. 397, figure 5.

U_2 and reach 4/5 utility already with $60. He will definitely select the position as shipping clerk if $80 is offered.

With the help of gambling each person can assign his utilities according to his own preferences. For instance: a utility of 4/5 is $80, but we know also that under different circumstances 4/5 utility is only $60. The "right" number is in each case determined by the shape of the utility curve. "The subject's preferences among alternatives and lotteries" have priority over the numerical characterization.[21] Each person carries his own utility thermometer with him. Strangely enough, the great number of thermometers is not a disadvantage; it marks progress beyond Bernoulli. Bernoulli could only use the logarithmical curve. Now many curves can be used for which the following formula is valid:

$$u(B) = p \cdot u(A) + (1-p) \cdot u(C);$$

u is utility; A, B, C are the three events. But this equation is not a sesame key.

Von Neumann, Morgenstern, and their followers know that their elegant deductions and formulas do not provide more than a foothold in the field of measuring.[22] Conditions and axioms restrict the validity of this solution.

The Recent Discussion

The achievements of von Neumann and Morgenstern were acclaimed by the mathematical economists, especially Friedman, Savage, and Samuelson. Outside this group the new construction was received with a mixed reaction. A debate emerged and is still going strong.[23] The discussion is as heated as the two old arguments about labor value and

[21] Luce-Raiffa, *Games and Decisions*, p. 22.
[22] Von Neumann and Morgenstern, *op.cit.*, p. 19.
[23] Hisatake, "A Reconsideration . . . ," p. 180.

about imputation; perhaps the arguments are still more confused today than they were in the past. The radical defenders of ordinalism are Ludwig von Mises and his group.[24] Sir Dennis Robertson maintains that cardinal numbers can be attached to all forms of preferences without introducing chances, and he also defends the cardinalist position of the time before 1943. The arguments are bandied back and forth between the extreme cardinalists and ordinalists. The views of both groups are given here in this antithetical table (on pages 216-217).

It seems that in this discussion the rebuttals are stronger than the critical remarks. On the other side, the result of the new method is very small. The greatest part of analysis needed for a workable theory must still be done. Morgenstern expresses a similar opinion. In the essays in honor of Edgar Salin he wrote, "A scientifical interpersonal comparison of utilities is for the time being not possible. . . . We have an idea of an existing social utility, but science has struggled with its explanation without success."[25] There is still a long way to go from the intrapersonal measuring under very restricted conditions to the interpersonal comparison and to social utility.

There is, however, one place where the theory even in its unfinished stage can be applied; this is the field of insurance. Bernoulli realized this. With the help of his calculation he criticized the insurance rates and asked for cheaper rates for sea transport from Amsterdam, Holland, to St. Petersburg, Russia.[26] Abstract speculations can have a very practical aspect.

[24] Ludwig von Mises, *Human Action*, pp. 105-18, 205-206; Murray N. Rothbard, "Toward a Reconstruction of Utility and Welfare Economics," pp. 239-43; Richard von Mises, *Probability, Statistics, and Truth*, p. 230.

[25] Oskar Morgenstern, pp. 85-86.

[26] Bernoulli, "Mensura Sortis," tr. Sommer *loc. cit.*, pp. 29-30.

ANTITHETICAL TABLE

Criticism	Rebuttal

1. *Unnecessary multiplication of proofs.*

The "additional evidence in favor of cardinalism which has been turned out" by the Neo-Cardinalists (von Neumann and Morgenstern) does not excite Sir Dennis Robertson, because he does not see the possibility of reaching an indifference point between the certain option and the lottery option. The Neo-Cardinalists forget the disequilibrating power of "the pleasures or pains of uncertainty per se."[27]

It is unlikely that cardinalism can be justified at this moment without the gambling hypothesis. Of course the pleasure and pain of uncertainty exists, but it is a factor shaping the utility function and not outside of it. Any increased aversion against risks will drive the curve to the left and up, while any enjoyment of gambling will drive the curve to the right and down.

2. *The constancy assumption.*

"The theory leans heavily on a constancy assumption so that utilities can be revealed by action over time."[28]

The constancy assumption is indeed fictitious and so is the ceteris paribus clause. I cannot see an essential difference between the two conditions: constancy and ceteris paribus clause. These declarations assure that the behavior pattern does not change in the time interval during which a sequence of events occurs. The theorist cannot prepare an analysis without accepting either the one or the other supposition. The logical positivist leans toward constancy, and the introspectionist is in favor of the ceteris paribus clause.

[27] Sir Dennis Robertson, "Utility and All What," pp. 665-78.
[28] Murray N. Rothbard, "Toward a Reconstruction . . . ," p. 240. Majundar denies that statistical recording of consumers' choices reveals preferences or indifferences. Majundar did not deny that the economist can operate with preferences or indifferences, but he believes that these terms are gained from reasoning and not from observation; therefore the behaviorist borrows his terminology from introspection. Tapas Majundar, "Behavioral Cardinalism in Utility Theory," p. 29.

3. *Probability and equally likely cases.*

Laplace gave the classical definition of probability: "Probability is the ratio of the number of favorable cases to the total number of equally likely cases."[29] Rothbard claimed that in economics equally likely cases do not exist, rather there are only specific individual events.[30] Under these circumstances probability cannot be applied in economics.

This argument surrenders economic analysis to history. We always create in theory equally likely cases, speaking about prices, money, interest, etc. In reality there are only unique prices, money systems, interest rates. Since the days of Adam Smith and Ricardo our concepts have been cleansed of historical circumstances; only the abstract concepts can be used for theoretical analysis.

4. *The indifference of utilities.*

An indifference situation does not exist in reality. The story of Buridan's ass who starved between two bundles of hay is a legend for asses and not for human beings. A man in a similar situation will choose and not submit to an indifference situation; the certain option cannot be balanced with the lottery option. Measuring is impossible.

On the surface this is by far the best argument. Everybody decides and selects. But a more subtle observation reveals the hesitating man who cannot decide whether or not he ought to give up his old position and start a new one. Several hundred dollars offered by the old or the future employer unbalances the value equilibrium which actually existed before.

5. *The complicated calculation.*

Few people are willing or able to go through the elaborate calculation. Therefore the whole approach is useless.

The assumption is correct, but not the conclusion. Although people are not able to solve such a difficult problem, the theory can be valuable. The economists want to know what ought to be done if people are guided strictly by their self-interest.[31] The measuring is a heuristic principle and not a generalization of observable facts.

[29] Richard von Mises, *Probability, Statistics, and Truth*, pp. 66-68.

[30] Rothbard, "Toward a Reconstruction . . . ," p. 240.

[31] William J. Baumol, *Economic Theory and Operational Analysis*, p. 340.

PART IV

EPILOGUE

CHAPTER XXI

THE CONTEMPORARY SITUATION

THE THREEFOLD ACHIEVEMENT

THE huge literature about measuring has historical significance, for it proves that some aspects of the value theory are very much alive. In spite of mounting criticism and declining interest in general, economists still care for the results of the value schools which are now ninety years old. The marginalists believe that their long lease on life is due to three great achievements: first, the marginal value is a more conclusive and consistent tool than the labor value theory; second, marginal utility is the pass key for the explanation of economic life and therefore the basis of economic analysis—price distribution and production are derivations of value; third, the marginalists, the Austrians especially, have created a science of the "right" household planning; it was described by Boulding as follows: "However, the marginal analysis, in its generalised form, is not an analysis of behavior but an analysis of advantage. It is not a psychology or an analysis of actual behavior. It is more akin to an ethic or an analysis of normative positions."[1]

The value theorists do not boast in vain; all these accomplishments exist, but they do not always represent the advanced stage of our science. The problems which the marginalists investigated will now be analyzed with tools which do not belong to the marginal theory; it must be remembered that the problems in which the marginalists

[1] Kenneth E. Boulding, *The Skills of the Economist* (Cleveland: Howard Allen, Inc., 1958), p. 60.

were interested are no longer as important as they were ninety years ago.

ENDURING ACHIEVEMENTS

Modern criticism of the three achievements is here investigated. The first view is that the labor value is no longer a tool of analysis outside the Iron Curtain. The whole controversy is obsolete. Marginal utility is challenged by new tools. The second claim of the value theory is exposed to two attacks at once. The price theory can be explained without marginal utility. Furthermore, utility is not the ultimate cause of price. The first line of attack has been opened by Johann von Neumann.

Twelve years before he cooperated on the general theory of games, Johann von Neumann had already developed an equilibrium model which is free from marginal utility elements.[2] D. G. Champernowne comments on von Neumann's theory as follows: "The orthodox analysis has distributed attention evenly between marginal utility and conditions of supply. . . . A price theory focusing attention on costs can give a very clear and yet an approximately true account."[3] "Consumers' tastes play, in fact, a comparatively minor role in the determination of equilibrium prices."[4]

Also in the later work, which von Neumann wrote together with Morgenstern, *The Theory of Games*, marginal

[2] Von Neumann, "Ueber ein ökonomisches Gleichungssystem und eine Verallgemeinerung des Brouwerschen Fixpunktsatzes," *Ergebnisse eines mathematischen Kolloquiums* (1938); von Neumann, "A Model of General Economic Equilibrium," *The Review of Economic Studies*, Vol. 13 (1945-46), p. 1.

[3] D. G. Champernowne, "A Note on John von Neumann's article on 'A Model of Economic Equilibrium,'" *Review of Economic Studies*, Vol. 13 (1945-46), p. 12; Kurt Singer, "The Logic of Pure Expansion," *Jahrbuch für Sozialwissenschaften*, Vol. 2 (Göttingen, 1960), especially p. 40.

[4] Singer, *ibid.*

utility plays at best a minor role. Von Neumann and Morgenstern are mainly interested in monopolistic competition. The gain expressed in money is the objective of producer's strategy.[5] Of course Oskar Morgenstern, the student of Hans Mayer, knows the connection between price and consumer valuation according to Austrian doctrine, but this causal relation is not even mentioned in his work. The economists of the Morgenstern circle will no longer be interested in the traditional relation between prices and marginal value. Writers outside this group, especially Galbraith, still ponder Boehm-Bawerk's dogma of the priority of marginal utility. The result of their thinking is unfavorable to Boehm-Bawerk.

John Kenneth Galbraith combines three great qualities: he writes pungent and powerful English; he unites original ideas with the ethical zeal of a Puritan; and he denies that in his society, the contemporary affluent society of the U.S.A., the consumer's scale of preference dictates shape and organization of production. Really, it is the other way around; production determines consumption. In this society production is a goal "of preeminent importance in our life."[6] Rooted in American tradition and social myth, production increase acquires a semi-divine character. The result of these efforts is an expanding national income. To consume these ever-increasing riches, consumer goods have to be changed as well as the consumer planning. To explain the expansion of consumption, Galbraith operates with marginal utility.[7] The law of diminishing utility tells us that first the goods with the highest utility will be consumed to the point where its marginal utility is very low.[8] When this stage is reached,

---

[5] Von Neumann and Morgenstern, *Theory of Games*, pp. 31ff.
[6] John Kenneth Galbraith, *The Affluent Society* (Cambridge, Mass., 1958), p. 137.
[7] *Ibid.*, p. 149.
[8] *Ibid.*, p. 146.

the slowing down of production can be prevented only if new wants and corresponding goods are created time and again. It is not that the consumer's needs create the new industry, but that the industry creates the consumer's wants. Boehm-Bawerk's causal nexus has been turned upside down.

Kurt Singer's arguments have some resemblance to Galbraith's reflections. "A shrewd onlooker could venture to define 'consumption' in the modern age, with or without planning, as service to the producer."[9] Singer claimed that demand is artificially created or suppressed following the requirements of mass production.

With regard to the third achievement, the results of household planning produced by the Austrian school have to compete with the research of the statistician, the sociologist, and the psychologist. In the same number of the *Jahrbuch für Sozialwissenschaft* in which Kurt Singer published his remarks, Eduard Kantzenbach[10] gave a condensed version of the newest stand of consumer research which, if accepted, might restrict still more the significance of marginal utility. He followed Veblen and Duesenberry, who had discovered that consumer motives are supposedly not identical with the direct utility of the consumer goods but with the needs for recognition and self-expression. Institutional and statistical investigations of consumer habits replace the a priori constructions of consumer strategy. These arguments against marginal utility theory are not new. Thirty-six years ago Werner Sombart in his *Modern Capitalism* presented ideas similar to those of Galbraith and Kantzenbach,[11] but the historical situation

---

[9] Singer, "The Logic of Pure Expansion," p. 39.

[10] Eduard Kantzenbach, "Bedürfnisstructur und Gesellschafts-ordnung," *Jahrbuch für Sozialwissenschaft*, Vol. 11 (1960), pp. 21ff.

[11] Werner Sombart, *Der moderne Kapitalismus* (Munich, 1927), Vol. 3, pp. 603ff.

changed. In 1927 Sombart, the last defender of historicism, met the opposition of the theorists. Today only small circles around Mises fight back vigorously, although in ninety years of discussion many arguments for the defense have been collected. But theorists are no longer as interested in the value theory in general as they were thirty years ago. The measuring controversy attracts greatest attention.

IMPACT OF JOHN M. KEYNES' GENERAL THEORY

The reason for the slackening interest is obvious. In 1936 Keynes' General Theory was published. English and American economists accepted it with more spontaneous enthusiasm and more readily than European economists after 1870 adopted marginal utility. The atmosphere of elation and the new zeal permeating American and British classrooms and seminars is best expressed by Samuelson, who quoted Wordsworth: "Bliss was it in that dawn to be alive, but to be young was very heaven."[12] But neither this enthusiasm which made out of Keynes the greatest economist of all times nor the denunciation of Keynes as the greatest quack helps us to understand why the General Theory stole the thunder from the schools of marginal utility.

If we exclude our emotions it is rather simple to understand why the economists lost interest in many aspects of the marginal utility theory. Let us start with a negative statement: the young economists did not stop to study the old consumer value because Keynes offered a newer and better value theory. Keynes dealt with individual preferences in the tradition of neo-classicism and the Viennese school. The balancing of the marginal propensity to save, to invest, and to consume are preference actions which can easily be marked on Vleugels' chart and on Pareto's indifference curve. It was not a new value theory but,

[12] Quoted by Mises, *Human Action*, p. 787 n. 4.

besides other considerations, the new analysis of unemployment and the policy suggested for the removing of this calamity lured young scholars away from the traditional outlook. Menger, Boehm-Bawerk, Wieser, and Marshall had no anti-social feelings, but they never faced an unemployment situation similar to that of the late 1920's and the early 1930's. Therefore, their books did not contain any remedies. The belief in the curative power of the unfettered free mechanism of the market economy was shared by several marginalists, but many younger British and American economists had lost faith in free competition. They even became tired of the methodical individualism which is considered by many older theorists to be the way of interpreting social interrelations. Methodical individualism means the dissolution of social aggregates into acts of choosing done by the individual.[13] Since the time of the Physiocrats some economists believed that aggregates are tools necessary for interpretation, and even the classicists operated with wage funds, price averages, balance of trade and payment, all of which are aggregate concepts. This approach, dealing with social entities, remained a secondary way of analysis for a long time.

Keynes made the macro-economic method the guiding technique of analysis. He and his followers created aggregate and average concepts, for instance, national income, multiplier, accelerator, economic growth, etc. These ideas are studied, new tools of the same kind are added every so often—and the interest in the consumer's preference decreases more and more. Paul A. Samuelson wrote a very popular textbook on principles; in the last edition of 836 pages, eleven pages (pp. 436-47) are dedicated to the explanation of marginal utility.[14] The

[13] Louis M. Spadaro, "Averages and Aggregates in Economics," *Essays in Honor of Ludwig von Mises*, p. 140; Ludwig von Mises, *Human Action*, p. 44.

[14] Paul Samuelson, *Economics* (New York, 1961).

theory of consumer preference has moved into a Cinderella position.

DEFENSE, REFORM, AND RETREAT

The older European economists and their American students are disturbed, but they have not capitulated; they fight back. For this battle they still can utilize the combined intelligence of three groups—the French economic-sociological group, the students of the game theory, and the Mises circle, besides non-committed free-lancers. Some of their finest representatives voiced their anti-Keynesian ideas in the three publications honoring Ludwig von Mises, Hans Mayer, and Alfred Amonn. They claim that the aggregate theory violates the principle of methodical individualism which is, according to their opinion, the essential assumption of every economic deduction (Wilhelm Weber, Mises); they claim further that the Austrians had already discovered the few correct insights of the reform (Hans Mayer), and that Keynes and his followers substitute mathematical evidence for the investigation of economic motivations (François Perroux).[15] These critical remarks are very often thought-provoking, but it seems that some writers did not understand the situation of economic thinking after 1936. Karl Borch, the subtle Norwegian interpreter of the game theory (who had the thankless job of teaching me some of the mathematics behind the theory of measuring), asked why there was a Keynesian revolution but not a von Neumann and Morgenstern revolution.[16] The situation which I sketched a few

[15] *Neue Beiträge zur Wirtschaftstheorie. Festschrift anlässlich des 70. Geburtstages von Hans Mayer* (Wien, 1949); *Wirtschaftstheorie und Wirtschaftspolitik. Festschrift für Alfred Amonn zum 70. Geburtstag* (Bern, 1953).

[16] Karl Borch, "Recent Developments in Economics and their Application to Insurance." Invited lecture to the Astin Colloquium, Juan-les-Pins, May, 1962. Mimeographed paper, p. 103.

pages ago makes it quite unlikely that the history of economics could have gone a different way. Other value theorists understood the historical conditions. We are indebted to Fritz Machlup for a lucid explanation of the multiplier and very valuable interpretations of foreign trade in the Keynesian manner. Wilhelm Röpke, a strong defender of the marginal utility principle, wrote a well-balanced and penetrating interpretation of Keynes' work.[17] Those like Machlup who seek a bridge between Menger and Keynes and those who fight shy of any compromise have to face a number of problems if they want to keep the value theory alive.

[17] Wilhelm Röpke, *Economics of the Free Society* (Chicago, 1963), pp. 221ff.

CHAPTER XXII

THE CHANCE OF SURVIVAL

THE ECONOMIC SYSTEM AND MARGINAL UTILITY

WILL the future theorist give up the study of value theory? It is possible, but it is not desirable. The neglect of marginal utility would deprive the theorist of an essential tool needed for economic analysis. Although some ill-founded claims of the value theorists have been discounted in the last chapter, essential achievements remain. These are a thorough analysis of consumer behavior and some valuable insights into the demand-structure. A substitute for utility theory does not exist.[1] The new attempts to interpret consumer habits—for instance, Duesenberry's statistical investigations and Galbraith's sociological descriptions—are very penetrating. But they are possible only on the basis of the marginal utility theory. The actual distribution of income between consumption and saving presupposes the consumer's preference decisions; the priority of production in the affluent society is explained with the help of the law of diminishing utility. The surviving marginalists, the game theorists, the French economic-sociological school, and the praxeologists should have no great difficulty in integrating these facts. This is a small part of the future work, for the main task is much more difficult. Future value theorists will have to write the final paragraphs to all the topical chapters of this study: they will have to attempt to solve the many problems which have been

[1] Frank H. Knight has written a penetrating study of this problem in his article "Value and Price," *Encyclopedia of the Social Sciences* (New York, 1938), Vol. 8, pp. 218-24.

discussed time and again since 1870. Progress surpassing these incomplete performances has been hindered in four ways.

The Four Controversial Points

First: from the beginning the great system builders of the Austrian school had a definite starting point, marginal utility. All concepts of theoretical analysis ought to be reduced to value problems, for value was the sesame key. The working out of this thought was confronted with hindrances. The value theorists spread their efforts too thin. It has been shown that the problems of price, imputation, and distribution can be solved without or with only small help from valuation. The inconclusive history of imputation shows the waste of effort caused by neglecting the inherent limitation of the preference theory. The core of the marginal utility theory ought to be consumption. Here is the field reserved for our theory.

Second: the simple utility maximum of the Robinson Crusoe economy is the favorite model of the Austrian theory, but its application is limited. It is valid only in a completely isolated economy. In the market economy, von Neumann and Morgenstern write, each participant attempts to maximize a function (his maximum) "of which he does not control all variables."[2] The consumer may not be able to equalize different marginal utilities. Von Neumann and Morgenstern have indicated the direction in which the problem may be solved.

Third: the Babylonian confusion has to be cleared away. Words are used as labels for many different phenomena. The meanings of the words utility, costs are many. Causality and teleology, hedonism and moral values, analysis and political programs have been mixed up. Unfortunately the situation of the value studies provokes this intellectual turmoil. Utility investigation reaches

[2] Von Neumann and Morgenstern, *Theory of Games*, p. 11.

into many disciplines. A value theorist has to be a mathematician, a psychologist, a philosopher, a theologian, and sometimes even an economist. No author can be sufficiently trained in all these fields. The value theorist has to accept the counsel provided by scholars from other branches of knowledge to clear away the fog of confusion.

Fourth: the verdict "I act thus and therefore everybody else acts this way" (So handle ich und das ist jedermann) is very bold. But boldness is not identical with correctness. Theoretical principles are gained from *introspection*, but the verification is dependent on *observations*. During the whole history of marginal utility, the theorists have not always checked their findings against observed cases and statistical evidence. In natural science every discovery is tested. Why have we done so little?

THE MARGINAL GAIN

It was my task to describe the history and not the future of a leading theory in economics. How much the reader has learned from this narration I do not know. I at least derived some pleasure from writing this study. I was thrilled by the discovery of new insights and the digging out of old documents. Furthermore, in a time like this it is sometimes agreeable to describe a philosophy of everyday life which does not define man as an exploited slave stumbling forward toward the holocaust of social revolution, which does not consider him a puppet dancing at the command of multiplier and accelerator, but which sees in man a person who selects his lunch, his dinner, his wardrobe, and his house. Certainly there was enough trouble struggling with a language which I had not spoken before I was thirty-seven years of age, with mathematics, and, still worse, with the intricacies of the rules of quotation. Yet, generally there was more enjoyment than annoyance, or, in the language of Friedrich von Wieser, marginal utility was greater than the opportunity costs.

SOURCES AND LITERATURE

FOR the history of a scientific concept the study of the books written about this subject is not enough. To gain a better insight into time and circumstances, to make sense of obscure writing, to gauge the intellectual influence, I had to interview surviving witnesses (Richard Schüller, Karl Menger, Jr.). I searched for letters, publications which had seldom been read, and for handwritten manuscripts and notes. The printed letters and journals are easily accessible and are catalogued here:

William St. Jevons. *Letters and Journals.* London, 1886.

Étienne Antonelli (ed.). "Léon Walras et Carl Menger à travers leur correspondance," *Économie appliquée*, Vol. 6, Nos. 2-3 (Paris, 1953), pp. 269-87. This document reveals the methodical differences between Léon Walras and Carl Menger. Unfortunately Menger's German letters are not correctly translated, as Professor Morton Jaffe told me.

Vilfredo Pareto. *Lettere a Maffeo Pantaleoni, 1890-1923*, Vol. 3, ed. Gabriele de Rosa. (Rome, 1960); *Carteggi Paretiani, 1892-1923*, Vol. 1, ed. Gabriele de Rosa. (Rome, 1962.) Pareto's letters were most generously presented to me by the Banca Nazionale del Lavoro. Unfortunately I received the four volumes too late for this publication.

The most exciting part of my investigation was the search for unpublished material. Visiting Menger's library at the Hitotsubashi University at Kunitachi, Tokyo, Japan, I had hunter's luck. The Menger Library is more than 100 years old. Carl Menger's father, a small-town lawyer in former Austrian Poland, collected the first 4,000 volumes. Carl Menger, who was an avid reader and a book collector, enlarged the collection to 25,000 volumes. After his death, the works dealing with the social sciences were acquired by the Japanese government and are now kept at the Hitotsubashi University, Kunitachi, Tokyo. The books by themselves are of great literary and scientific value; they are especially important for the historian of economic thought, because they contain essential parts of Menger's scientific legacy.

Menger's collection reflects his working habits, his thinking, and his personality. He wrote corrections, short notes, and fragmentary essays on the flyleaves, margins, and other empty spots of the books he owned. More often than not, these notes have only an indirect connection with the printed text. They are monologues by which he clarified and developed his own thoughts. Most important are his notes in Rau's *Grundsätze der Volkswirthschaftslehre* and in his copy of his own *Principles* of 1871. Menger's remarks in Rau's handbook (abbreviated: Rm.) contain an early version of his theories of value, price, and money. Menger's hand copy of his theory of 1871 (abbreviated: fragment) includes an unfinished correction of this work which was planned as an introduction for a four-volume handbook. He wrote his corrections on inserted sheets as well as on the printed pages. I have transcribed the two manuscripts. The following list gives a selection of those books in which I found Menger's comments. It also indicates that the search is not finished; ample material still has to be investigated.

Selection of Menger's annotated books
  Books investigated.

Joseph Kudler. *Die Grundlehren der Volkswirthschaft.* Wien, 1846, Vol. 1. Apparently used by Menger for his state-examination, 1860-1863. (Menger Library Comp. 168.)

Karl Friedrich Rau. *Grundsätze der Volkswirthschaftslehre*. 7th ed., Leipzic, 1863. Menger remarked twice (title page and page 1) that he started his study of Rau in September, October of 1867. (Mlb. Comp. 266.) (title abbreviated Rm. Published as a mimeographed book: *Carl Mengers Erster Entwurf zu seinem Hauptwerk "Grundsätze" geschrieben Als Anmerkungen zu den "Grundsätzen Der Volkswirthschaftslehre" Von Karl Heinrich Rau*. Tokio, Hitotsubashi Universität. 1963.

Carl Menger. *Grundsätze der Volkswirthschaftslehre*. Wien, 1871. The author's copy. Menger changed the title to *Allgemeine theoretische Volkswirthschaftslehre*. Attached newspaper clippings indicate that Menger started to work about 1873. He may have stopped writing on this manuscript after 1892, because a note on the cover asks the honest finder to deliver the book to Menger for the reward of 100 Kronen. The crown currency was introduced in Austria in 1892. (Abbreviated title: Fragment.) Published as a mimeographed book: *Carl Mengers Zusätze zu "Grundsätze der Volkswirthschaftslehre."* Tokyo: Bibliothek der Hitotsubashi Universität, 1961.

John Stuart Mill. *Grundsätze der politischen Oekonomie*. German translation by Adolph Soetbeer, Hamburg, 1864. Read by Menger after he had published his *Principles*. Important notes about price and the law of diminishing return. (Mlb. Eng. 983.)

Friedrich Ueberweg. *Grundriss der Geschichte der Philosophie der Neuzeit*. Berlin, 1872. Read before he published his methods of social sciences. See Kauder, "Menger and his Library," *The Economic Review*, Hitotsubashi University, Vol. 10, No. 1 (January, 1959).

Hermann Heinrich Gossen. *Entwickelung der Gesetze des menschlichen Verkehrs*. Braunschweig, 1854. Rare first edition. (Comp. 99.) Menger read this book in the summer of 1886. See remark in ink on title page which is very important for Menger's attitude toward Gossen.

Rudolf Auspitz und Richard Lieben. *Zur Theorie des Preises*. Leipzig, 1887. (Mlb. Mon 91.) This is the only mathematical treatise in the whole library which Menger had thoroughly studied.

Menger's remarks to Knapp. *Staatliche Theorie des Geldes*. According to a letter by Oskar Morgenstern, Ludwig von Mises deposited this book at the University library, Geneva, Switzerland. I own a microfilm.

Books, pamphlets and other material existing but not available.

Notes on the theory of value 1867, mentioned in F. A. von Hayek, "Carl Menger," *The Collected Works of Carl Menger*, Vol. 1, The London School of Economics and Political Science, London, 1934, p. xi, footnote. I could not find out whether or not these notes are identical with the Rm.

Preface intended for a second edition of the *Principles*, partly published in Carl Menger, *Grundsätze der Volkswirhtschaftslehre*, 2nd posthumous ed.; Wien, 1923. Preface by Richard Schüller, ed. Karl Menger (son). (Abbr. Sch.M.), pp. viiff.

Carl Menger's paper "Kritik von Wundts Logik." (Sch.M.), p. xiii. Owned by Karl Menger?

Correspondence Carl Menger and Boehm-Bawerk. Partly published Sch.M. xii and Economisk Tidskrift. Upsala, 1921, pp. 87ff.

Original manuscripts of the Sch.M. Property of Karl Menger?

I did not find another treasure trove. The search for documents, letters, and unpublished manuscripts of Menger's successors was almost a complete failure. Only the letters of the young Friedrich von Hayek to Wesley C.

Mitchell could be located at Columbia University, Seligman room.

Before I finish this survey, I must mention a curiosum to which Professor Fritz Machlup drew my attention. For his seventieth birthday Carl Menger desired that each economist of the whole earth should be photographed and have a picture sent to him. Everyone except Gustav Schmoller and Lujo Brentano did so. Apparently, the leaders of the historical school could neither forgive nor forget. These old-fashioned pictures made by real "Hofphotographen" (photographers to the court by imperial and royal appointment) date from a time when marginal utility theory had a growing influence and when the dignity of a professor was exactly measured by the length of his beard. The whole collection is in the Economics Department of the Johns Hopkins University, Baltimore, Maryland.

AUTHOR INDEX